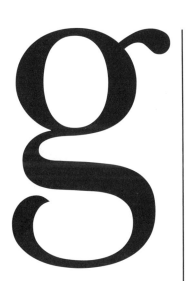

READING COMPREHENSION & ESSAYS

GRE Verbal Strategy Guide

This volume provides students with a comprehensive approach to the GRE's Reading Comprehension passages and questions. Included are practical techniques for grasping difficult content and rapidly perceiving passage structure. Plus, an additional Essays section equips test-takers with handy analytical tools to compose excellent responses.

Reading Comprehension & Essays GRE Strategy Guide, Second Edition

10-digit International Standard Book Number: 1-935707-52-3
13-digit International Standard Book Number: 978-1-935707-52-3
eISBN: 978-0-984178-09-4

8 GUIDE INSTRUCTIONAL SERIES

Math GRE Preparation Guides

Algebra
(ISBN: 978-1-935707-47-9)

Fractions, Decimals, & Percents
(ISBN: 978-1-935707-48-6)

Geometry
(ISBN: 978-1-935707-49-3)

Number Properties
(ISBN: 978-1-935707-50-9)

Word Problems
(ISBN: 978-1-935707-54-7)

Quantitative Comparisons & Data Interpretation
(ISBN: 978-1-935707-51-6)

Verbal GRE Preparation Guides

Reading Comprehension & Essays
(ISBN: 978-1-935707-52-3)

Text Completion & Sentence Equivalence
(ISBN: 978-1-935707-53-0)

Manhattan GRE

March 15th, 2011

Dear Student,

Thank you for picking up one of the Manhattan GRE Strategy Guides—we hope that it ends up being just what you need to prepare for the new GRE.

As with most accomplishments, there were many people involved in the book that you're holding. First and foremost is Zeke Vanderhoek, the founder of MG Prep. Zeke was a lone tutor in New York when he started the Company in 2000. Now, ten years later, the Company has Instructors and offices nationwide and contributes to the studies and successes of thousands of students each year.

Our Manhattan GRE Strategy Guides are based on the continuing experiences of our Instructors and our students. On the Company side, we are indebted to many of our Instructors, including but not limited to Roman Altshuler, Chris Berman, Faruk Bursal, Jen Dziura, Dmitry Farber, Stacey Koprince, David Mahler, Seb Moosapoor, Stephanie Moyerman, Chris Ryan, Michael Schwartz, Tate Shafer, Emily Sledge, Tommy Wallach, and Ryan Wessel, all of whom either wrote or edited the books to their present form. Dan McNaney and Cathy Huang provided their formatting expertise to make the books as user-friendly as possible. Last, many people, too numerous to list here but no less appreciated, assisted in the development of the online resources that accompany this guide.

At Manhattan GRE, we continually aspire to provide the best Instructors and resources possible. We hope that you'll find our dedication manifest in this book. If you have any comments or questions, please e-mail me at dan@manhattangre.com. I'll be sure that your comments reach our curriculum team—and I'll read them too.

Best of luck in preparing for the GRE!

Sincerely,

Dan Gonzalez
Managing Director
Manhattan GRE

HOW TO ACCESS YOUR ONLINE STUDENT CENTER

If you...

> ## are a registered Manhattan GRE student

and have received this book as part of your course materials, you have AUTOMATIC access to ALL of our online resources. To access these resources, follow the instructions in the Welcome Guide provided to you at the start of your program. Do NOT follow the instructions below.

> ## purchased this book from the Manhattan GRE Online store or at one of our Centers

1. Go to: http://www.manhattangre.com/studentcenter.cfm

2. Log in using the username and password used when your account was set up. Your one year of online access begins on the day that you purchase the book from the Manhattan GRE online store or at one of our centers.

> ## purchased this book at a retail location

1. Go to: http://www.manhattangre.com/access.cfm

2. Log in or create an account.

3. Follow the instructions on the screen.

Your one year of online access begins on the day that you register your book at the above URL.

You only need to register your product ONCE at the above URL. To use your online resources any time AFTER you have completed the registration process, login to the following URL:
http://www.manhattangre.com/studentcenter.cfm

Please note that online access is non-transferable. This means that only NEW and UNREGISTERED copies of the book will grant you online access. Previously used books will not provide any online resources.

> ## purchased an e-book version of this book

1. Create an account with Manhattan GRE at the website:
   https://www.manhattangre.com/createaccount.cfm

2. Email a copy of your purchase receipt to books@manhattangre.com to activate your resources. Please be sure to use the same email address to create an account that you used to purchase the e-book.

For any technical issues, email books@manhattangre.com or call 646-254-6479.

TABLE OF CONTENTS

g

Chapter 1
of
READING COMPREHENSION & ESSAYS

INTRODUCTION &
THE REVISED GRE

In This Chapter . . .

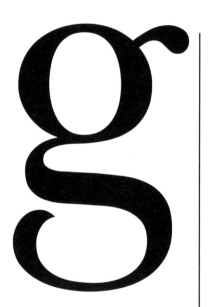

- Introduction, and How to Use Manhattan GRE's Strategy Guides
- The Revised GRE
- Question Formats in Detail

Introduction, and How to Use Manhattan GRE's Strategy Guides

We know that you're looking to succeed on the GRE so that you can go to graduate school and do the things you want to do in life.

We also know that you might not have done math since high school, and that you may never have learned words like "adumbrate" or "sangfroid." We know that it's going to take hard work on your part to get a top GRE score, and that's why we've put together the only set of books that will take you from the basics all the way up to the material you need to master for a near-perfect score, or whatever your score goal may be. You've taken the first step. Now it's time to get to work!

How to Use These Materials

Manhattan GRE's materials are comprehensive. But keep in mind that, depending on your score goal, it may not be necessary to "get" absolutely everything. Grad schools only see your overall Quantitative, Verbal, and Writing scores—they don't see exactly which strengths and weaknesses went into creating those scores.

You may be enrolled in one of our courses, in which case you already have a syllabus telling you in what order you should approach the books. But if you bought this book online or at a bookstore, feel free to approach the books—and even the chapters within the books—in whatever order works best for you. *For the most part, the books, and the chapters within them, are independent; you don't have to master one section before moving on to the next.* So if you're having a hard time with something in particular, you can make a note to come back to it later and move on to another section. Similarly, it may not be necessary to solve every single practice problem for every section. As you go through the material, continually assess whether you understand and can apply the principles in each individual section and chapter. The best way to do this is to solve the Check Your Skills and Practice Problems throughout. If you're confident you have a concept or method down, feel free to move on. If you struggle with something, make note of it for further review. Stay active in your learning and oriented toward the test—it's easy to read something and think you understand it, only to have trouble applying it in the 1–2 minutes you have to solve a problem.

Study Skills

As you're studying for the GRE, try to integrate your learning into your everyday life. For example, vocabulary is a big part of the GRE, as well as something you just can't "cram" for—you're going to want to do at least a little bit of vocab every day. So, try to learn and internalize a little bit at a time, switching up topics often to help keep things interesting.

Keep in mind that, while many of your study materials are on paper (including ETS's most recent source of official GRE questions, *The Official Guide to the GRE revised General Test*), your exam will be administered on a computer. Because this is a computer-based test, you will NOT be able to underline portions of reading passages, write on diagrams of geometry figures, or otherwise physically mark up problems. So get used to this now. Solve the problems in these books on scratch paper. (Each of our books talks specifically about what to write down for different problem types).

Again, as you study stay focused on the test-day experience. As you progress, work on timed drills and sets of questions. Eventually, you should be taking full practice tests (available at www.manhattangre.com) under actual timed conditions.

The Revised GRE

As of August 1, 2011, the Quantitative and Verbal sections of the GRE will undergo a number of changes. The actual body of knowledge being tested won't change, but the *way* it is tested will. Here's a brief summary of what to expect, followed by a more comprehensive assessment of the new exam.

Overall, the general format of the test will change. The length of the test will increase from about 3.5 hours to about 4 hours. There will be two scored math sections and two scored verbal sections rather than one of each, and a new score scale of 130–170 will be used in place of the old 200–800 scale. More on this later.

The Verbal section of the GRE will change dramatically. The Analogies and Antonym questions will disappear. The Sentence Completions and Reading Comprehension will remain, to be expanded and remixed in a few new ways. Vocabulary will still be important, but only in the context of complete sentences. That is, you'll no longer have to worry about vocabulary words standing alone. So for those who dislike learning vocabulary words, the changes will provide partial relief. For those who were looking forward to getting lots of points just for memorizing words, the Manhattan GRE verbal strategy guides will prepare you for the shift.

The Quant section of the GRE prior to August 1, 2011 is composed of multiple choice problems, Quantitative Comparisons, and Data Interpretation questions (which are really a subset of multiple choice problems). The revised test will contain two new problem formats in addition to the current problem formats. However, the type of math, and the difficulty of the math, will remain unchanged.

Additionally, a small four-function calculator with a square root button will appear on-screen. Many test takers will rejoice at the advent of this calculator! It is true that the GRE calculator will reduce emphasis on computation—but look out for problems, such as percents questions with tricky wording, that are likely to foil those who rely on the calculator too much. *In short, the calculator may make your life a bit easier from time to time, but you will never <u>need</u> the calculator to solve a problem.*

Finally, don't worry about whether these new problem types are "harder" or "easier." You are being judged against other test takers, all of whom are in the same boat. So if the new formats are harder, they are harder for other test takers as well.

Exam Structure

The revised test has six sections. You will get a ten-minute break between the third and fourth sections and a one-minute break between the others. The Analytical Writing section is always first. The other five sections can be seen in any order and will include:

- Two Verbal Reasoning sections (approximately 20 questions each in exactly 30 minutes per section)

- Two Quantitative Reasoning sections (approximately 20 questions each in exactly 35 minutes per section)

- Either an "unscored" section or a "research" section

An unscored section will look just like a third Verbal or Quantitative Reasoning section, and you will not be told which of them doesn't count. If you get a research section, it will be identified as such.

Section Type	# Questions	Time	Scored?
Analytical Writing	2 essays	30 minutes each	Yes
Verbal #1	Approx. 20	30 minutes	Yes
Quantitative #1	Approx. 20	35 minutes	Yes
Verbal #2	Approx. 20	30 minutes	Yes
Quantitative #2	Approx. 20	35 minutes	Yes
Unscored Section (verbal or quant)	Approx. 20	30 or 35 min	No
Research Section	Varies	Varies	No

10 min break →

order varies

one or the other, but not both {

Later in the chapter, we'll look at all the question formats in detail.

Using the Calculator

The addition of a small, four-function calculator with a square root button means that those taking the revised test can forget re-memorizing their times tables or square roots. However, the calculator is not a cure-all; in many problems, the difficulty is in figuring out what numbers to put into the calculator in the first place. In some cases, using a calculator will actually be less helpful than doing the problem some other way. Let's look at an example:

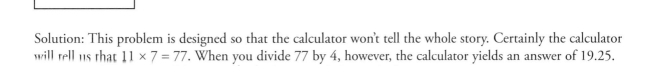

If x is the remainder when (11)(7) is divided by 4 and y is the remainder when (14)(6) is divided by 13, what is the value of $x + y$?

Solution: This problem is designed so that the calculator won't tell the whole story. Certainly the calculator will tell us that $11 \times 7 = 77$. When you divide 77 by 4, however, the calculator yields an answer of 19.25. The remainder is *not* 0.25 (a remainder is always a whole number).

You might just go back to your pencil and paper, and find the largest multiple of 4 that is less than 77. Since 4 DOES go into 76, we can conclude that 4 would leave a remainder of 1 when dividing into 77. (Notice that we don't even need to know how many times 4 goes into 76, just that it goes in. One way to mentally "jump" to 76 is to say, *4 goes into 40, so it goes into 80 … that's a bit too big, so take away 4 to get 76.*) You could also multiply the leftover 0.25 times 4 (the divisor) to find the remainder of 1.

However, it is also possible to use the calculator to find a remainder. Divide 77 by 4 to get 19.25. Thus, 4 goes into 77 nineteen times, with a remainder left over. Now use your calculator to multiply 19 (JUST 19, not 19.25) by 4. You will get 76. The remainder is $77 - 76 = 1$. Therefore, $x = 1$.

Use the same technique to find y. Multiply 14×6 to get 84. Divide 84 by 13 to get 6.46... Ignore everything after the decimal, and just multiply 6 by 13 to get 78. The remainder is therefore $84 - 78 = 6$. Therefore, $y = 6$.

Since we are looking for $x + y$ and $1 + 6 = 7$, the answer is 7.

You can see that blind faith in the calculator can be dangerous. Use it responsibly! And this leads us to...

Practice Using the Calculator!

On the new GRE, the on-screen calculator will slow you down or lead to incorrect answers if you're not careful! If you plan to use the thing on test day (which you should), you'll want to pactice first.

We have created an online practice calculator for your use. To access this calculator, go to www.manhattangre.com and sign in to the student center using the instructions on the "How to Access Your Online Student Center" page found at the front of this book.

In addition to the calculator, you will see instructions for how to use the calculator. Be sure to read these instructions and work through the associated exercises. Throughout our math books, you will see the  symbol. This symbol means "use the calculator here!" As much as possible, have the online practice calculator up and running during your review of our math books. You'll have the chance to use the on-screen calculator when you take our practice exams as well.

Navigating the Questions in a Section

Another change for test takers on the new GRE is the ability to move freely around the questions in a section... you can go forward and backward one-by-one and can even jump directly to any question from the "review list." The review list provides a snapshot of which questions you have answered, which ones you have tagged for "mark and review," and which are incomplete, either because you didn't select enough answers or because you selected too many (that is, if a number of choices is specified by the question). You should double-check the review list for completion if you finish the section early. Using the review list feature will take some practice as well, which is why we've built it into our online practice exams. Here's some introductory advice.

The majority of test takers will be pressed for time. Thus, for most of you, it won't be feasible to "go back to" multiple problems at the end of the section. Generally, if you can't get a question the first time, you won't be able to get it the second time around either. With this in mind, here's how we recommend using the new review list feature.

1. Do the questions in order as they appear.

2. When you encounter a difficult question, do you best to eliminate answer choices you know are wrong.

3. If you're not sure of an answer, take an educated guess from the choices remaining. Do <u>NOT</u> skip it and hope to return to it later.

4. Using the "mark" button at the top of the screen, mark up to three questions per section that you think you might be able to solve with more time. Mark a question only after you have taken an educated guess.

5. If you have time at the end of the section, click on the review list, identify any questions you've marked and return to them. If you do not have any time remaining, you will have already taken good guesses at the tough ones.

What you want to avoid is "surfing"—clicking forward and backward through the questions searching for the easy ones. This will eat up valuable time. Of course, you'll want to move through the tough ones quickly if you can't get them, but try to avoid skipping stuff.

Again, all of this will take practice. Use our practice exams to fine-tune your approach.

Scoring

Two things have changed about the scoring of the Verbal Reasoning and Quantitative Reasoning sections: (1) how individual questions influence the score and (2) the score scale itself.

For both the Verbal Reasoning and Quantitative Reasoning sections, you will receive a raw score, which is simply how many questions you answered correctly. Your raw score is converted to a scaled score, accounting for the difficulties of the specific questions you actually saw.

The old GRE was question-adaptive, meaning that your answer to each question (right or wrong) determined, at least somewhat, the questions that followed (harder or easier). Because you had to commit to an answer to let the algorithm do its thing, you weren't allowed to skip questions or go back to change answers. On the revised GRE, the adapting will occur from section to section (e.g., if you do well on the first verbal section, you will get a harder second verbal section) rather than from question to question. The only change test takers will notice is one most will welcome: you can now move freely about the questions in a section, coming back to tough questions later, changing answers after "ah-ha!" moments, and generally managing your time more flexibly.

The scores for the revised GRE Quantitative Reasoning and Verbal Reasoning will be reported on a 130 to 170 scale in 1-point increments, whereas the old score reporting was on a 200 to 800 scale in 10-point increments. You will receive one 130–170 score for verbal and a separate 130–170 score for quant. If you are already putting your GRE math skills to work, you may notice that there are now 41 scores possible (170 – 130, then add one before you're done), whereas before there were 61 scores possible ([800 – 200]/10, then add one before you're done). In other words, a 10 point difference on the old score scale actually indicated a smaller performance differential than a 1 point difference on the new scale. However, the GRE folks argue that perception is reality: the difference between 520 and 530 on the old scale could simply seem greater than the difference between 151 and 152 on the new scale. If that's true, then this change will benefit test-takers, who won't be unfairly compared by schools for minor differences in performance. If not true, then the change will be moot.

Important Dates

Registration for the GRE revised General Test opens on March 15, 2011, and the first day of testing with the new format is August 1, 2011.

Perhaps to encourage people to take the revised exam, rather than rushing to take the old exam before the change or waiting "to see what happens" with the new exam long after August 1, 2011, ETS is offering a 50% discount on the test fee for anyone who takes the revised test from August 1 through September 30, 2011. Scores for people who take

the revised exam in this discount period will be sent starting in mid- to late-November. This implies that you may have to wait up to 3.5 months to get your score during this rollout period!

By December 2011, ETS expects to resume normal score reporting schedules: score reports will be sent a mere 10-15 days after the test date.

IMPORTANT: If you need GRE scores before mid-November 2011 to meet a school deadline, take the "old" GRE no later than July 31, 2011! Waiting to take the revised test not only would require you to study for a different test, but also would delay your score reporting.

Question Formats in Detail

Essay Questions

The Analytical Writing section consists of two separately timed 30-minute tasks: Analyze an Issue and Analyze an Argument. As you can imagine, the 30-minute time limit implies that you aren't aiming to write an essay that would garner a Pulitzer Prize nomination, but rather to complete the tasks adequately and according to the directions. Each essay is scored separately, but your reported essay score is the average of the two rounded up to the next half-point increment on a 0 to 6 scale.

Issue Task—This essay prompt will present a claim, generally one that is vague enough to be interpreted in various ways and discussed from numerous perspectives. Your job as a test taker is to write a response discussing the extent to which you agree or disagree and support your position. Don't sit on the fence—pick a side!

For some examples of Issue Task prompts, visit the GRE website here:

http://www.ets.org/gre/revised_general/prepare/analytical_writing/issue/pool

Argument Task—This essay prompt will be an argument comprised of both a claim(s) and evidence. Your job is to dispassionately discuss the argument's structural flaws and merits (well, mostly the flaws). Don't agree or disagree with the argument—evaluate its logic.

For some examples of Argument Task prompts, visit the GRE website here:

http://www.ets.org/gre/revised_general/prepare/analytical_writing/argument/pool

Verbal: Reading Comprehension Questions

Standard 5-choice multiple choice reading comprehension questions will continue to appear on the new exam. You are likely familiar with how these work. Let's take a look at two *new* reading comprehension formats that will appear on the new test.

Select One or More Answer Choices and Select-in-Passage

For the question type, "Select One or More Answer Choices," you are given three statements about a passage and asked to "select all that apply." Either one, two, or all three can be correct (there is no "none of the above" option). There is no partial credit; you must select all the correct choices and none of the incorrect choices.

Strategy Tip: On "Select One or More Answer Choices," don't let your brain be tricked into telling you "Well, if two of them have been right so far, the other one must be wrong," or any other arbitrary idea about how many of the choices "should" be correct. Make sure to consider each choice independently! You cannot use "Process of Elimination" the same way as you do on "normal" multiple-choice questions.

For the question type "Select-in-Passage," you are given an assignment such as "Select the sentence in the passage that explains why the experiment's results were discovered to be invalid." Clicking anywhere on the sentence in the passage will highlight it. (As with any GRE question, you will have to click "Confirm" to submit your answer, so don't worry about accidentally selecting the wrong sentence due to a slip of the mouse.)

Strategy Tip: On "Select-in-Passage," if the passage is short, consider numbering each sentence (that is, writing 1 2 3 4 on your paper) and crossing off each choice as you determine that it isn't the answer. If the passage is long, you might write a number for each paragraph (I, II, III), and tick off each number as you determine that the correct sentence is not located in that paragraph.

Now let's give these new question types a try!

The sample questions below are based on this passage:

> Physicist Robert Oppenheimer, director of the fateful Manhattan Project, said "It is a profound and necessary truth that the deep things in science are not found because they are useful; they are found because it was possible to find them." In a later address at MIT, Oppenheimer presented the thesis that scientists could be held only very nominally responsible for the consequences of their research and discovery. Oppenheimer asserted that ethics, philosophy, and politics have very little to do with the day-to-day work of the scientist, and that scientists could not rationally be expected to predict all the effects of their work. Yet, in a talk in 1945 to the Association of Los Alamos Scientists, Oppenheimer offered some reasons why the Manhattan project scientists built the atomic bomb; the justifications included "fear that Nazi Germany would build it first" and "hope that it would shorten the war."

For question #1, consider each of the three choices separately and select all that apply.

1. The passage implies that Robert Oppenheimer would most likely have agreed with which of the following views:

    [A] Some scientists take military goals into account in their work
    [B] Deep things in science are not useful
    [C] The everyday work of a scientist is only minimally involved with ethics

2. Select the sentence in which the writer implies that Oppenheimer has not been consistent in his view that scientists have little consideration for the effects of their work.

[Here, you would highlight the appropriate sentence with your mouse. Note that there are only four options.]

Solutions:

1. {A, C} Oppenheimer says in the last sentence that one of the reasons the bomb was built was scientists' "hope that it would shorten the war." Thus, Oppenheimer would likely agree with the view that "Some scientists take military goals into account in their work." B is a trap answer using familiar language from the passage. Oppenheimer says that scientific discoveries' possible usefulness is not why scientists make discoveries; he does not say that the discoveries aren't useful. Oppenheimer specifically says that ethics has "very little to do with the day-to-day work of the scientist," which is a good match for "only minimally involved with ethics."

   Strategy Tip: On "Select One or More Answer Choices," write ABC on your paper and mark each choice with a check, an X, or a symbol such as ~ if you're not sure. This should keep you from crossing out all three choices and having to go back (at least one of the choices must be correct). For example, let's say that on a different question you had marked

   > *A. X*
   > *B. X*
   > *C. ~*

   The one you weren't sure about, (C), is likely to be correct, since there must be at least one correct answer.

2. The correct sentence is: **Yet, in a talk in 1945 to the Association of Los Alamos Scientists, Oppenheimer offered some reasons why the Manhattan project scientists built the atomic bomb; the justifications included "fear that Nazi Germany would build it first" and "hope that it would shorten the war."** The word "yet" is a good clue that this sentence is about to express a view contrary to the views expressed in the rest of the passage.

Verbal: Text Completion Questions

Text Completions are the new, souped-up Sentence Completions. They can consist of 1–5 sentences with 1–3 blanks. When Text Completions have two or three blanks, you will select words for those blanks independently. There is no partial credit; you must make every selection correctly.

Because this makes things a bit harder, the GRE has kindly reduced the number of possible choices per blank from five to three. Here is an old two-blank Sentence Completion, as it would appear on the old GRE:

Old Format:

> Leaders are not always expected to _____ the same rules as are those they lead; leaders are often looked up to for a surety and presumption that would be viewed as _____ in most others.

> A. obey ... avarice
>
> B. proscribe ... insalubriousness
>
> C. decree ... anachronism
>
> D. conform to ... hubris
>
> E. follow ... eminence

And here's how this same sentence would appear on the new exam.

New Format:

Leaders are not always expected to (i) _____ the same rules as are those they lead; leaders are often looked up to for a surety and presumption that would be viewed as (ii) _____ in most others.

Blank (i)	Blank (ii)
decree	hubris
proscribe	avarice
conform to	anachronism

On the new GRE, you will select your two choices by actually clicking and highlighting the words you want.

Solution:

In the first blank, we need a word similar to "follow." In the second blank, we need a word similar to "arrogant." Only choice D works in the old format; in the new format, the answer is still "conform to" and "hubris," but you'll make the two choices separately.

Note that in the "Old Format" question, if you knew that you needed a word in the second blank that meant something like "arrogant," and you knew that "hubris" was the only word in the second column with the correct meaning, you could pick correct answer choice D without even considering the first word in each pair. In the new format, this strategy is no longer available to us.

Also note that, in the "Old Format" question, "obey," "conform to," and "follow" mean basically the same thing. On the new GRE, this can't happen: since you select each word independently, no two choices can be synonyms (otherwise, there would be two correct answers).

Strategy Tip: As on the old GRE, do NOT look at the answer choices until you've decided for yourself, based on textual clues actually written in the sentence, what kind of word needs to go in each blank. Only then should you look at the choices and eliminate those that are not matches.

Let's try an example with three blanks.

For Kant, the fact of having a right and having the (i) _____ to enforce it via coercion cannot be separated, and he asserts that this marriage of rights and coercion is compatible with the freedom of everyone. This is not at all peculiar from the standpoint of modern political thought—what good is a right if its violation triggers no enforcement (be it punishment or (ii) _____)? The necessity of coercion is not at all in conflict with the freedom of everyone, because this coercion only comes into play when someone has (iii)_____ someone else.

Blank (ii)	Blank (ii)	Blank (iii)
technique	amortization	questioned the hypothesis of
license	reward	violated the rights of
prohibition	restitution	granted civil liberties to

Manhattan **GRE** Prep

Solution:

In the first sentence, use the clue "he asserts that this marriage of rights and coercion is compatible with the freedom of everyone" to help fill in the first blank. Kant believes that "coercion" is "married to" rights and is compatible with freedom for all. So we want something in the first blank like "right" or "power." Kant believes that rights are meaningless without enforcement. Only the choice "license" can work (while a "license" can be physical, like a driver's license, "license" can also mean "right").

The second blank is part of the phrase "punishment or _____," which we are told is the "enforcement" resulting from the violation of a right. So the blank should be something, other than punishment, that constitutes enforcement against someone who violates a right. (More simply, it should be something bad!) Only "restitution" works. Restitution is compensating the victim in some way (perhaps monetarily or by returning stolen goods).

In the final sentence, "coercion only comes into play when someone has _____ someone else." Throughout the text, "coercion" means enforcement against someone who has violated the rights of someone else. The meaning is the same here. The answer is "violated the rights of."

The complete and correct answer is this combination:

Blank (i)	Blank (ii)	Blank (iii)
license	restitution	violated the rights of

In theory, there are $3 \times 3 \times 3 = 27$ possible ways to answer a 3-blank Text Completion—and only one of those 27 ways is correct. The guessing odds will go down, but don't be intimidated. Just follow the basic process: come up with your own filler for each blank, and match to the answer choices. If you're confused by this example, don't worry! We'll start from the beginning in our *Text Completion & Sentence Equivalence* strategy guide.

Strategy Tip: As on the old GRE, do NOT "write your own story." The GRE cannot give you a blank without also giving you a clue, physically written down in the passage, telling you what kind of word or phrase MUST go in that blank. Find that clue. You should be able to give textual evidence for each answer choice you select.

Verbal: Sentence Equivalence Questions

In this question type, you are given one sentence with a single blank. There are six answer choices, and you are asked to pick TWO choices that fit the blank and are alike in meaning.

Of the new question types, this one depends the most on vocabulary and also yields the most to strategy.

No partial credit is given on Sentence Equivalence; both correct answers must be selected. When you pick two of six choices, there are 15 possible combinations of choices, and only one is correct. However, this is not nearly as daunting as it sounds.

Think of it this way—if you have six choices, but the two correct ones must be "similar in meaning," then you have, at most, three possible PAIRS of choices. Maybe fewer, since not all choices are guaranteed to have a "partner." If you can match up the "pairs," you can seriously narrow down your options.

Here is a sample set of answer choices:

[A] tractable

[B] taciturn

[C] arbitrary

[D] tantamount

[E] reticent

[F] amenable

We haven't even given you the question here, because we want to point out how much you can do with the choices alone, if you have studied vocabulary sufficiently.

TRACTABLE and AMENABLE are synonyms (tractable, amenable people will do whatever you want them to do). TACITURN and RETICENT are synonyms (both mean "not talkative"). ARBITRARY (based on one's own will) and TANTAMOUT (equivalent) are not similar in meaning and therefore cannot be a pair. Therefore, the ONLY possible answers are {A, F} and {B, E}. We have improved our chances from 1 in 15 to a 50/50 shot without even reading the question!

Of course, in approaching a Sentence Equivalence, we do want to analyze the sentence the same way we would with a Text Completion—read for a textual clue that tells you what type of word MUST go in the blank. Then look for a matching pair.

Strategy Tip: If you're sure that a word in the choices does NOT have a partner, cross it out! For instance, if A and C are partners, and E and F are partners, and you're sure B and D are not each other's partners, cross out B and D completely. They cannot be the answer together, nor can either one be part of the answer.

The sentence for the answer choice above could read,

> Though the dinner guests were quite _____ , the hostess did her best to keep the conversation active and engaging.

Thus, B and E are the best choices. Let's try an example.

While athletes usually expect to achieve their greatest feats in their teens or twenties, opera singers don't reach the _____ of their vocal powers until middle age.

[A] harmony

[B] zenith

[C] acme

[D] terminus

[E] nadir

[F] cessation

Solution:

Those with strong vocabularies might go straight to the choices to make pairs. ZENITH and ACME are synonyms, meaning "high point, peak." TERMINUS and CESSATION are synonyms, meaning "end." NADIR is a low point and HARMONY is present here as a trap answer reminding us of opera singers. *Cross off A and E, since they do not have partners.* Then, go back to the sentence, knowing that your only options are a pair meaning "peak" and a pair meaning "end."

The answer is {B, C}.

Math: Quantitative Comparison

This format is a holdover from the old exam. Here's a quick example:

Quantity A	**Quantity B**
x	x^2

(A) Quantity A is greater.
(B) Quantity B is greater.
(C) The two quantities are equal.
(D) The relationship cannot be determined from the information given.

Solution: If $x = 0$, the quantities are equal. If $x = 2$, quantity B is greater. Thus, we don't have enough information.

The answer is D.

Let's look at the new math question formats.

Math: Select One or More Answer Choices

According to the *Official Guide to the GRE Revised General Test*, the official directions for "Select One or More Answer Choices" read as follows:

> Directions: Select one or more answer choices according to the specific question directions.
>
> If the question does not specify how many answer choices to select, select all that apply.
>
> The correct answer may be just one of the choices or as many as all of the choices, depending on the question.
>
> No credit is given unless you select all of the correct choices and no others.
>
> If the question specifies how many answer choices to select, select exactly that number of choices.

Note that there is no "partial credit." If three of six choices are correct and you select two of the three, no credit is given. It will also be important to read the directions carefully.

That said, many of these questions look *very* similar to those on the "old" GRE. For instance, here is a question that could have appeared on the GRE in the past:

If $ab = |a| \times |b|$, which of the following *must* be true?

I. $a = b$
II. $a > 0$ and $b > 0$
III. $ab > 0$

A.   II only
B.   III only
C.   I and III only
D.   II and III only
E.   I, II, and III

Solution: If $ab = |a| \times |b|$, then we know ab is positive, since the right side of the equation must be positive. If ab is positive, however, that doesn't necessarily mean that a and b are each positive; it simply means that they have the same sign.

I.   It is not true that a must equal b. For instance, a could be 2 and b could be 3.
II. It is not true that a and b must each be positive. For instance, a could be -3 and b could be -4.
III. True. Since $|a| \times |b|$ must be positive, ab must be positive as well.

The answer is B (III only).

Note that, if you determined that statement I was false, you could eliminate choices C and E before considering the remaining statements. Then, if you were confident that II was also false, you could safely pick answer choice B, III only, without even trying statement III, since "None of the above" isn't an option. That is, because of the multiple choice answers, it is sometimes not necessary to consider each statement individually. This is the aspect of such problems that will change on the new exam.

Here is the same problem, in the new format.

If $ab = |a| \times |b|$, which of the following *must* be true?

Indicate <u>all</u> such statements.

[A] $a = b$
[B] $a > 0$ and $b > 0$
[C] $ab > 0$

Strategy Tip: Make sure to fully "process" the statement in the question (simplify it or list the possible scenarios) before considering the answer choices. This will save you time in the long run!

Here, we would simply select choice C. The only thing that has changed is that we can't do process of elimination; we must always consider each statement individually. On the upside, the problem has become much more straightforward and compact (not every real-life problem has exactly five possible solutions; why should those on the GRE?).

Math: Numeric Entry

This question type requires the text taker to key a numeric answer into a box on the screen. You are not able to "work backwards" from answer choices, and in many cases it will be difficult to make a guess. However, the principles being tested are the same as on the old GRE.

Here is a sample question:

If $x*y = 2xy - (x - y)$, what is the value of 3*4?

Solution:

We are given a function involving two variables, x and y, and asked to substitute 3 for x and 4 for y:

$$x*y = 2xy - (x - y)$$
$$3*4 = 2(3)(4) - (3 - 4)$$
$$3*4 = 24 - (-1)$$
$$3*4 = 25$$

The answer is 25.

Thus, you would type 25 into the box.

Okay. You've now got a good start on understanding the structure and question formats of the new GRE. Now it's time to begin fine-tuning your skills.

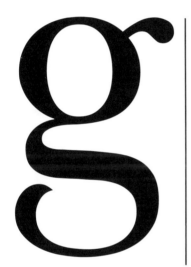

Chapter 2
of
READING COMPREHENSION & ESSAYS

READING COMPREHENSION PRINCIPLES

In This Chapter . . .

LOGISTICS OF READING COMPREHENSION

You are probably already familiar with Reading Comprehension from other standardized tests. You are given a passage to read, and you are asked questions about the substance and structure of the passage.

About half of the GRE Verbal Reasoning questions will be Reading Comprehension questions. This means you can expect about five passages per section. Each passage will be accompanied by one to four questions, for a total of ten Reading Comprehension questions per section.

Reading Comprehension Practice Formats

Long passages, which consist of about 460 words in three to five paragraphs, take up about 75–85 lines on the computer screen (or 25–30 printed lines in *The Official Guide to the GRE Revised General Test*). Since only about 25 lines fit on the screen, you will have to scroll three to four times just to read the passage. Each long passage will have about **four questions** associated with it (while *The Official Guide to the GRE Revised General Test* states that long passages can have up to six associated questions, official tests released by ETS always present long passages with only four associated questions). You can expect to see **one long passage** on your exam. There are only two examples of long passages in *The Official Guide to the GRE Revised General Test*, on pages 66 and 312.

Short passages, which consist of about 160 words in one or two paragraphs, take up about 25–33 lines on the computer screen (or 8–15 printed lines in *The Official Guide to the GRE Revised General Test*). Usually, you will have to scroll once to reveal the very bottom of a short passage. Most short passages will have one to three questions associated with it on the GRE, though it is possible to have as many as four. You can expect to see five to six short passages on your exam. Two examples of short passages on the GRE appear on pages 57 and 315 of *The Official Guide to the GRE Revised General Test*.

Argument Structure Passages (ASPs) consist of between 25 and 75 words in one paragraph, take up between five and eight lines on the computer screen (or two to five lines in *The Official Guide to the GRE Revised General Test*), and are sometimes no longer than a single sentence! You won't need to scroll to see the entire passage, and there will ALWAYS be only one associated question. You can expect to see about three of these passages per exam. While the GRE still considers ASPs part of Reading Comprehension, they are significantly different from short and long passages. Short and long passages give you information about a topic, with associated questions relevant either to the structure of the passage or its content. Argument Structure Passages will instead feature a short argument about which you will be asked the only salient question that the passage would allow. In other words, the passage has been written with only ONE question in mind. Because of this disparity, the recommended approach for ASPs is quite different from that for long and short passages.

All Reading Comprehension questions appear one at a time on the right side of the computer screen. The passage will always be visible on the left side of the screen while you answer the questions associated with that passage. On the new GRE, you are able to quickly click through and preview all the questions associated with a given passage. This kind of previewing can be helpful, but make sure you give the passage a start-to-finish read before attempting to answer any individual question. This is critical for your overall comprehension.

Reading Comprehension Question Formats

There are three question formats associated with Reading Comprehension passages:

> **1) Multiple Choice, Select One:** This is a traditional multiple-choice format, in which you must select ONLY ONE of five possible answer choices (labelled A–E, with circular buttons). It is recommended that you read all of the answer choices before making a decision. All questions associated with argument structure passages will be in this format.

2) Multiple Choice, Select-All-That-Apply: This format is also multiple-choice, only now there are just three possible answer choices (labelled A–C, with square-shaped buttons), and you must pick ALL OF THEM that apply. At least one must be correct, and it is just as likely that all three will be correct as that any one or two of them will be. This type of question makes guessing more difficult, as there are technically 7 different combinations of answers (A, B, C, A–B, A–C, B–C, and A–B–C), and there is no partial credit given for half-right answers. Make sure to evaluate each answer choice on its own; this question format should almost feel like three different questions in one.

3) Select-in-Passage: This question format asks you to click on the sentence in the passage that correctly answers a given question. For longer passages, the question will specify only one or two paragraphs with an arrow, and you will be unable to highlight anything in the rest of the passage. From a guessing perspective, the larger the specified area, the harder this type of question becomes.

Challenges of Reading Comprehension

The GRE makes Reading Comprehension difficult in several ways.

The content is demanding. Passages focus on specific and often unfamiliar topics in physical science (physics, astronomy, geology, chemistry), biological science (biology, ecology), social science, history, and other humanities (literature, art, music). No specialized knowledge beyond high school is assumed, but the passages are written for an educated post-college audience. In fact, at least some of the passages seem to be adapted from journals published in particular fields for educated laypeople. You might be neither knowledgeable nor enthusiastic about these fields.

You have to read on the screen. You cannot print the passage out and mark it up. Instead, you have to scroll a window up and down to see all of a long passage. Furthermore, reading on a computer screen is difficult on the eyes.

You have to read quickly. You should only take at most three minutes to read a passage and understand it (about one and a half minutes for a short or AS passage, about three minutes for a long passage). You may find Reading Comprehension frustrating for precisely this reason. If you had enough time, you could master almost any passage and answer almost any question correctly. But you do not have that luxury.

You have to stay with it. Reading Comprehension demands that you answer multiple questions about the same block of content. With other question types, if you get completely stuck on the content of a particular question, you can always take a guess and move on to another question about something completely different without incurring too drastic a penalty. But you cannot afford to give up so easily on a short or long Reading Comprehension passage, which have multiple associated questions. This means you must "tough it out" and wring a decent level of understanding out of every passage, no matter what.

Two Extremes and a Balanced Approach

One response to the challenges of Reading Comprehension is to become a **Hunter**. Hunters avoid the first read-through altogether, reasoning that most questions require some kind of detailed look-up anyway—so why not just skip the initial reading and go right to the questions? As their name implies, Hunters simply go "hunting" for the answer in a passage they have never read.

This strategy seems to save time up front, but you have to spend a lot more time per question. More importantly, this approach leads to many wrong answers. Without a good general understanding of the passage, Hunters can fall prey to trap answers.

At the other extreme, some GRE test-takers become **Scholars.** Scholars do a very careful first read-through, paying attention to details. "After all," Scholars worry, "I could be asked about any aspect of the passage—and if I skim over anything, how can I be sure that that one clause was not important, even critical, to my overall understanding?"

One obvious problem with this method is that it takes far too much time. More importantly, if you read <u>too</u> slowly and pay <u>too</u> much attention to all the details, you can easily lose sight of the big picture: the gist and structure of the whole passage. And the big picture is what you absolutely need to take away from the first read.

The middle ground between Hunters and Scholars is occupied by **Big Picture Readers**, who take a balanced approach. Before trying to answer the questions, they read the passage with an eye toward structure. At the beginning of the passage, Big Picture Readers go slowly, ensuring a solid grasp of the basics. But they go quickly at the end, keeping minor details at arm's length. They read ACTIVELY but EFFICIENTLY.

The goal of Big Picture Reading is to avoid finishing a passage and feeling that you just wasted your time—either because you got lost in the weeds, or because you skimmed over the passage at too removed a level to grasp any content.

How do you become a Big Picture Reader on the GRE? Here are **Seven Principles of Active, Efficient Reading** to guide you. Keep in mind that these rules apply more directly to long and short passages than to ASPs, which do not feature nearly as much "content," in terms of either length or detail.

Principle #1: Engage with the Passage

The first principle has to do with your <u>emotional attitude</u> toward the passage. The maxim *Engage with the Passage* is not as warm and fuzzy as it seems. It is based on a simple truth about your brain: you simply cannot learn something that you actively loathe or viscerally reject. So getting over your dread of the passage is not just a feel-good exercise. It is a prerequisite. You do not have to fall madly in love with medieval Flemish poetry or the chemistry of zinc, but you do have to stop keeping the topic at arm's length.

One quick and effective method is to **pretend that you really like this stuff**. Say to yourself, "This is great! I get to spend the next six minutes thinking about *sea urchins*!" Who knows—you might actually like them, learn something along the way, and do well on the questions (the most important thing).

Another way to help yourself get into the passage psychologically is to **identify good guys and bad guys**. If the sea urchins are threatened by environmental damage, get a little angry on their behalf. If you engage your emotions, you will both enjoy the passage more and recall it better than otherwise.

If you cannot stomach these steps, **simply acknowledge that you do not find the passage thrilling.** Allow yourself a moment of disappointment. Then hunker down and get back into it. Whatever you do, do not let yourself be pushed around by the passage. Love it or hate it, you have to own it.

The next six principles have to do with your <u>cognitive processes</u>: what you do with your brain as you do a Big Picture Read. To illustrate these processes, we will construct an analogy. Imagine, if you will, that your brain is a <u>company's headquarters</u>.

Recruiting for Your Working Memory, Inc.

More precisely, a <u>part</u> of your brain is like a company's headquarters: your **working memory**, where you store active thoughts. Your attention lives here. When you are thinking about sea urchins, your ideas about sea urchins live in your working memory. Only a few items fit at a time. Your working memory is the most valuable real estate in your brain.

Your job is to be the recruiter for the headquarters in your brain. A recruiter has two tasks: (1) to let <u>in</u> all the talented, important people AND (2) to keep <u>out</u> all the people who will not contribute.

As you read the passage, you have to act like a selective recruiter. You have to let the important parts into your working memory, but you also have to skim over the unimportant parts, so that you do not distract yourself with every last detail.

The next six principles explain how to be a good recruiter for your brain.

Principle #2: Look for the Simple Story

Every GRE passage has a **simple story—the gist or core meaning of the passage**. You must find this simple story on the first read-through.

How do you identify this simple story? Here are three different methods. Also, for now, do not worry about whether, or how, you write down the simple story as you read a passage. Just focus on finding that story.

1. Text It To Me. As you read, ask yourself this question: how would you retell all this stuff to an intelligent but bored teenager in just a couple of sentences? Can you give him or her just 5–10 words to describe a paragraph? You will find yourself cutting out the trivia.

Simplifying does not contradict the principle of being engaged with the content of the passage. You should be extremely interested in the passage, so you know what is important.

2. Make a Table of Contents. Alternatively, you can create a short table of contents. Use five words or fewer for the headline of each paragraph. As written, these headlines may not sound exactly like a story, but they outline the same narrative.

3. Look for Content and Judgment. The parts of a simple story can generally be classified as Content or Judgment, as follows:

> <u>Content</u>: **the scientific, historical, or artistic subject matter of the passage.**
>
> >   (a) Causes (effects, evidence, logical results)
> >
> >   (b) Processes (steps, means, ends)
> >
> >   (c) Categories (examples, generalities)
>
> <u>Judgment</u>: **what the author and any other people believe about the Content.**
>
> >   (a) Theories and Hypotheses
> >
> >   (b) Evaluations and Opinions
> >
> >   (c) Comparisons and Contrasts
> >
> >   (d) Advantages and Disadvantages

You can think of the simple story in a few different ways. However you approach the issue, remember the **KISS Principle: Keep It Simple, Stupid!**

Reminder: Don't Forget the Twist. Even as you look for the simple story, realize that on the GRE, there will often be some important <u>qualification</u> or <u>contrast</u>—a **key twist** or two in the road. A "qualification" is a restriction or a limiting factor. After all, such twists help the GRE ask difficult questions. Be ready to incorporate a key twist or even two in your simple story.

For example, a passage might be about the worldwide decline in the population of bees. In describing various theories, the passage might emphasize a distinction between the pessimistic theories shared by most scientists and the optimistic theory of one Scientist X, who believes that the decline is taking place within a natural oscillation.

The simple story might go like this:

> The number of bees in the world is falling fast. There are a few possible explanations, including pollution, climate change, and loss of habitat. Most scientists think this decline is a serious problem caused by human activity, but Scientist X thinks it's part of a natural cycle and the bees will come back soon on their own.

Manhattan GRE® Prep
the new standard

Here, the contrast is between what most scientists believe about the bee decline and what Scientist X believes.

Principle #3: Link to What You Already Know

When you read words on a page, they typically activate pre-existing knowledge in your head. This is a crucial part of comprehending what you are reading. Every word that you know in the English language is naturally tied to a web of memories and ideas. In fact, if a word does NOT activate ideas when you read it, it might as well be *zzyrglbzrch*!

Normally, your brain wakes up these ideas and memories as a natural part of reading. However, under stress, your eyes can pass over words and even recognize them, but no ideas come to life in your brain. You are too distracted and overwhelmed, and the words on the page remain "just words."

In this case, try **concretizing**. That is, **actively *imagine* what the words are referring to**. Re-explain the original text to yourself. Visualize what it represents. Indulge in simplifications, even stereotypes. Make up examples and use any other
mental handles that you can.

Of course, there is a danger in actively concretizing part of a GRE passage—you might introduce outside ideas. However, that danger is small in comparison to the worse problem of *not understanding at all* what you are reading, especially at the start of a passage.

Consider the following sentence, which could be the opening of a passage:

> Most exobiologists—scientists who search for life on other planets or moons—agree that carbon probably provides the backbone of any extraterrestrial biological molecules, just as it does of terrestrial ones, since carbon is unique among the elements in its ability to form long, stable chains of atoms.

Ideally, you can read this sentence and grasp it without any problems. Under exam pressure, however, you might need some help understanding the sentence.

In your mind, you might concretize this sentence in the following manner:

Words	Concretized Ideas
...exobiologists–scientists...	smart folks in white coats
...who search for life on other planets or moons...	who peer through telescopes looking for little green men
...carbon probably provides the backbone of extraterrestrial biological molecules...	carbon: charcoal, key element in living things backbone: like a spine to a little molecule
...its ability to form long, stable chains of atoms.	carbon can make long, stable chains like bones in a backbone or links in a physical chain

You should NOT write this concretization down (except as an exercise during your preparation). The process should happen quickly in your head. Moreover, as you read further into the passage, the need to concretize should diminish. In fact, if you do too much concretizing along the way, you might introduce too many outside ideas and lose track of what is actually written in the passage. However, concretizing can help you make sense of a difficult opening paragraph, so you should practice this technique.

Principle #4: Unpack the Beginning

You must understand the first few sentences of every passage, because they supply critical context for the entire passage. If you do not grasp these sentences at first, you have two choices. Either you can take more time with them right away, or you can read a little further and gather more context. In the latter case, you MUST go back and re-acquire those initial sentences later.

All too often, GRE students satisfy themselves with an "impressionistic" sense of the beginning of a passage. However, **forming an impression is not the same as comprehending the passage**. Given the importance of the initial sentences, you should make sure you grasp 100% of the beginning of any passage (even if you only grasp 40% of the end). That is far better than comprehending 70% of the text throughout.

Complicating matters, the GRE often opens passages with long, opaque sentences. How do you make sure you understand them, either now or later? The process of concretizing can help. You can also use the **unpacking** technique. Academic language is often dense with long noun phrases formed out of simple sentences. **To unpack an academic-style sentence, turn it into a few simple sentences** that express essentially the same meaning.

In general, you should NOT write this unpacking out (except as an exercise) or apply it throughout the passage. Like concretizing, unpacking is a powerful tool to smash open resistant language, especially at the start of the passage. Use this technique judiciously.

The steps to unpacking a complex sentence are as follows:

1. Grab a concrete noun first. Pick something that you can touch and that causes other things to happen. Do not necessarily pick something at the start of the sentence.

2. Turn actions back into verbs. In academic language, verbs are often made into noun or adjective phrases. Re-create the verbs. Also, feel free to start with *There is* or *There was*.

3. Put only ONE simple thought in a sentence. One subject, one verb.

4. Link each subsequent sentence to the previous one, using *this* or *these*. For instance, *This resulted in…* This process mimics speech, which is usually easy to understand.

5. Simplify or "quote off" details. If a jargon word is used in an important way, put quotes around it. Think to yourself
"*…whatever that means…*" and keep going. If the term is necessary, you will figure it out from context later.

Consider this example opening of a passage:

> In a diachronic investigation of possible behavioral changes resulting from accidental exposure
> in early childhood to environmental lead dust, two sample groups were tracked over decades.

1. Grab a concrete noun first, especially a cause. A good candidate is *lead dust*. The first sentence could simply be this: *There was lead dust in various environments.*

2. Turn other parts of speech, such as action nouns and adjectives, back into verbs. For instance, *exposure* becomes *were exposed. Behavioral* becomes *behaved.*

3. Put only one thought in a sentence, such as *There was lead dust in various environments.*

4. Link each sentence to the previous with *this/these*. So the second sentence could read *Young children in these environments were exposed to this dust by accident.*

5. Simplify or "quote off" details or jargon. For instance, the term *"diachronic"* needs a pair of quotes, so that you do not focus on it. You might even think of it just as *"d-something."*

The final list of a few simple sentences could come out this way:

(1) There was lead dust in various environments.

(2) Young children in these environments were exposed to this dust by accident.

(3) This exposure may have changed how the children behaved.

(4) This whole matter was investigated.

(5) In this "diachronic" investigation, two sample groups were tracked over time.

This unpacked "story" is easier to dive into and understand than the original sentence—even though the story contains nearly twice as many words! Also note that the subject and verb of the original sentence do not appear until the end. This phenomenon is very common. Often, it is easiest to understand the outer "frame" of the original sentence *last.*

Again, it is often not practical to employ such an elaborate process in real time on the GRE. However, knowing how to break down a complex sentence into its component ideas can help you read more efficiently in general. In addition, you can use this technique if you are stuck on one of the early sentences, although it will require some effort.

Incidentally, the ten-dollar word *diachronic* means "happening over time" in certain technical settings. If you needed to know that word, you would be able to infer its meaning from context. For instance, the passage might contrast this decades-long *diachronic* investigation with a *synchronic* study of a cross-section of people all examined at one time. For GRE passages, you need to have an educated adult's working vocabulary, but you will not need advanced knowledge of truly specialized jargon. For more on this issue, see the *Vocabulary and Idioms chapter at the end of the book.*

Principle #5: Link to What You Have Just Read

As you read further, you must continue to ask yourself about the **meaning** and **purpose** of what you are reading. What does this sentence mean, in relation to everything else I have read? Why is this sentence here? What function does it serve in relation to the previous text?

In the unpacking technique, we saw the power of linking. Complicated ideas can be made digestible by breaking them into pieces and hooking them together. In writing, we do not always use *this* and *these*, but we often put references to old information at the beginnings of sentences, even complex ones, to hook them to previous material. Likewise, we tend to save new information for the ends of sentences.

What kinds of relationships can a sentence have to the previous text? In general, you should think about these possibilities:

(1) Is the new sentence **expected or surprising**?

(2) Does it **support or oppose** earlier material?

(3) Does it **answer or ask** a question?

More specifically, the **Content/Judgment** framework that we encountered before can guide you. Do NOT use this framework as a checklist. Rather, simply be aware of the various possible relationships.

Content: the scientific or historical subject matter of the passage.

(a) Causes   (effects, evidence, logical results)

(b) Processes   (steps, means, ends)

(c) Categories   (examples, generalities)

<u>Judgment</u>: what the author and any other people believe about the Content.

    (a) Theories and Hypotheses

    (b) Evaluations and Opinions

    (c) Comparisons and Contrasts

    (d) Advantages and Disadvantages

Do not over-analyze as you read. You have been linking sentences together and making sense of them as a whole for many years—in fact, you are doing so now, as you read this chapter. We are just describing the process.

Principle #6: Pay Attention to Signals

To help link new material to previous text that you have read, you should be aware of various language signals.

First of all, **paragraph breaks** are important. They indicate something new. The sentences in the simple story often correspond to different paragraphs in the passage. If you take a "Table of Contents" approach to the simple story, your headlines correspond to the different paragraphs.

This does not mean that paragraphs cannot shift direction internally; they occasionally do. But paragraph breaks are not random. Each one marks a new beginning of some kind.

Second, **signal words** indicate relationships to previous text. Here are a number of such relationships, together with their common signals.

Relationship	Signal
Focus attention	As for; Regarding; In reference to
Add to previous point	Furthermore; Moreover; In addition; As well as; Also; Likewise; Too
Provide contrast	On one hand / On the other hand; While; Rather; Instead; In contrast; Alternatively
Provide conceding contrast (author unwillingly agrees)	Granted; It is true that; Certainly; Admittedly Despite; Although
Provide emphatic contrast (author asserts own position)	But; However; Even so; All the same; Still; That said Nevertheless; Nonetheless; Yet; Otherwise; Despite
Dismiss previous point	In any event; In any case
Point out similarity	Likewise; In the same way
Structure the discussion	First, Second, *etc.*; To begin with; Next; Finally; Again
Give example	For example; In particular; For instance
Generalize	In general; To a great extent; Broadly speaking
Sum up, perhaps with exception	In conclusion; In brief; Overall; Except for; Besides
Indicate logical result	Therefore; Thus; As a result; So; Accordingly; Hence
Indicate logical cause	Because; Since; As; Resulting from
Restate for clarity	In other words; That is; Namely; So to speak
Hedge or soften position	Apparently; At least; Can, Could, May, Might, Should; Possibly; Likely
Strengthen position	After all; Must, Have to; Always, Never, etc.
Introduce surprise	Actually; In fact; Indeed
Reveal author's attitude	Fortunately; Unfortunately; *other adverbs*; So-called

Principle #7: Pick Up the Pace

As you read the passage, go faster after the first few sentences. In your working memory, hold the growing jigsaw puzzle that is the big picture of the passage. As you read text later in the passage, ask whether what you are reading adds anything truly significant to that jigsaw puzzle. Toward the end, only dive into information that is clearly part of the big picture.

Do NOT get lost in details later on in the passage. Do NOT try to master every bit of content. You must read the whole
passage—but keep later parts at arm's length.

Only pay close attention to the following elements later on in a long passage:

> (1) **Beginnings of paragraphs**. The first or second sentence often functions as a topic sentence, indicating the
> content and/or purpose of the paragraph.

> (2) **Big surprises** or changes in direction.

> (3) **Big results**, answers or payoffs.

Everything else is just detail. Do not skip the later text entirely. You must pass your eyes over it and extract *some* meaning, so that if you are asked a specific question, you remember that you saw something about that particular point, and you know (sort of) where to look. Moreover, those big surprises and results can be buried in the middle of paragraphs. You must actually read the later paragraphs and make some sense of them.

Nevertheless, do not try to grasp the whole passage deeply the first time through. Your attention and your working memory are the most valuable assets you have on the GRE in general and on Reading Comprehension in particular. Allocate these assets carefully.

Summary: The 7 Principles of Active, Efficient Reading

To become a Big Picture Reader of GRE Reading Comprehension passages, follow these principles.

> (1) **Engage with the Passage**
>
> (2) **Look for the Simple Story**
>
> (3) **Link to What You Already Know**
>
> (4) **Unpack the Beginning**
>
> (5) **Link to What You Have Just Read**
>
> (6) **Pay Attention to Signals**
>
> (7) **Pick up the Pace**

Will you consciously go through each of these principles every time you read? Of course not. You need to practice them so that they become a natural part of your reading.

Practice on Non-GRE Material

Reading Comprehension may seem difficult to improve, especially in a short period of time. However, you can accelerate your progress by applying these principles to what you read *outside* of the GRE, as part of your daily life. Actively engage with the material, especially if you are not initially attracted to it. Look for the simple story. Link what you read to what you already know and to what you have just read. Unpack and/or concretize language if necessary. Pay attention to signals. And pick up the pace as you read, in order to avoid getting lost in details.

These principles work on a wide range of expository writing—a company's annual report, a book review in the newspaper, an article in your college alumni magazine. By applying these principles outside of a testing or test-prep environment, you will become much more comfortable with them.

Granted, some outside material is more GRE-like than other material. You should read major journals and newspapers, such as *The New Yorker, The Economist, The Wall Street Journal, The Atlantic,* and *The New York Times,* to become better informed about the world in general. However, these publications are somewhat *too* digestible. The paragraphs are too short, and neither the topics nor the writing itself is quite as boring as what you find on the GRE.

In this regard, **university alumni magazines** are good sources of articles that resemble Reading Comprehension passages in style and substance. (No offense to our alma maters!) Also, if you are not naturally attracted to science topics, then you should consider reading a few articles in *Scientific American* or similar publications that popularize the latest advances in science and technology. In this way, you can gain familiarity with science writing aimed at an educated but non-specialized audience.

You might also find appropriate online resources. For instance, the website www.aldaily.com (Arts and Letters Daily) is an excellent source of articles with high intellectual content. Reading Arts and Letters Daily is an excellent way to prepare for the Reading Comprehension portion of the exam while also filling your brain full of information that might come in handy for the GRE Issue Essay. Make sure to look up any words you don't know, and practice reading with an eye for the main idea, tone, and structure of an argument or article.

Problem Set

In problems #1–4, **concretize** each sentence. Focus on specific terms that you can visualize. Associate these terms with your knowledge and memories, and create a "mind's-eye" view of each sentence. Spend no more than 15–20 seconds per sentence. Then write down this concretization. (We do not suggest that you write down concretizations on the GRE, but by writing them down now as part of this exercise, you can compare them to the sample answers and develop your ability to concretize.)

1. Computer models of potential terrestrial climate change over the next century must take into account certain assumptions about physical and chemical processes.

2. Various popular works of art, from pulp novels to blockbuster films have been influenced by syncretic religious traditions such as candomblé, santeria, and voodoo but few such works treat these traditions with appropriate intelligence or sensitivity.

3. Given the complexity of the brain's perceptual and cognitive processes, it is not surprising that damage to even a small set of neurons can interfere with the execution of seemingly simple tasks.

4. The rise of Athenian democracy in ancient times can be considered a reaction to class conflict, most importantly between a native aristocracy and the inhabitants of nearby towns incorporated politically into the growing city-state.

In problems #5–8, **unpack** each complex sentence. That is, find a few simple sentences that convey the same information as the original sentence. Do the unpacking in your head first, then write down the unpacked sentences. (Do not write down unpacked sentences during the GRE, but by writing them down now as part of this exercise, you can compare them to the sample answers and develop your ability to unpack.)

5. The simplistic classification of living things as plant, animal, or "other" has been drastically revised by biologists in reaction to the discovery of microorganisms that do not fit previous taxonomic schemes.

6. Despite assurances to the contrary by governments around the world, the development of space as an arena of warfare is nearly certain, as military success often depends on not ceding the "high ground," of which outer space might be considered the supreme example.

7. Since the success of modern digital surveillance does not obviate the need for intelligence gathered via old-fashioned human interaction, agencies charged with counter-terrorism responsibilities must devote significant effort to planting and/or cultivating "assets"—that is, spies—within terrorist organizations that threaten the country.

8. Students learning to fly fixed-wing aircraft are taught to use memory devices, such as the landing checklist GUMPS ("gas, undercarriage, mixture, propeller, switches"), that remain constant even when not every element of the device is relevant, as in the case of planes with non-retractable landing gear.

Read the following passage, and then complete the exercises on the next page.

Passage: Pro-Drop Languages

In many so-called "pro-drop" or pronoun-drop languages, verbs inflect for subject number and person. That is, by adding a prefix or suffix or by changing in some other way, the verb itself indicates whether the subject is singular or plural, as well as whether the subject is first person (*I* or *we*), second person (*you*), or third person (*he*, *she*, *it*, or *they*). For example, in Portuguese, at least partially a pro-drop language, the verb *falo* means "I speak": the *–o* at the end of the word indicates first person, singular subject (as well as present tense). As a result, the subject pronoun *eu*, which means "I" in Portuguese, does not need to be used with *falo* except to emphasize who is doing the speaking. In this regard, Portuguese can also be called a null-subject language, since no word in the sentence *falo português* ("I speak Portuguese") plays the precise role of subject. Some pro-drop languages omit object pronouns as well.

It should be noted that not every language that drops its pronouns inflects its verbs for subject characteristics. Neither Chinese nor Japanese verbs, for instance, change form at all to indicate the number or person of the subject; however, personal pronouns in both subject and object roles are regularly omitted in both speech and writing, leaving the meaning to be inferred from contextual clues. Despite these similarities, Chinese and Japanese verbs are extremely different in other respects, since Chinese is an analytic language, in which words typically carry only one morpheme, or unit of meaning, whereas Japanese is an agglutinative language, in which individual words are often composed of many glued-together morphemes.

It should also be noted that not every language that inflects its verbs for subject person and number drops subject pronouns in all non-emphatic contexts. Linguists argue about the pro-drop status of the Russian language, but there is no doubt that, although the Russian present-tense verb *govoryu* ("I speak") unambiguously indicates a first person, singular subject, it is common for Russian speakers to express "I speak" as *ya govoryu*, in which *ya* means "I," without indicating either emphasis or contrast.

Nevertheless, Russian speakers do frequently drop subject and object pronouns; one study of adult and child speech indicated a pro-drop rate of 40-80%. Moreover, personal pronouns must in fact be dropped in some Russian sentences in order to convey particular meanings. It seems safe to conjecture that languages whose verbs inflect unambiguously for the person and number of the subject permit the subject pronoun to be dropped, if only under certain circumstances, in order to accelerate communication without loss of meaning. After all, in these languages, both the subject pronoun and the verb inflection convey the same information, so there is no real need both to include the subject pronoun and to inflect the verb.

9. Unpack the first two sentences of the first paragraph. That is, break them down into a series of simple linked sentences.

10. How does the second sentence of the first paragraph relate to the first sentence? What words indicate this relationship? Use the Content/Judgment framework, if it is helpful:

    Content: (a) Causes (effects; evidence; logical result)
                   (b) Processes (steps; means; end)
                   (c) Categories (example; generality)
    Judgment: (d) Theories/Hypotheses
                   (e) Evaluations/Opinions
                   (f) Comparisons/Contrasts
                   (g) Advantages/Disadvantages
                   (h) General Judgments (support/oppose; expected/surprising; answer/ask questions)

11. How do the third and fourth sentences of the first paragraph relate to what came before? Use the Content/Judgment framework.

12. Analyze the second paragraph, using the Content/Judgment framework. What does this paragraph say, in brief? How does this paragraph relate to the first paragraph? Where are the big surprises and big results, if any?

13. Perform the same analysis on the third paragraph.

14.   What is the simple story of this passage? Try one or more of these different styles:

      (a) Full Sentences

           • Summarize each paragraph in just a couple of sentences.

      (b) "Text It To Me"

           • Summarize each paragraph in 5–10 words or abbreviations.

           • Use symbols (such as = to equate two things).

           • Still try to express full thoughts.

      (c) Table of Contents

           • Give each paragraph a title or headline of no more than five words.

           • Do not try to express full thoughts.

Concretizations

These concretizations are specific examples. Your own concretizations will likely be different. Again, on the GRE, you will *never* write down full concretizations such as these. Rather, you need to practice the process so that you can carry it out quickly in your head.

1.

Words	Concretized Ideas
Computer models of potential terrestrial climate change over the next century...	Big computers in some laboratory running programs about <u>potential terrestrial climate change</u> (how the Earth's weather might change) over the next 100 years...
...must take into account certain assumptions about physical and chemical processes.	These programs must know, or assume, how physics and chemistry work: how water heats up and evaporates, for instance.

2.

Words	Concretized Ideas
Various popular works of art, from pulp novels to blockbuster films...	*Make up actual examples.* The latest Dan Brown book and James Bond movie.
...have been influenced by syncretic religious traditions such as candomblé, santeria, and voodoo...	These books & movies show a voodoo ritual or something.
...but few such works treat these traditions with appropriate intelligence or sensitivity.	These books and movies disrespect *real* voodoo and related religions. [*If you've seen Live & Let Die, you get the picture!*]

3.

Words	Concretized Ideas
Given the complexity of the brain's perceptual and cognitive processes...	The brain is complex. It does complex things, like a computer in your skull. <u>perceptual</u>: how we see and hear <u>cognitive</u>: how we think and reason Given all that...
...It is not surprising that damage to even a small set of neurons...	...it is not surprising that just a little brain damage (say, caused by a small stroke), frying some wires in the computer...
...can interfere with the execution of seemingly simple tasks.	...can mess up how you do even "simple" things (say, speaking aloud or riding a bike). After all, your computer would probably stop working completely if you opened it up and ripped out "just a few" wires.

4.

Words	Concretized Ideas
The rise of Athenian democracy in ancient times...	<u>Athenian democracy in ancient times</u>: Socrates, Plato, Pericles, etc. voting in a public square. Marble statues and pillars everywhere.
...can be considered a reaction to class conflict...	You can think of all that as the result of <u>class conflict</u>: different economic and social groups struggling with each other. The workers versus the nobles.
...most importantly between a native aristocracy and the inhabitants of nearby towns incorporated politically into the growing city-state.	<u>Native aristocracy</u>: the rich & powerful people of Athens. They are struggling with the people from the provinces who are now under Athens' thumb. The map of "greater Athens" grows.

<u>Unpacking</u>

Like the concretizations, these unpacked sentences are simply examples of the process. Your versions will likely differ. Note that unpacking often involves some concretizing as well. Again, you should not write down unpacked sentences during the GRE. This exercise is meant to develop your mental muscles, so you can take apart complex academic language.

5.   Living things can be classified as plant, animal, or "other."
This classification is simplistic.
In fact, it has been drastically revised by biologists.
Why? Because certain microorganisms (say, bacteria) have been discovered.
These microorganisms do not fit previous "taxonomic" schemes (that is, classifications).

6.   Space could be developed as an arena of warfare.
In fact, that's nearly certain to happen.
(Even though governments say otherwise.)
That's because to win wars, you often have to hold the "high ground."
And outer space may be the best "high ground" around.

7.   There is something called "modern digital surveillance" (say, spy bugs in cell phones).
This kind of surveillance has been successful.
But we still need people to gather "intelligence" by talking to other people.
So, the CIA etc. has to work hard to put "assets" (spies) inside Al Qaeda etc.

8.   There are people who learn to fly "fixed-wing aircraft."
These students learn memory devices.
An example of a memory device is GUMPS, which is a landing checklist.
These memory devices stay the same no matter what.
In fact, they stay the same even when part of the memory device does not apply.
An example is planes with "non-retractable" landing gear.

Passage: "Pro-Drop Languages"

9. The first two sentences could be unpacked in the following way:

> There are languages called "pronoun-drop" languages.
> In many of these languages, verbs "inflect" for number and person.
> That is, you change the verb itself somehow.
> This change shows who is doing the action (I, you, or someone else).
> The verb tells us whether that subject is singular or plural.
> The verb also tells us whether that subject is first, second, or third person.

10. The second sentence restates and **explains** the first sentence. A clear clue is given by the first three words: *In other words.* The second sentence provides **specific examples** to help the reader understand a general assertion in the first sentence: *verbs inflect for number and person.* Also, the second sentence is **neutral in tone** and attitude.

11. The third and fourth sentences provide an **even more specific example** of the phenomenon described in the first two sentences (*verbs inflect for number and person*). A clear clue is given at the start of the third sentence: *For example.* In the third sentence, we read about how the Portuguese verb *falo* is inflected. In the fourth sentence, we are told that the pronoun *eu* does not need to be used with *falo.* Again, the third and fourth sentences are **neutral in tone** and attitude.

12. The second paragraph provides **qualification and contrast** to the first paragraph. The second paragraph also provides **specific examples** to support this contrast.

In brief, the second paragraph makes these points:
- NOT every pro-drop language has verb inflections.
  - Example of Chinese & Japanese: pro-drop but not inflected.
- NOT every inflected-verb language drops its pronouns, either!
  - Example of Russian: inflected but not pro-drop.

Logically, the categories of (A) "pro-drop" and (B) "inflected verbs" can be seen as overlapping circles on a Venn diagram. The assertion in the first paragraph is that these two circles overlap. In other words, *some A = B.* The second paragraph counters that these circles do not completely overlap, nor does one circle completely contain the other. That is, *NOT all A = B, and NOT all B = A.*

The "big surprises" and results are these two qualifications. You do not have to master the examples, although you should read them and make some sense of them. Moreover, at this stage, you might not grasp the nuances of the complicated Russian example. This is okay, as long as you understand the big picture of this paragraph.

13. In the first two sentences, the third paragraph provides a **contrast to the contrast** by continuing with the example of Russian, which turns out to be at least somewhat pro-drop.

Then the third paragraph proposes a **hypothesis** (inflected-verb languages are at least partially prodrop) that follows from the Russian example. Finally, the paragraph offers a **rationale** for that hypothesis.

In brief, the third paragraph makes these points:

- Actually, Russian IS sometimes pro-drop.
- Hypothesis: Inflected-verb languages are at least partially pro-drop.
- Why? The inflection and the subject pronoun are redundant.

The switchback at the beginning might be considered a "big surprise." You need to grasp that the author is qualifying the example of the Russian language. Fortunately, you are given a clue in the very first word of the sentence, *Nevertheless*, which highlights a contrast to what came immediately prior. What follows *Nevertheless* is a position that the author wants to espouse.

The "big result" is the hypothesis in the third sentence. Note that this is the first time that the author goes beyond straight reporting and makes a claim: he or she states that *it is safe to conjecture* something.

14. The simple story of the passage can be expressed in at least three different styles.

> Full Sentences
> (1)   Many "pronoun-drop" languages have verbs that "inflect," or change.
> • The inflected verb tells you something about the subject.
> • So you can drop the subject pronoun.
> • Portuguese is an example.
>
> (2)   NOT every pro-drop language has verb inflections.
> • Chinese & Japanese are examples.
> Likewise, NOT every inflected-verb language is pro-drop!
> • Russian is an example.
>
> (3)   BUT, Russian is actually sort of pro-drop.
> SO I think inflected-verb languages are all sort of pro-drop.
> • Why? The inflected verb and the pronoun tell you the same thing.
>
> Text It To Me
> (1)   Pro-drop = inflect verbs. No subj.
>
> (2)   Not all pro-drop = inflect. Not all inflect = pro-drop, either.
>
> (3)   But actually, inflect = sort of pro-drop. Why repeat yrself.
>
> Table of Contents
> (1)   "Pronoun-Drop" Languages & Inflected Verbs
>
> (2)   Exceptions Both Way
>
> (3)   Inflected Verbs − Pro-Drop Anyway

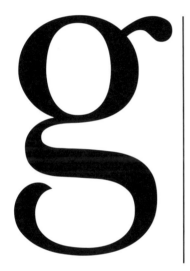

Chapter 3
of
READING COMPREHENSION & ESSAYS

INTRODUCTION TO SHORT & LONG PASSAGES

In This Chapter . . .

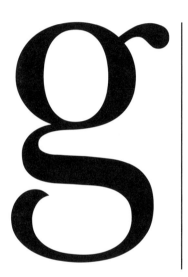

- Short vs. Long
- Components of Passages
- Foreshadowing

SHORT VS. LONG

In the next four chapters, we'll look at Short and Long Passages. Any general rules laid out in these chapters should be taken to apply ONLY to Short and Long Passages. Argument Structure Passages will be discussed later in this book.

Short and Long Passages are quite similar in both their overall content and their associated question types. However, there are a few important differences between the two.

1) **Length.** Long passages aren't just slightly longer than short passages. They're SIGNIFICANTLY longer. A long passage can be as much as three times as long as a short passage. This means you'll need to take far more time not only to read and outline the passage, but also to answer specific questions that require you to search through the passage for an answer. Keep this in mind when you're pacing yourself on the test. Only one of your verbal sections should have a long passage. If you struggle to finish your verbal sections in the time alotted, you might consider searching out and dealing with the long passage FIRST. Just remember, long passages generally have four associated questions, and the last thing you want to do is miss all of them because you didn't pace yourself well.

2) **Number of Questions.** Again, long passages will generally, but not always, have four associated questions. Short passages will usually have between one and three. Obviously, the more questions associated with a passage, the more essential it is that you grasp the passage.

3) **Complexity of detail.** Because of the length disparity between short and long passages, you should expect far more detail in a long passage. Generally the first paragraph will be some kind of introduction, and the next two to three paragraphs will be full of dense details requiring significant unpacking. It may take multiple reads to fully understand these details.

4) **Complexity of argument.** Because long passages tend to be 3–4 paragraphs, it's possible to create complex arguments. But in a longer passage, it's possible to begin by positing an old theory, then twisting to reveal a new theory, then twisting AGAIN to present problems with the new theory. Your outline for long passages should reflect this increased complexity. In a 1–2 paragraph short passage, there is only room for one twist.

Components of Passages

Reading Comprehension passages cover a wide range of topics and are structured in many different ways. However, all passages are made up of certain components. By understanding and looking for these components, you can more easily grasp the meaning and structure of the passage.

Any Reading Comprehension passage has four possible components:

(1) The Point
(2) Background
(3) Support
(4) Implications

We will consider each of these components in turn.

The Point

The Point is **the most important message of the passage**. In other words, the author has written the passage in order to convey the Point, even if nothing else gets through to the reader. The Point explains why the passage is interesting, at least in the author's opinion.

Every passage, long or short, contains a Point. Perhaps surprisingly, the Point is sometimes made explicit in a single sentence. In the "Pro-Drop Languages" passage from last chapter, the Point is the hypothesis put forward in the third paragraph:

> It seems safe to conjecture that **languages whose verbs inflect unambiguously for person and number permit pronoun dropping**, if only under certain circumstances, in order to accelerate communication without loss of meaning.

The author wants us to remember this Point. Of course, the author also wants us to understand how pro-drop languages work in general, how some pro-drop languages do not inflect their verbs, and so forth. But the most important message is this hypothesis, which is also the most important claim that the author puts forward.

How does the Point relate to the simple story of the passage, as discussed in Chapter 1? Very simply, **the Point is the crux of the simple story**. After all, the Point is the most important message that the author wants to convey. We can also relate the Point to the Content/Judgment framework. The Point contains the most important Judgment made by the author about the central Content of the passage.

Thus, a crucial task for you as reader is to **find the Point**! By the end of your first read-through, you should think about the simple story you have constructed. Use it to identify the Point.

Where is the Point in the passage? It can be almost anywhere. The way to find the Point is to ask "what is the most important message that the author is trying to convey in this passage? If I had to choose, what would be the one thing I should take away from reading this passage?"

The Point may be any kind of important message, but across sample passages, we observe a few common varieties that sometimes overlap:

(a) **Resolution:** resolves an issue or a problem
(b) **Answer:** answers a question (similar to Resolution)
(c) **New Idea:** describes a surprising new idea, theory or research result
(d) **Reason:** explains an observation

During the GRE, you will *not* have to classify the Point as one of the preceding types. Rather, this list is meant to help you identify and understand the Point as you read a variety of passages.

Notice that **the Point is related to a passage's purpose**. The point is what the author wants to *convey*. The purpose of a passage is generally to convey that Point. However, the purpose can often be described more broadly or abstractly as well. For instance, the purpose of the "Pro-Drop Languages" passage is to describe how languages may be categorized as pro-drop and as verb-inflecting, and to discuss the complex relationship between these two types of languages.

Also note that the Point may not make a lot of sense on its own. For instance, in order to understand and be convinced that *languages whose verbs inflect unambiguously for person and number permit pronoun dropping*, you need to understand the rest of the "Pro-Drop Languages" passage.

Occasionally, the Point is spread across two sentences, or it may be less than explicit. However, most passages have a clear Point within a single sentence.

Note that passages do not always make impassioned arguments or take strong positions, so the Point of a passage might be less of a "claim" than the conclusion of an argument. Sometimes the Point of a passage is just the most

interesting and general fact about the topic. The author may simply wish to inform the reader of this fact, rather than convince the reader of a debatable position.

Simply looking for the Point as you read will make you a more active reader. You will find that your comprehension of each passage will improve as a result.

Background, Support, and Implications

The other components all relate to the Point in some way.

1. **The Background is information you need to understand the Point.** The context and the basic facts about the topic are given in the Background. This component may be brief.

2. **The Support is evidence, assertions, and opinions FOR the Point.** The Support might include concessions to the other side of the argument. This component is always present and often constitutes a substantial portion of the passage.

The Background and the Support may be intertwined. It is never important to determine whether a particular sentence is Background or Support. A sentence can provide background information and support the Point at the same time.

3. **The Implications result from the Point.** In other words, the author now assumes that you are convinced of the Point and so begins to enumerate the consequences. Implications are not always present, but when they are, they tend to be important.

Although you do not have to separate Background and Support in every case, you should understand what you are reading in terms of the four components:

- Is this the main message? If so, this is the Point.
- Is this just background information? If so, this is Background.
- Is this supporting evidence for the main message? If so, this is Support.
- Is this an implication of the main message? If so, this is an Implication.

Foreshadowing

Some part of the Background or the Support may also function as foreshadowing. **Foreshadowing sets up the Point.** It often does so by standing in contrast to the Point.

Foreshadowing		Point
Problem....................	leads to	Resolution
Question....................	leads to	Answer
Old Idea....................	leads to	New Idea
Observation..............	leads to	Reason or New Idea

An Old Idea might be a typical expectation or way of thinking (e.g., *Traditionally, lower returns on investments correlate with lower risk*). An Observation often expresses not only a fact but also an opinion about that fact (e.g., *The decision about where to store high-level nuclear waste for millennia has unfortunately not been resolved*). Note that in both of these examples, an adverb (*traditionally, unfortunately*) sets up a contrast that will be made explicit with the Point.

Note that just as you will never have to classify the Point on the GRE, you will not have to classify the foreshadowing. This list is only meant to help you identify and understand the relationships between any foreshadowing and the Point.

Foreshadowing is not always present. Do not rely on foreshadowing to identify the Point. However, if foreshadowing is present, it can help you to find the Point more quickly and easily.

Problem Set

Answer the questions below by referring to the following passage.

Passage: Rock Flour

Although organic agriculture may seem to be the wave of the future, some experts believe that the next stage in agricultural development requires the widespread adoption of something very inorganic: fertilizer made from powdered rocks, also known as rock flour. The biochemical processes of life depend not only on elements commonly associated with living organisms, such as oxygen, hydrogen, and carbon (the fundamental element of organic chemistry), but also on many other elements in the periodic table. Specifically, plants need the so-called "big six" nutrients: nitrogen, phosphorus, potassium, calcium, sulfur, and magnesium. In modern industrial agriculture, these nutrients are commonly supplied by traditional chemical fertilizers. However, these fertilizers omit trace elements, such as iron, molybdenum and manganese, that are components of essential plant enzymes and pigments. For instance, the green pigment chlorophyll, which turns sunlight into energy that plants can use, requires iron. As crops are harvested, the necessary trace elements are not replaced and become depleted in the soil. Eventually, crop yields diminish, despite the application or even over-application of traditional fertilizers. Rock flour, produced in abundance by quarry and mining operations, may be able to replenish trace elements cheaply and increase crop yields dramatically.

It may also be possible to restore forest health through the application of rock flour. Near Asheville, North Carolina, as part of a greenhouse study, hundreds of red spruce and Fraser fir trees were planted in depleted mountain soils that were remineralized with rock flour to varying degrees. Rock-dusted trees not only grew significantly faster than controls, at rates correlating with the application amount, but also manifested improved resistance to disease, demonstrated by increased survival rates. Preliminary field trials have also indicated that remineralization helps alleviate the deleterious effects of acid rain, which drains key nutrients from forest soils.

Not all rock flour would be suitable for use as fertilizer. Certain chemical elements, such as lead and cadmium, are poisonous to humans; thus, applying rock flour containing significant amounts of such elements to farmland would be inappropriate, even if the crops themselves do not accumulate the poisons, because human contact could result directly or indirectly (e.g., via soil runoff into water supplies). However, most rock flour produced by quarries seems safe for use. After all, glaciers have been creating natural rock flour for thousands of years as they advance and retreat, grinding up the ground underneath. Glacial runoff carries this rock flour into rivers; downstream, the resulting alluvial deposits are extremely fertile. If the use of man-made rock flour is incorporated into agricultural practices, it may be possible to make open plains as rich as alluvial soils. Such increases in agricultural productivity will be necessary to feed an ever more crowded world.

1. What is the Point of this passage? Justify your choice. Categorize the Point: (a) Resolution, (b) Answer, (c) New Idea, or (d) Reason. (The Point may fall into more than one category.)

2. Identify the other components of the passage, if present: Background, Support, and Implications. Again, justify your assignments.

3. Identify any foreshadowing, if present. If there is foreshadowing, categorize it: (a) Problem, (b) Question, (d) Old Idea, or (d) Observation. (Like the Point, foreshadowing may fall into more than one category.)

4. What is the simple story of this passage?

1. The Point of this passage is contained in the first sentence of the first paragraph: *Some experts believe that the next stage in agricultural development requires the widespread adoption of something very inorganic: fertilizer made from powdered rocks, also known as "rock flour."* This is the most important message that the author intends to convey.

Two other candidates for the Point say nearly the same thing, as they extol the potential benefits of rock flour. In fact, these other sentences are perhaps even more emphatic than the Point itself, but they are slightly narrower in scope.

(a) Last sentence, first paragraph: *Rock flour... may be able to replenish trace elements cheaply and increase crop yields dramatically.* This sentence explains <u>how</u> rock flour may be able to help us achieve *the next stage in agricultural development*. Thus, this sentence is Support for the Point.

(b) Second to last sentence, second paragraph: *If the use of man-made rock flour is incorporated into agricultural practices, it may be possible to make open plains as rich as alluvial soils.* This sentence practically restates the Point in concrete terms. However, those concrete terms (*open plains, alluvial soils*) are more specific than the Point. Thus, this sentence should also be classified as Support for the Point.

Categorization of the Point:
The Point is a New Idea: a new type of fertilizer that may seem surprising initially. Alternatively, the Point can be considered the Resolution to a Problem (the depletion of trace elements essential for plant growth). As was mentioned in the text, it is not important for you to determine whether the Point is a New Idea or a Resolution; it could be both. These categories are only there to help you recognize and understand the Point.

2. The other parts of the passage can be labeled thus.

Background: First paragraph
           First clause, first sentence: *Although organic agriculture... future,*
           Second sentence: *The biochemical processes... periodic table.*
           Third sentence: *Specifically,... magnesium.*
           Fourth sentence: *In modern... traditional chemical fertilizers.*

These sentences give information, but they do not delineate the problem that must be solved.

Support: First paragraph
           Fifth sentence: *However, these fertilizers omit... pigments.*
           all the way through to
           Second paragraph
           Second to last sentence: *If the use... alluvial soils.*

This Support begins from the *However*, which introduces the problem. The rest of that paragraph explains the problem that rock flour solves.

Note that the Support includes the qualifications and concessions in the first half of the second paragraph.

Implications: Second paragraph
           Last sentence: *Such increases... more crowded world.*

This sentence tells us the result of the Point. That is, if you accept the Point, then with the *resulting increases in agricultural productivity*, we may able to *feed the world!*

3. The first clause of the first sentence (*Although organic agriculture may seem to be the wave of the future*) is foreshadowing. This foreshadowing sets up the Point by telling us what may <u>seem</u> to be the solution (implying that something else IS the solution). Note that this foreshadowing is immediately followed by the Point itself. This juxtaposition is not unusual.

The category of foreshadowing is Old Idea (the old "new idea" of *organic agriculture*, as the author implies). Thus, we can now see that the Point is really New Idea: an idea that may solve a problem, of course, but we do not learn about that problem in the foreshadowing.

4. As we saw in the last chapter, the simple story of the passage can be expressed in at least three different styles.

<u>Full Sentences</u>
(1) Some think the future of agriculture depends on rock flour (= powdered rock).
- Plants require certain elements.
- Normal fertilizers do not give you the <u>trace</u> elements such as iron.
- Rock flour might fill the gap.
(2) Some rock flour is bad, even poisonous.
BUT most would be fine.
Glaciers make natural rock flour which is good for the soil.
If we use rock flour, maybe we can feed the world.

<u>Text It To Me</u>
(1) Agricult. future = rock flour (= powder). Gives plants missing trace elems.
(2) Some flour = bad. But glaciers make it & it's good. Might feed the world.

<u>Table of Contents</u>
(1) Rock Flour as Future of Agriculture
(2) Concerns; Reassuring Glaciers

Chapter 4
of
READING COMPREHENSION & ESSAYS

SHORT
PASSAGES

In This Chapter . . .

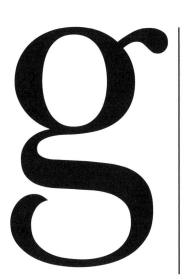

- Short Passages: An Overview
- Don't Just Read, Do Something!
- The Headline List
- Common Notations
- Using Your Headline List
- Timing for Short Passages
- Model Short Passage: **Insect Behavior**
- Model Headline List: **Insect Behavior**

SHORT PASSAGES

As noted in Chapter 1, short passages consist of about 160 words in one to two short paragraphs, usually with one to three associated questions. If you struggle with pacing on the GRE, you might want to do a quick preview of the number of questions associated with a given passage. If it's only one, you might be able to afford skipping or skimming that passage. If it's three, you absolutely can't afford anything but total comprehension. Previewing also helps you know what to pay special attention to while reading the passage.

To approach short passages, recall the Seven Principles of Active, Efficient Reading:

> (1) Engage with the Passage
>
> (2) Look for the Simple Story
>
> (3) Link to What You Already Know
>
> (4) Unpack the Beginning
>
> (5) Link to What You Have Just Read
>
> (6) Pay Attention to Signals
>
> (7) Pick up the Pace

Imagine that you are taking the GRE and up pops a new Reading Comprehension passage. How do you apply these reading principles? Let us imagine two scenarios:

> <u>Positive Scenario</u>: you are feeling good about your performance on the GRE overall and on the Verbal section in particular. You are on pace or even ahead of pace. You are focused and energetic. Even better, the passage is about killer whales—and you happen to have majored in marine biology, a subject close to your heart.

> <u>Negative Scenario</u>: you are feeling anxious about your performance on the GRE overall and on the Verbal section in particular. You are short on time. You are tired and scatterbrained. Making matters even worse, the passage is about killer whales—and you happen to hate biology. You even dislike the ocean.

In the Positive Scenario, it will be easy for you to apply the Seven Principles. You love the subject, you already know something about it, and you are in good shape on the exam. In this case, what you should do is **simply read the passage**. Enjoy it as you quickly digest it; simply be sure not to bring in outside knowledge. In the Positive Scenario, you can read the passage rapidly, easily, and effectively, and you can then move to answering the questions, a subject we will cover later in this book.

The Negative Scenario might happen to you during the GRE. In fact, it is likely that you will be stressed at least some of the time during the exam. Moreover, even in the best of circumstances, you *might* find that only one or two passages fall on your "home turf" of topics. The others will probably be unfamiliar territory. In addition, the GRE makes otherwise interesting passages as boring and tedious as possible by using dry, clinical language and overloading the passages with details.

So how do you apply the Seven Principles in the Negative Scenario: that is, when the passage is unfriendly and you are stressed out?

Don't Just Read, Do Something!

The temptation will be simply to read the passage and then jump into the questions. The problem with this approach is that your grasp of the passage will be superficial. Moderately difficult questions will trick or stump you. You will have to reread the passage non-systematically. In fact, you might even answer every question without feeling that you *ever* understood this passage!

When the passage is unfriendly, you should NOT *just* read it!

There is a better way. We use three general methods to learn something new:

>   (1) We read, as when we read a college textbook (or this guide).
>   (2) We write, as when we take notes during a college lecture.
>   (3) We listen, as during a lecture in a college course.

You can build your comprehension more quickly and effectively—*especially* when the passage is unfriendly—by using more than one learning method. Under normal circumstances you cannot have someone read the passage aloud to you. Nor can you read the passage aloud to yourself (although you might benefit from mouthing it or *quietly* mumbling to yourself). Thus, **you should make use of WRITING**, which activates a second learning process that facilitates comprehension.

Identifying <u>and writing down</u> key elements of the passage will force you to read ACTIVELY as opposed to passively. If you write in the right way, your comprehension of unfriendly passages will improve dramatically. Indeed, you should develop a writing strategy for *every* passage during practice, because you need that strategy to be robust under all circumstances.

Of course, it is not possible to rewrite an entire passage in the time allocated for Reading Comprehension questions. But even writing and summarizing key elements will help you understand the structure and content of a passage while saving you time for questions.

Now, what you write during the GRE must be different from other kinds of notes you have taken (e.g., during a college lecture). In college, you take notes in order to study from them later. In contrast, **you take notes during the GRE in order to create comprehension right there and then.** This is a very different goal. In fact, you should take notes that, in theory, you could *crumple up and throw away* before answering any questions, if you were forced to. Why take notes, then? To force your mind to carry out the Seven Principles of Active, Effective Reading—*not* to study for some later test. So you must fundamentally change your approach to taking notes.

You should NOT plan to use your notes afterwards very much, because then you will be tempted to write too much down. If you write too much down, you will get lost in the details, and you will spend too much time. *Knowing* that you are spending too much time, you will become even more stressed. Thus, your level of comprehension will decrease. Eventually, you may abandon note-taking altogether. If you do so, you will not have an effective strategy for unfriendly passages. So, **imagine that you have limited ink**. Everything that you write down should pass a high bar of importance.

What kinds of notes should you take? **You should take notes that allow you to grasp the simple story of the passage**.

That does not mean that you should necessarily write down the simple story in full sentences. Generally, you should try to be more abbreviated. Use the "Text It To Me" style (a full thought in 5-10 words) or the "Table of Contents" style (a headline of five words or fewer). We call these notes of the simple story the HEADLINE LIST of the passage.

When you encounter a short passage, create a Headline List of the passage during your first reading.

A Headline List serves several purposes:

>   (1) It fosters an understanding of the content and purpose of the passage by using writing to enable active reading.

(2) It provides a general structure without getting you bogged down in details.

(3) It promotes a fast first reading of a passage that still gives you enough time to answer questions.

The Headline List

To create a Headline List, follow these steps:

1. A headline summarizes and conveys the main idea of a newspaper article. Likewise, **your Headline List should summarize or indicate the main idea of each paragraph.**

Most paragraphs have one topic sentence. Generally, the topic sentence is the first or second sentence, although it can also be a combination of the two.

Read the first sentence or two of the first paragraph. Identify the topic sentence and summarize it concisely on your scratch paper in the form of a headline. Use either the "Text It To Me" style or the "Table of Contents" style (a headline of 5 words or fewer). If you cannot identify a topic sentence, then your headline should summarize the main idea or purpose of the
paragraph in your own words.

2. Read the rest of the paragraph with an eye for big surprises and results.

As you read the rest of the paragraph, briefly summarize anything else that is very important or surprising in the paragraph. Often, this will consist of simply jotting down a word or two. You may in fact not add anything to the original topic sentence if the paragraph fits neatly within the scope of that sentence.

3. If there is a second paragraph, follow the same process.

Each paragraph may introduce a whole new idea. Therefore, your approach to any second paragraph should be the same as with the first paragraph. As you create your Headline List, make it coherent. The parts should relate to each other.

How much do you read before stopping to take notes? It depends. If the passage is really tough, slow down and go sentence by sentence. If the passage is easier and you think you are getting it, read more (even a whole paragraph) before taking notes on that chunk. Stopping to take notes can take you out of the "flow." At the same time, you should force yourself to stop periodically and consider adding to your Headline List.

4. Once you have finished the passage, identify the passage's Point.

After you have finished reading the passage and creating the Headline List, glance back over your notes and over the passage. Make sure you know what the Point of the passage is. If it is not in your Headline List already, be sure to add it. Then, label or mark the Point, so that you articulate it to yourself. This way, you are certain of the author's most important message. Now proceed to the first question.

Common Notations

To create your Headline List as quickly as possible, consider the following notations:

(1) Abbreviate long terms, particularly proper nouns.

(2) Use arrows (e.g. →) to indicate cause-effect relationships or changes over time.

(3) If a passage contains speakers, writers, points-of-view, arguments, etc., keep them organized by placing the person with the opinion before a given opinion with a colon. For example: **Historians: econ. interests → war.**

(4) If you write down examples, mark them with parentheses or "Ex." For example: **Insects = inflexible (sphex wasp)**.

(5) Number each paragraph. Paragraph breaks are important to remember.

You will have your own note-taking style. For instance, if you are a visual thinker, you may draw pictures or use graphs to show relationships. Regardless of the notations you use, practice them and keep them CONSISTENT.

Using Your Headline List

How do you use your Headline List to answer questions about the passage? As mentioned above, you should avoid having to use the Headline List at all! You should already understand the simple story of the passage. Thus, you should be able to answer all GENERAL questions without referring either to your notes or to the passage. General questions pertain to the passage's main idea, its purpose, or its structure overall.

As for SPECIFIC questions, you will have to return to the passage to find particular details. Do not depend on your memory, as the GRE knows how to take advantage of this. PROVE your answer in the text. In many cases, you will be able to find the relevant details on your own. But you can also use your Headline List as a search tool, so that you can locate the detail. You may have even jotted the detail down, if it struck you as important at the time.

Timing for Short Passages

To determine how much time to spend on a passage, use this rule: **you have about 1.5 minutes per Reading Comprehension question, total.** The total number of minutes includes time for reading the passage, creating a Headline List, and answering all the questions. So, if a short passage has two questions associated with it, you would have roughly **three minutes** to read and sketch the short passage and then answer the two associated questions.

Out of this three-minute period, you should spend approximately 1.5 minutes reading the passage and generating your Headline List. Then you should spend an average of 45 seconds actually answering each question. You should try to answer General questions in about 30 seconds. Specific questions will be more time-consuming, since they demand that you review the text of the passage. You should allocate up to 60 seconds for any Specific question.

You can best learn to create Headline Lists with repeated practice. Study the model below, then do the In-Action exercises. Later, for more practice, create Headline Lists for passages from the ETS Guide.

Model Short Passage: *Insect Behavior*

Insect behavior generally appears to be explicable in terms of unconscious, inflexible stimulus–response mechanisms. For instance, a female sphex wasp leaves her egg sealed in a burrow alongside a paralyzed grasshopper, which her larvae can eat upon hatching. Before she deposits the grasshopper in the burrow, she inspects the burrow; if the inspection reveals no problems, she drags the grasshopper inside by its antennae. As thoughtful as this behavior appears, it reveals its mechanistic character upon interference. Darwin discovered that prior removal of the grasshopper's antennae prevents the wasp from depositing the grasshopper, even though the legs or ovipositor could also serve as handles. Likewise, Fabre moved the grasshopper a few centimeters away from the burrow's mouth while the wasp was inside inspecting. The wasp returned the grasshopper to the edge of the burrow and then began a new inspection. Fabre performed this disruptive maneuver forty times; the wasp's response never changed.

Model Headline List for *Insect Behavior*

Insect behav. = unconsc. stim/resp. = inflexible ← Point
-- Ex: wasp

D: w. won't drag g. w/o ant.
F: endless cycle

The Headline List summarizes the topic sentence of the paragraph, and the example is briefly listed. Likewise, the two experiments are simply bullet-points. Note that single letters can stand for whole words (w = wasp, g = grasshopper). Remember that you are not taking notes that you need to study from later!

In this example, the Point of the passage is the first sentence of the paragraph. The rest of the passage is Support for the Point.

Problem Set

1. Read the following passage and create a Headline List within 2.5–3 minutes (note that this is a bit more time than you'll want to spend on the actual exam). After answering the questions below the passage, compare your Headline List to the sample in the answer key. How well did your Headline List succeed in pushing you to read actively? How well did it capture the simple story of the passage without getting bloated with details?

Passage: Arousal and Attraction

In 1974, psychologists Dutton and Aron discovered that male subjects who had just crossed a precarious wire-suspension bridge reacted to an attractive female interviewer differently than subjects who had instead crossed a low, solid bridge. Specifically, in response to a questionnaire that secretly measured sexual arousal, subjects from the wire-suspension bridge revealed significantly more sexual imagery than the others; moreover, a far greater fraction of wire-suspension subjects than of solid-bridge subjects contacted the interviewer afterward. Dutton and Aron explained their results in terms of misattribution. In their view, subjects crossing the wobbly bridge experienced physiological fear reactions, such as increased heart rate. Such reactions with ambiguous or suppressed causes are easily reinterpreted, in the presence of a potential partner, as sexual attraction. However, Foster and others later found that an unattractive interviewer is actually perceived as much less attractive by subjects physiologically aroused by fearful situations. Thus, the arousal is reinterpreted either as attraction or as repulsion, but in either case, the true cause is masked.

2. What is the Point of this passage? Justify your choice.

3. Identify the other components of the passage, if present: Background, Support, and Implications. Again, justify your assignments.

4. Based on the passage, which of the following could be reasonably assumed about passengers of a particularly turbulent flight? Select *all* that apply.

    A They would be likely to misattribute the cause of a sexual attraction they felt to a fellow passenger during a long lull in turbulence

    B They would be likely to misattribute the cause of a sexual attraction they felt to a fellow passenger a few days after the flight

    C They would be more likely to find themselves viscerally disgusted by a baggage handler at their arrival gate whom they typically would have found merely unappealing

5. Read the following passage and create a Headline List in 1.5 minutes. After answering the questions below the passage, compare your Headline List to the sample in the answer key and provide critiques.

Passage: Animal Treatment

   In the early nineteenth century, educated Britons came to accept the then-novel notion that animals must be treated humanely, as evidenced by the outlawing of certain forms of domestic animal abuse, as well as the founding of the Society for the Prevention of Cruelty to Animals in 1824. This trend may be regarded as part of a broader embrace of compassionate ideals, such as abolitionism and alleviation of poverty. For instance, in 1785 a Society for the Relief of Persons Imprisoned for Small Sums persuaded Parliament to restrict that archaic punishment, and similar societies focused on various issues of humane treatment emerged around this time. However, a deeper explanation should be traced to socioeconomic conditions related to ongoing industrialization. Those protesting cruelty to animals were city-dwellers who viewed animals as pets rather than as livestock, despite the ubiquity of horse transport. In fact, nature was no longer considered menacing, since society's victory over wilderness was conspicuous. Animals were to some extent romanticized as emblems of a bucolic, pre-industrial age.

6. What is the Point of this passage? Justify your choice.

7. Identify the other components of the passage, if present: Background, Support, and Implications. Again, justify your assignments.

8. Based on the passage, which of the following is true about the first few decades of the 19th century? Select *all* that apply.

   A English society was becoming more compassionate towards some oppressed animals and humans

   B England was entering a more bucolic age of industry

   C Some viewed industrialization as a victory over wilderness

9. Select the sentence that, according to the author, would best explain the early 19th century trends towards womre humane treatment of animals.

1. <u>Arousal and Attraction</u> — Headline List

> Psychs D+A:
> — Wire bridge: aroused → attr.
> Expl: misattrib. physiol. fear AS attractn
> BUT actually: attr. OR repuls. masks the cause   ← Point

2. The Point of the passage is in the last sentence: *Thus, the arousal is reinterpreted either as attraction or as repulsion, but in either case, the true cause is masked.* The author is taking a little stand here. Everything in the passage leads up to this Point.

3. The paragraph is all Background and Support, leading up to the Point at the end.

4. C. This is a select-all-that-apply question that asks you to extrapolate out from the bridge example to an example involving an airplane. This isn't nearly as complicated as it sounds, as a turbulent flight would be almost exactly like crossing a wobbly bridge.

> A. The passage states that those crossing the wobbly bridge experience "physiological fear reactions" and that these reactions are "easily reinterpreted…as sexual attraction." During a long lull in turbulence, there would not be physiological fear reactions, so it is unlikely that there would be misattribution.

> B. The passage stresses the manner in which the researchers interviewed subjects IMMEDIATELY after crossing the bridge, when the "physiological fear reactions" were still fresh. A few days after a turbulent flight, passengers would be unlikely to continue to experience those reactions.

> C. CORRECT. This example is analogous to the one given in the passage. A passenger coming off of a turbulent flight would likely still be experiencing "physiological fear reactions," which we are told can cause repulsion as easily as attraction. We are also told directly that an "unattractive interviewer is actually perceived as much less attractive by subjects physiologically aroused by fearful situations."

5. <u>Animal Treatment</u> — Headline List

> 19th c.: Educ B's say animal cruelty = bad
> Why: Part of broader embrace of compassn. Ex's   ← Point
> Deeper Why: Industzn → citydwellers   ← Point
> — Nature romanticized

6. The Point here is complicated; it needs to be synthesized from key ideas spread throughout the paragraph. The main message of the author can be written thus:

> *19th c. British rejection of cruelty to animals, part of a broader embrace of compassion, actually stemmed from a romanticization of nature by city dwellers.*

7. The paragraph begins with Background (rejection of animal cruelty), then moves to Support (causes of this rejection).

8. A and C. This is a select-all-that-apply question asking about the beginning of the 19th century. The passage mentions a few dates, all of which will be useful in determining what was true at the dawn of the 19th century.

> A. CORRECT. The passage states that "ongoing industrialization" provides an explanation for the changing treatment of animals. Later in the passage, this industrialization is taken as "society's victory over wilderness," at least by those who viewed animals as pets rather than livestock.

B. The last sentence says that in the 19th century, animals became emblems of a "bucolic, pre-industrial age." The point is that that bucolic age was coming to an end at this time. England was not "entering" that age.

C. CORRECT. The passage says that in 1785, some kind of law was passed to "restrict" an "archaic punishment" related to people being imprisoned for small sums. Thus it stands to reason that fewer people were imprisoned at the beginning of the 19th century than had been imprisoned at the beginning of the 18th century.

10. This is another select-in-passage question asking for examples. The second sentence states, "This trend may be regarded as part of a broader embrace of compassionate ideals, such as abolitionism and alleviation of poverty." This sentence provides one possible explanation, but the author presents a "deeper explanation" later on. "However, a deeper explanation should be traced to socioeconomic conditions related to ongoing industrialization." This is the correct sentence.

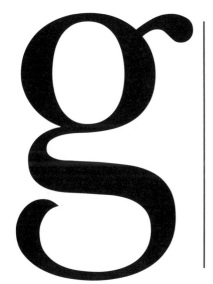

Chapter 5
of
READING COMPREHENSION & ESSAYS

LONG
PASSAGES

In This Chapter . . .

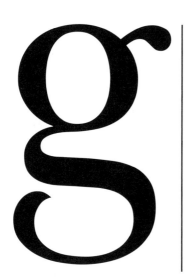

LONG PASSAGES

As noted in Chapter 1, long passages consist of 450–475 words in three to five paragraphs, streching 75 to 85 lines on the computer screen. Most likely, you will see one long passage per GRE exam (one verbal section will have a long passage, and one will not). Each long passage will likely have four questions associated with it, so your previewing of the questions will ONLY be useful in terms of getting a feel for what you'll be asked.

Long passages present much the same challenge as short passages, but because of their increased length and complexity, must be viewed as slightly more difficult. They are also more important, because of the increased number of associated questions. However, the individual questions associated with long passages will not be any harder, aside from the fact that there's more passage to be referenced, and thus more you're expected to understand.

As discussed in the case of short passages, what really makes the difference between an easy or "friendly" passage and a difficult or "unfriendly" one is your background (*How much do you like this topic? What do you already know about this topic?*), as well as your status on the exam at that moment (*Are you ahead of pace or lagging behind? How are you feeling about how you are doing? How is your energy level, your focus, your processing speed?*).

If the long passage turns out to be friendly, then simply read it. Feel free to take any notes you like (indeed, it is a good habit to take notes every time), but you probably do not need to do so. You are off to the races with a passage you like and a brain that is firing on all cylinders.

On the other hand, when the passage is unfriendly (as, in fact, the majority of long passages are likely to be), you need a **robust note-taking process** that you can carry out under any conditions, in order to read actively, rapidly, and effectively. Also, remember that a passage that looks friendly at first glance may turn ugly in the middle. Your default approach should always be to take notes. Skipping it may save you time, but it will almost certainly cost you some amount of comprehension.

For a long passage, we will approach our notes slightly differently—by creating a SKELETAL SKETCH. As with the Headline List for short passages, a Skeletal Sketch serves several purposes:

(1) It fosters an understanding of the content and purpose of the passage by using writing to enable active reading.

(2) It provides a general structure without getting you bogged down in details.

(3) It promotes a fast first reading of a long, complex passage that still gives you enough time to answer questions.

The Skeletal Sketch

The creation of a Skeletal Sketch has several key elements:

1. The top of a skeleton (the skull) is its most defined feature. Likewise, the first paragraph of every long passage gives shape to the text. As such, **your Skeletal Sketch requires a defined "skull."**

One of the primary differences between a long passage and a short passage is that, with a long passage, the first paragraph is often substantially more important than the other paragraphs, setting the tone and more often than not describing what the rest of the passage will be about. Thus, you should take extra time to summarize the first paragraph, making sure that you thoroughly understand it.

To form the skull, be prepared to both read at your absolute best, and to take more detailed notes than you will for the rest of the passage. Use the same notations and abbreviations as you do for Headline Lists of short passages.

As with short passages, you must decide how frequently you stop to take notes: after each sentence, after a couple of sentences, or after the entire paragraph. Again, the answer is that it depends on how well you are grasping the content and purpose of the text, as well as the length of the paragraph at issue. The more difficult the passage, the more frequently you should stop to process what you have read.

2. The limbs of your Skeletal Sketch are short headlines or one-sentence summaries of each of the remaining paragraphs.

The subsequent paragraphs of a long passage are generally not as important as the first, in terms of anything but the structure. These paragraphs are likely to be thick with detail that may or may not be important, based on the questions you are asked. As a result, you should read and notate these paragraphs differently than you read and notate the first paragraph.

Read each body paragraph to determine its point or structural purpose. Pay special attention to the first one or two sentences of the paragraph, since this is where the paragraph's topic is usually found. Read the remaining sentences quickly, intentionally skimming over details and examples. There is no point in trying to absorb the nitty-gritty details in these sentences during this initial reading. If you are asked a question about a specific detail, you will need to reread these sentences anyway. In fact, it is often *counter-productive* to try to absorb these details, since doing so takes you away from the main goal of your initial reading and sketching. Also, remember not to depend on your memory when answering detail questions. There's too much detail in a long passage for you to hope to remember it all after one read.

That said, you should not be skipping over the content of a paragraph; read everything. Be on the lookout for big surprises or important results. Sometimes, the GRE buries such surprises or results within the body of a later paragraph, and you must be ready to add them to your Skeletal Sketch.

If you focus on constructing the simple story, then you will read with the appropriate level of attention: not too close, not too far away, but just right.

3. Once you have finished the passage, identify the Point.

In a long passage, it is most likely that you will identify the point before you move beyond the first paragraph, as the vast majority of long passages reference the main idea right at the beginning. Thus, before you move onto the second paragraph, be sure you didn't miss the point. Either way, however, make sure you've written down the point before you start looking at any answer choices. There's nothing more important on Reading Comprehension than an understanding of the main idea of a passage.

Using Your Skeletal Sketch

How do you use your Skeletal Sketch to answer questions about the passage? The same way you use a Headline List for a short passage: you should avoid having to use it at all! The purpose of the Sketch is to facilitate your comprehension of the passage. You should be able to answer all GENERAL questions without referring either to your notes or to the passage.

As for SPECIFIC questions, you will need to find the details in the passage. You can often find these details on your own. But you can also use your Skeletal Sketch as a search tool. This is particularly helpful in an epic five-paragraph passage.

Timing for Long Passages

Recall from our discussion of short passages the following rule to determine how much time to spend on a particular reading passage: **you have 1.5 minutes per question, total,** including time to read the passage, create a Skeletal Sketch, and answer all the questions.

Typically, each long passage has four questions associated with it. Thus, you have roughly **six minutes** to read and sketch the long passage and then answer the associated questions.

Out of this six-minute period, you should spend approximately three minutes reading and generating your Skeletal Sketch. Then you should spend between 45 and 60 seconds actually answering each question, taking more time for Specific questions and less time for General questions, as noted in the previous chapter.

You can best learn to create Skeletal Sketches by repeated practice. Study the model given at the end of this chapter, and do the In-Action exercises. Also create Skeletal Sketches of Official Guide passages as you practice later.

Common Structures of Long Passages

Long passages often have more of a **narrative** to their simple story than short passages do. Here are a couple abstracted narratives contained within some long passages on the GRE. Of course, there can be many others! Do NOT impose these narratives on every passage.

1. A Theory

   Here is an area of scientific or historical **research**.
   Here is a **theory** about that area of research.
   Here is **support** for that theory.
   (Possibly) Here are **implications** of that theory.
   Point: EITHER the theory itself OR an assertion about the theory, e.g. **Theory X can now be tested**. In the latter case, support for the assertion is given.

2. A Couple of Theories

   Here is a **phenomenon** in some area of scientific or historical research.
   Here are a couple of **theories** about that phenomenon.
   Here is **support** for each of those theories.
   Point: **Theory X is best** OR **they all fall short**.

Model Long Passage: *Electroconvulsive Therapy*

Electroconvulsive therapy (ECT) is a controversial psychiatric treatment involving the induction of a seizure in a patient via the passage of electricity through the brain. While beneficial effects of electrically induced seizures are evident and predictable in most patients, a unified mechanism of action has not yet been established and remains the subject of numerous investigations. According to most, though not all, published studies, ECT has been shown to be effective against several conditions, such as severe depression, mania, and some acute psychotic states, that are resistant to other treatments, although, like many other medical procedures, ECT has its risks.

Since the inception of ECT in 1938, the public has held a strongly negative conception of the procedure. Initially, doctors employed unmodified ECT. Patients were rendered instantly unconscious by the electrical current, but the strength of the muscle contractions from induced, uncontrolled motor seizures often led to compression fractures of the spine or damage to the teeth. In addition to the effect this physical trauma had on public sentiment, graphic examples of abuse were documented in nonfiction or loosely fictional books and movies, such as Ken Kesey's One Flew Over the Cuckoo's Nest, which portrayed ECT as punitive, cruel, overused, and violative of patients' legal rights. Indeed, the alternative term "electroshock" has a negative connotation, tainted by these depictions in the media.

In comparison with its earlier incarnation, modern ECT is virtually unrecognizable. The treatment is modified by the muscle relaxant succinylcholine, which renders muscle contractions virtually nonexistent. Additionally, patients are given a general anesthetic. Thus, the patient is asleep and fully unaware during the procedure, and the only outward sign of a seizure may be the rhythmic movement of the patient's hand or foot. ECT is generally used in severely depressed patients for whom psychotherapy and medication prove ineffective. It may also be considered when there is an imminent risk of suicide, since antidepressants often require several weeks to show results. Exactly how ECT exerts its influence on behavior is not known, but repeated applications affect several important neurotransmitters in the brain, including serotonin, norepinephrine, and dopamine.

The consensus view of the scientific and medical community is that ECT has been proven effective, but the procedure remains controversial. Though decades-old studies showing brain cell death have been refuted in recent research, many patients do report retrograde amnesia (of events prior to treatment) and/or anterograde amnesia (of events during or shortly after treatment). Patients have also reported that their short-term memories continue to be affected for months after ECT, though some doctors argue that this memory malfunction may reflect the type of amnesia sometimes associated with severe depression. A recent neuropsychological study at Duke University documents a significant decline in performance on memory tests, ironically accompanied at times by self-reports of improved memory function; however, the researchers recommended only that these potential detriments be weighed against the potential benefits of ECT in any particular case.

Model Skeletal Sketch: *Electroconvulsive Therapy*

1) ECT controv. psych. treat: Electr. into brain → seizure
   -- Beneficial, but mech not understood
   ** Very effective for some conditions; has risks

2) Since 1938, public dislikes ECT

3) Modern ECT totally diff

4) ECT effective but still controv   ← Point

Notice that the "skull" of the sketch includes the most detail, as it carefully outlines the major points of the first paragraph.

The limbs of the sketch are each very concise, consisting only of a brief summary of the main idea of each body paragraph. Note that for each of the body paragraphs, the main idea is found in the first one or two sentences of the paragraph. This is often the case.

The Point of the passage is the first sentence of the last paragraph: *ECT has proven effective, but it remains controversial*. This is the most important message that the author wants to convey. Of course, we need the rest of the passage to supply context (e.g., to explain what ECT is in the first place). In fact, the last sentence of the first paragraph is very similar to the Point, but notice that *risks* are not quite the same thing as *controversy*.

The Point comes last (in the last paragraph). What comes before the Point is Background (explaining what ECT is) and Support, both for the controversial side of ECT (paragraph 2) and the effective side of ECT (paragraph 3).

Notice that the narrative here does NOT exactly fit one of the patterns mentioned earlier. The narrative here might best be expressed as "A Judgment about a Method": *Here is a method. It is effective but controversial.*

Problem Set

1. Read the following passage and create a Skeletal Sketch in 2–3 minutes. Afterward, using the sample given, critique your Skeletal Sketch by identifying ways in which it succeeds, as well as ways in which it could be improved.

Passage: Ether's Existence

In 1887, an ingenious experiment performed by Albert Michelson and Edward Morley severely undermined classical physics by failing to confirm the existence of "ether," a ghostly massless medium that was thought to permeate the universe. Although the implications of this experimental failure were not completely evident for many years, they ultimately paved the way for Einstein's special theory of relativity.

Prior to the Michelson–Morley experiment, nineteenth-century physics conceived of light as a wave of electric and magnetic fields. These fields were governed by Maxwell's equations, which predicted that these waves would propagate at a particular speed c. The existence of ether was hypothesized in part to explain the propagation of light waves, which was believed to be impossible through empty space. Moreover, the ether provided the theoretical baseline for the speed of light predicted by Maxwell's equations: light was to travel at speed c relative to the ether. Physical objects, such as planets, were also thought to glide frictionlessly through the unmoving ether.

The Michelson–Morley experiment relied on the concept that the Earth, which orbits the Sun, would be in motion relative to the fixed ether. Just as a person on a motorcycle experiences a "wind" caused by the cycle's motion relative to the air, the Earth would experience an "ethereal wind" caused by its motion through the ether. Such a wind would affect our measurements of the speed of light. If the speed of light is fixed with respect to the ether, but the earth is moving through the ether, then to an observer on Earth light must appear to move faster in a "downwind" direction than in an "upwind" direction.

In 1887 there were no clocks sufficiently precise to detect the speed differences that would result from an ethereal wind. Michelson and Morley surmounted this problem by using the wavelike properties of light itself to test for such speed differences. In their apparatus, known as an interferometer, a single beam of light is split in half. Mirrors guide each half of the beam along a separate trajectory before ultimately reuniting the two half-beams into a single beam. If one half-beam has moved more slowly than the other, the reunited beams will be out of phase with each other. In other words, peaks of the slower half-beam will not coincide exactly with peaks of the faster half-beam, resulting in an interference pattern in the reunited beam. However, this interference pattern failed to appear. No matter how they positioned the arms of the interferometer in relation to the theoretical ethereal wind, Michelson and Morley detected only a tiny degree of interference in the reunited light beam—far less than what was expected based on the motion of the Earth. This null result helped demolish the ether construct and replace it, in the end, with a far stranger view of time and space.

2. What is the Point of this passage? Justify your choice.

3. Identify the other components of the passage, if present: Background, Support, and Implications. Again, justify your assignments.

4. Where is the Point of this passage positioned, and why? What is the abstract narrative of this passage?

5. Select the sentence in the final two paragraphs that explains why Michelson and Morley had to depend on interference patterns to test their theory.

6. Which of the following would the author of the passage be likely to agree with? Select *all* that apply.

[A] Michelson and Morley's experiment was clever.

[B] The lack of precise stopwatches did not significantly impact Michelson and Morley's eventual results.

[C] 20th century physics would not necessarily have progressed as quickly as it did without Michelson and Morley's experiment.

7. Read the following passage and create a Skeletal Sketch in 2–3 minutes. Afterward, using the sample given, critique your Skeletal Sketch by identifying ways in which it succeeds, as well as ways in which it could be improved.

Passage: Prescription Errors

In Europe, medical prescriptions were historically written in Latin, for many centuries the universal medium of communication among the educated. A prescription for eye drops written in Amsterdam could be filled in Paris, because the abbreviation *OS* meant "left eye" in both places. With the disappearance of Latin as a lingua franca, however, abbreviations such as *OS* can easily be confused with *AS* ("left ear") or *per os* ("by mouth"), even by trained professionals. Such misinterpretations of medical instructions can be fatal. In the early 1990s, two infants died in separate but identical tragedies: they were each administered 5 milligrams of morphine, rather than 0.5 milligrams, as the dosage was written without an initial zero. The naked decimal (.5) was subsequently misread.

The personal and economic costs of misinterpreted medical prescriptions and instructions are hard to quantify. However, anecdotal evidence suggests that misinterpretations are prevalent. While mistakes will always happen in any human endeavor, medical professionals, hospital administrators, and policymakers should continually work to drive the prescription error rate to zero, taking simple corrective steps and also pushing for additional investments.

Certain measures are widely agreed upon, even if some are difficult to enforce, given the decentralization of the country's healthcare system. For instance, the American Medical Association and other professional organizations have publicly advocated against the use of Latin abbreviations and other relics of historical pharmacology. As a result, incidents in which *qd* ("every day"), *qid* ("four times a day"), and *qod* ("every other day") have been mixed up seem to be on the decline. Other measures have been taken by regulators who oversee potential areas of confusion, such as drug names. For instance, the FDA asked a manufacturer to change the name of Levoxine, a thyroid medication, to Levoxyl, so that confusion with Lanoxin, a heart failure drug, would be reduced. Likewise, in 1990 the antacid Losec was renamed Prilosec at the FDA's behest to differentiate it from Lasix, a diuretic. Unfortunately, since 1992 there have been at least a dozen reports of accidental switches between Prilosec and Prozac, an antidepressant. As more drugs reach the market, drug-name "traffic control" will only become more complicated.

Other measures are controversial or require significant investment and consensus-building. For instance, putting the patient's condition on the prescription would allow double-checking but also reduce patient privacy; thus, this step continues to be debated. Computerized prescriber order entry (CPOE) systems seem to fix the infamous problem of illegible handwriting, but many CPOE systems permit naked decimals and other dangerous practices. Moreover, since fallible humans must still enter and retrieve the data, any technological fixes must be accompanied by substantial training. Ultimately, a multi-pronged approach is needed to address the issue.

8. What is the Point of this passage? Justify your choice.

9. Identify the other components of the passage, if present: Background, Support, and Implications. Again, justify your assignments.

10. Where is the Point of this passage positioned, and why? What is the abstract narrative of this passage?

11. Select the sentence in the middle two paragraphs that gives a reason why prescription errors could become more common in the future.

12. Which of the following could help reduce the number of prescription errors made by doctors?

[A] A reduction in the use of anachronistic terminology

[B] A law forcing drug companies to name their products in ways that make confusion with pre-existing drugs less likely

[C] Better training for nurses and nurse practitioners who enter prescriptions into databases

1. <u>Ether's Existence</u> — Skeletal Sketch

    (1) 1887, <u>M+M experim. undermined class. physics</u>   ← Point
        → No ether (ghostly medium thru-out univ)
        — not apparent right away, but led to Einstein's rel.
    (2) Before: light = wave of e + m fields in ether
    (3) M+M used Earth's motion in ether (like wind)
    (4) → looked for speed diffs, found alm nothing

The "skull" of this sketch summarizes the brief first paragraph. The limbs are the summarized main ideas of each of the subsequent three paragraphs.

Notice that you have to pull more from the last paragraph than just the first sentence. You do not have to master how an interferometer works, but you have to have read everything in that last paragraph to get to the main idea, which is distributed throughout.

2. The Point of the passage is contained in the first sentence of the passage: *In 1887, an ingenious experiment performed by Albert Michelson and Edward Morley severely undermined classical physics by failing to confirm the existence of "ether,"....* (Of course, you should not copy this word for word into your Skeletal Sketch, but instead abbreviate it dramatically, as is shown above.) Everything else in this passage is secondary to this assertion.

3. The first paragraph gives Background on the ether (*a ghostly massless medium that was thought to permeate the universe*) and also gives an Implication (*Although the implications... theory of relativity*). The rest of the passage is a combination of Background knowledge and Support for the assertion made in the Point.

4. The Point comes at the top. In fact, the Point is the very first sentence. By placing the Point first in this passage, the author plants a stake in the ground, asserting the importance of the topic from the get-go (*...severely undermined classical physics...*) and providing the reader a sense of direction necessary for such a technical topic that requires a lot of Background. The narrative might be called "An Experiment": *M+M's shook physics, paved the way for Einstein. Here is what people used to think existed. Here is what M+M did to look. Here is what they found: Nothing!*

5. This is a select-in-passage question asking for a particular detail. We can look to where "interference" is mentioned, and then try to work backwards to figure out why Michelson and Morley needed it. The first sentence of the final paragraph states, "In 1887 there were no clocks sufficiently precise to detect the speed differences that would result from an ethereal wind." Because they couldn't simply time the light, Michelson and Morley had to depend on the interference patterns of split light beams.

6. A, B, and C. This is a very general select-all-that-apply question, which could draw from information provided anywhere in the passage.

    A. CORRECT. The first sentence says that the experiment "was ingenious," meaning clever.

    B. CORRECT. We are told in the final paragraph that Michelson and Morley "surmounted" the problem of not having precise enough clocks. That means that the lack of such clocks did not significantly impact their results.

    C. CORRECT. The second sentence of the first paragraph tell us that the results of the experiment "paved the way for Einstein's special theory of relativity." This means that, without the experiment, it is POSSIBLE that physics would not have progressed as quickly.

7. <u>Prescription Errors</u> — Skeletal Sketch

    (1) Eur: Rx in Latin, educ. Same in G, F.
        BUT now easy to confuse abbrev.
        — Can be fatal. Ex: 2 babies.
    (2) Cost Rx mistakes = hard to quant, but prevalent
        Med prof, admin, pol should elim errors   ← Point
    (3) Some steps = agreed.
    (4) Other steps harder. Need multi-prong.

Incidentally, Rx is an abbreviation for "prescription," probably originating from Latin. If you happen to encounter a passage on prescription drugs, feel free to use this abbreviation; otherwise, use it to locate a pharmacy when traveling abroad.

8. The Point is the last sentence of the second paragraph: *While mistakes will always happen in any human endeavor, medical professionals, hospital administrators, and policymakers should continually work to drive the prescription error rate to zero, taking simple corrective steps and also pushing for additional investments.* This is the strongest and most general claim made by the author.

9. What comes before the Point is a mixture of Background (e.g., the use of Latin on medieval prescriptions) and Support (e.g., the explanation of the fatal tragedies). After the Point is mostly Implications (various potential steps with pros and cons). The last two paragraphs could be interpreted as judgments on specific tactics, *given* that we all want to drive the error rate down to zero.

10. The Point is positioned in the middle, possibly because the author wants to set up the Point with Background and Support stories first, generating outrage about the infant deaths. Then the author can assert the Point, which does not require much more subsequent support.

11. This is a select-in-passage question that is quite specific. Notice that it doesn't ask for problems with the prescription-writing process, but a reason why the problem could get worse. The final sentence of the third paragraph states that, "As more drugs reach the market, drug-name 'traffic control' will only become more complicated." While other sentences mention other CURRENT problems with drug-name confusion, this is the only sentence giving a reason why things might get WORSE in the future.

12. A and B. This is a select-all-that-apply question of a slightly more specific variety. Notice that the question specifies "doctors." Try to pick up on aspects of the question that narrow the range of possible answers.

    A. CORRECT. The third paragraph describes the confusion caused by the use of the terms "qd", "qid", and "qod". Clearly the phasing out of this terminology could reduce prescription errors.

    B. CORRECT. The third paragraph describes "a dozen reports of accidental switches between Prilosec and Prozac." If these two products had more distinctive names, prescription errors could be reduced.

    C. While better training for nurses and nurse practitioners could conceivably lower the rate at which patients are misprescribed, it wouldn't actually affect the number of errors "made by doctors," as the question stipulated.

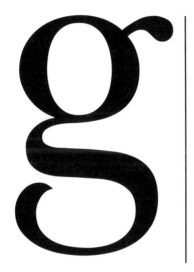

Chapter 6
of

READING COMPREHENSION & ESSAYS

STRATEGIES FOR SHORT AND LONG PASSAGES

In This Chapter . . .

- Question Types
- General Questions
- Specific Questions
- Strategies for All Reading Comprehension Questions
- The Seven Strategies for Reading Comprehension

QUESTION TYPES

As discussed earlier, GRE Reading Comprehension questions come in a variety of forms on long and short passages, but they can be placed into two major categories:

   (1) GENERAL questions

   (2) SPECIFIC questions

In this chapter, you will learn Seven Strategies for answering Reading Comprehension questions for short and long passages. The first of these strategies will help you answer General questions. The second and third strategies will help you answer Specific questions. The last four strategies are applicable to both General and Specific questions.

General Questions

General questions deal with the main idea, purpose, or structure of a passage. Typical general questions are phrased as follows:

   The primary purpose of the passage is...?

   The author is chiefly concerned with...?

   A good title for the passage would be...?

   The passage as a whole can best be characterized as which of the following?

The correct answer to general questions such as *What is the primary purpose of this passage?* should relate to as much of the passage as possible.

Your understanding of the passage gained through generating a Headline List or a Skeletal Sketch provides the key to answering general questions. You should be able to answer general questions without having to reread the entire passage. In fact, rereading the entire passage can actually be distracting. An incorrect answer choice may pertain only to a detail in a body paragraph. As you reread, you might spot that attractive detail and choose the wrong answer.

So, instead of rereading, **dive right into the answer choices and start eliminating.** If you need to, **review the Point** so that you are certain in your knowledge of the author's main message. Armed with the Point, you should be able to eliminate two or three choices quickly.

The last four strategies described in this chapter will help you get to the final answer. Occasionally, though, you may still find yourself stuck between two answer choices on a general question. If this is the case, use a Scoring System to determine which answer choice relates to more paragraphs in the passage. Assign the answer choice two points if it relates to the first paragraph. Give one more point for each additional related paragraph. The answer choice with more points is usually the correct one. In the event of a tie, select the answer choice that pertains to the first paragraph over any choices that do not.

> **STRATEGY for GENERAL Q's: If you are stuck between two answer choices, use a SCORING SYSTEM to assign a value to each one.**

Specific Questions

Specific questions deal with details, inferences, assumptions, and arguments. Typical specific questions are phrased as follows:

> According to the passage...?

> It can be inferred from the passage that...?

> All of the following statements are supported by the passage EXCEPT...?

> Which of the following would weaken the assertion in the passage...?

In contrast to your approach to General questions, you will need to reread and grasp details in the passage to answer Specific questions. First, read the question and focus on the key words you are most likely to find in the passage. Then, look back over the passage to find those key words. Use your Headline List or Skeletal Sketch as a search tool, if necessary. Do NOT look at the answer choices. Four out of five of them are meant to mislead you.

> **STRATEGY for SPECIFIC Q's: Identify the KEY WORDS in the question. Then, go back to the passage and find those key words.**

Consider the limbs of the sample Skeletal Sketch below:

1) Standardized tests = not valid predict.
2) Timing test implies → "fast = smart" BUT not true
3) Tests = also biased ag. non-native spkrs

Imagine that you are presented with this question: *Robinson raises the issue of cultural bias to do which of the following?* You would start scanning the passage looking for *cultural bias*. Since you just created the sketch, you would probably head toward the third paragraph anyway, but if necessary, the sketch would remind you to look there.

Sometimes, you will need to find a synonym for the key words in the question. For example, if the question addresses *weapons of mass destruction*, you may need to find a paragraph that addresses *nuclear* or *chemical* or *biological weapons*.

Once you find the key words, you should reread the surrounding sentence or sentences to answer the question. You may have to do a little thought work or take a few notes to figure out what the sentences mean. That is expected: after all, you did not master those details the first time through. In fact, do not look at the answer choices until you **boil down the relevant sentence or sentences into a "mantra"**—five words of truth. Then you can bring back that mantra and hold it in your head as you scan the five answer choices, eliminating the four lies and matching your mantra to the truth.

> **STRATEGY for SPECIFIC Q's: Find one or two PROOF SENTENCES to defend the correct answer choice.**

Only a handful of specific questions require more than two proof sentences.

the new standard

Strategies for All Reading Comprehension Questions

You should implement the following strategies for all Reading Comprehension questions.

> ### STRATEGY: JUSTIFY every word in the answer choice.

In the correct answer choice, **every word must be completely true** and within the scope of the passage. If you cannot justify *every* word in the answer choice, eliminate it. For example, consider the answer choices below:

(A) The colonists resented the king for taxing them without representation.
(B) England's policy of taxation without representation caused resentment among the colonists.

The difference in these two answer choices lies in the word *king* versus the word *England*. Although this seems like a small difference, it is the key to eliminating one of these answer choices. If the passage does not mention the *king* when it discusses the colonists' resentment, then the word *king* cannot be justified, and the answer choice should be eliminated.

> ### STRATEGY: AVOID EXTREME words if possible.

Avoid Reading Comprehension answer choices that use extreme words. These words, such as *all* and *never*, tend to broaden the scope of an answer choice too much or make it too extreme. **The GRE prefers moderate language and ideas**. Eliminate answer choices that go too far. Of course, occasionally you are justified in picking an extreme choice, but the passage must back you up 100%.

> ### STRATEGY: INFER as LITTLE as possible.

Many Reading Comprehension questions ask you to infer something from the passage. An inference is an informed deduction. Reading Comprehension inferences rarely go far beyond what is stated in the passage. In general, you should infer so
little that the inference seems obvious. It is often surprising how simplistic GRE inferences are. If an answer choice answers the question AND can be confirmed by language in the passage, it will be the correct one. Conversely, you should eliminate answer choices that require any logical stretch or leap. When you read *The passage suggests...* or *The passage implies...*, you should rephrase that language: *The passage STATES JUST A LITTLE DIFFERENTLY....* **You must be able to prove the answer, just as if the question asked you to look it up in the passage**.

> ### STRATEGY: PREVIEW the question.

As stated earlier, you will always see one question on the screen next to the passage. Because you are able to skip questions on the revised GRE test, you could theoretically preview all of the questions you'll be asked before you read the passage. However, previewing all of the questions is not a good use of time. Instead, we recommend quickly clicking through to see how many questions are associated with the passage, and then going back to the first question. Before reading the passage, read the first question. Previewing the first question will give you a good sense for what you can expect in the passage. So, to review, first check the number of questions associated with the passage, then preview the first question, then read the passage.

The Seven Strategies for Reading Comprehension

You now have seven effective strategies to use on Reading Comprehension questions on the GRE. Make sure that you know them and practice them frequently.

For GENERAL questions:

> (1) Use a **SCORING SYSTEM** when stuck between two answer choices.

For SPECIFIC questions:

> (2) Match **KEY WORDS** in specific questions to key words (or synonyms) in the passage.

> (3) Defend your answer choice with one or two **PROOF SENTENCES**.

For ALL questions:

> (4) **JUSTIFY** every word in your answer choice.

> (5) **AVOID** answer choices that contain **EXTREME** words.

> (6) Choose an answer choice that **INFERS** as **LITTLE** as possible.

And do not forget to:

> (7) **PREVIEW** the first question before reading the passage.

Chapter 7
of
READING COMPREHENSION & ESSAYS

QUESTION TYPE ANALYSIS

In This Chapter . . .

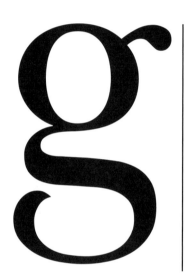

- Question Type Analysis

- Types of Wrong Answer Choices

- Model Short Passage Revisited: **Insect Behavior**

- Model Long Passage Revisited: **Electroconvulsive Therapy**

QUESTION TYPE ANALYSIS

As you begin a Reading Comprehension question, you should classify it right away as General or Specific. This distinction determines your fundamental approach to the question. With General questions, you dive right into eliminating answer choices, but with Specific questions, you go back to the passage and find proof sentences before looking at the answer choices.

That said, we can identify several common subtypes as follows. You should not spend any time during the exam classifying questions into these subtypes. We provide this further classification simply so that you can become more familiar with the variety of possible questions on the GRE.

1. Main Idea

Asks you about the main idea of the passage. This question type is always General.

Typical wordings:

"The author is primarily concerned with…"

"Which of the following best states the author's main point?"

"Which of the following would be the most appropriate title for the passage?"

2. Lookup Detail

Asks you for a detail that you can look up exactly "according to the passage." This question type is always Specific.

Typical wordings:

"According to the passage, X resulted primarily from which of the following…"

"According to the passage, as the process of X continues, all of the following may occur EXCEPT"

"According to the passage, person X indicates that all of the following were true of Y EXCEPT"

"The author provides information that would answer which of the following questions? "

"Which of the following is NOT cited in the passage as…"

Notice that Lookup Detail questions can be made harder with "EXCEPT." With an EXCEPT variation, you have to find the one answer that *isn't* true. The primary way to do so is by process of elimination: knock out the 4 answer choices that *are* true according to the passage.

3. Infer about Facts

Asks you to make a clear, unshakeable deduction about facts presented in the passage. This deduction should be almost mathematical or dictionary-like in nature. For instance, if the passage tells you that there is less calcium in water than in milk, then you can infer that there is more calcium in milk than in water. This question type is always Specific.

Typical wordings:

"It can be inferred from the passage that slower X than those discussed in the passage…"

"The author implies that a major element of X is…"

"Which of the following statements concerning X is most directly suggested in the passage."

"The quality of X described in lines 10–15 is most clearly an example of…"

"The passage supports which of the following statements about X?"

Occasionally, you will need to make an inference connecting two parts of the passage. Regardless, you must not make any new assumptions or draw on knowledge from outside the passage.

4. Infer about Opinions

Asks you to make a clear, unshakeable deduction about an opinion or attitude. This opinion or attitude may be of someone referred to in the passage, or it may be of the author himself or herself. No matter what, you must find clear justification in the passage. This justification might come in the form of just one word, such as "regrettably" or "understandably." This question type is usually Specific, but it might occasionally be General.

Typical wordings:

"The author's attitude toward X, as discussed in the passage, is best described as…" [answer choices are adjectives]

"In the first paragraph of the passage, the author's attitude toward X can best be described as…"

"It can be inferred from the passage that person X chose Y because X believed that…"

"It can be inferred from the passage that the author believes which of the following about X?"

5. Author's Purpose

Asks you *why* or *for what purpose* the author has written something or constructed the passage in a certain way. These questions address the role, structure, and function of particular words, phrases, sentences, paragraphs, and even the passage as a whole. In the last case, the question would be General, but usually this question type is Specific.

Typical wordings:

"The author refers to X (line 45) primarily in order to…"

"Which of the following phrases best expresses the sense of word X as it is used in lines 20–21 of the passage?"

6. Minor Types

You may be asked to Extrapolate the Content of the passage (e.g., "what would be the best sentence to add onto the end of the passage") or to evaluate what would Strengthen or Weaken a claim (e.g., "which of the following pieces of evidence would most strengthen the claim made in lines 13–15?"). These questions are almost always Specific.

Types of Wrong Answer Choices

Wrong answers on Reading Comprehension questions tend to fall into one of five broad categories. Caution: on the real test, you should NOT try to classify wrong answers right away. You should not waste precious time or attention classifying an answer choice that is obviously wrong. Rather, use this classification in the last stage of elimination, if you are stuck deciding among answer choices that all seem attractive. However, while practicing Reading Comprehension, you should attempt to categorize all the wrong answers, if not while doing the question, then while reviewing it.

1. Out of Scope

- **Introduces an unwarranted assertion** supported nowhere in the passage.
- Might be "Real-World Plausible." That is, the answer might be true or seem to be true in the real world. However, if the answer is not supported in the passage, it is out of scope.

2. Direct Contradiction

- **States the exact opposite** of something asserted in the passage.
- Paradoxically attractive, because it relates to the passage closely. If you miss one contrast or switchback in the trail, you can easily think a Direct Contradiction is the right answer.

3. Mix-Up
- **Scrambles together disparate content** from the passage.
- Tries to trap the student who simply matches language, not meaning.

4. One Word Wrong
- **Just one word (or maybe 2) is incorrect.** Includes extreme words.
- More prevalent in General questions.

5. True But Irrelevant
- True according to the passage, but does not answer the given question.
- May be too narrow or simply unrelated.

This framework can be particularly helpful as you analyze the patterns in wrong answers that you incorrectly choose during practice (whether under exam-like conditions or not). If you frequently choose Direct Contradiction answers, for instance, then you might incorporate one more double-check into your process to look for that particular sort of error. Again, however, **you should not attempt to classify wrong answers as a first line of attack**. This strategy is inefficient and even distracting.

Differences Between Question Formats

All three of the different question formats associated with Long and Short Passages test your understanding of the passage. However, there are some things you want to keep in mind when taking on the two non-traditional formats (as opposed to Select-one questions).

1. Select-all-that-apply

   It is unlikely that you'll be asked structural questions (main idea, author's purpose), because questions like that could really only have one answer. Instead, expect to see mostly inference questions, though they can be either specific or general. Select-all-that-apply questions are a bit like three inference questions in one. Because each of the answer choices can be correct, all three have to be considered in isolation.

2. Select-in-Passage

   These questions can only be specific (as they must relate to only ONE sentence in the passage), and they can be deceptively difficult. Remember that the correct answer needs to be relevant to every aspect of the requested prompt, but that the correct sentence is allowed to do or say more than just what the prompt demands. So don't ignore a sentence if part of it seems out of scope. If it contains the details requested by the prompt, it doesn't matter what else is discussed within it.

In the rest of this chapter, we will review two of the passages used as examples in the previous chapters covering short and long passages.

Note: For the purpose of practice and exposure to different question types, we will be reviewing six questions on the short passage and seven questions on the long passage. However, on the GRE, a short passage will typically have only one to three questions associated with it, and a long passage will typically have only four questions associated with it.

Reread the first passage, reproduced on the following page for your convenience. As you read, create a Headline List. Do not try to reproduce the earlier version; simply make your own. On the pages that follow, try to answer each question in the appropriate amount of time (between 45 and 60 seconds) BEFORE you read the accompanying explanation.

Model Short Passage Revisited: *Insect Behavior*

> Insect behavior generally appears to be explicable in terms of unconscious, inflexible stimulus–response mechanisms. For instance, a female sphex wasp leaves her egg sealed in a burrow alongside a paralyzed grasshopper, which her larvae can eat upon hatching. Before she deposits the grasshopper in the burrow, she inspects the burrow; if the inspection reveals no problems, she drags the grasshopper inside by its antennae. As thoughtful as this behavior appears, it reveals its mechanistic character upon interference. Darwin discovered that prior removal of the grasshopper's antennae prevents the wasp from depositing the grasshopper, even though the legs or ovipositor could also serve as handles. Likewise, Fabre moved the grasshopper a few centimeters away from the burrow's mouth while the wasp was inside inspecting. The wasp returned the grasshopper to the edge of the burrow and then began a new inspection. Fabre performed this disruptive maneuver forty times; the wasp's response never changed.

Your Headline List:

1. The primary purpose of the passage is to _____.

(A) prove, based on examples, that insects lack consciousness
(B) argue that insects are unique in their dependence on rigid routines
(C) analyze the maternal behavior of wasps
(D) compare and contrast the work of Darwin and Fabre
(E) argue that insect behavior relies on rigid routines which appear to be unconscious

This is a GENERAL question (subtype: Main Idea), so we should be able to answer the question using the understanding of the passage that we gained through creating our Headline List. For questions asking about the main idea of the passage, be sure to refer to the opening paragraph, which either articulates the Point of the passage or sets up the necessary context.

We can eliminate **(A)** based upon the topic sentence of the paragraph. The passage does not claim to prove that insects lack consciousness; it merely suggests, rather tentatively, that insect behavior *appears to be explicable* in terms of unconscious mechanisms. The word *prove* is too extreme in answer choice **(A)**. [One Word Wrong]

Answer choice **(B)** reflects the language of the passage in that the passage does indicate that insects depend on rigid routines. However, it does not address the question of whether there are any other animals that depend on such routines, as is stated in answer choice **(B)**. The passage makes no claim about whether or not insects are *unique* in this respect. Remember that every word in an answer choice must be justified from the text. [Out of Scope]

We can eliminate answer choice **(C)** using our Headline List. It is clear that the sphex wasp's maternal behavior is used as an example to illustrate a more general idea; this behavior is not itself the Point of the passage. [True But Irrelevant]

Fabre and Darwin are simply mentioned as sources for some of the information on wasps. Moreover, their results are not contrasted; rather, their experiments are both cited as evidence to support the Point. Answer choice (**D**) is incorrect. [Out of Scope]

(**E**) **CORRECT**. The passage begins with a topic sentence that announces the author's Point. The Point has two parts, as this answer choice correctly indicates: (1) insect behavior relies on rigid routines, and (2) these routines appear to be unconscious. The topic sentence does not use the term *rigid routine*, but it conveys the idea of rigidity by describing insect behavior as *inflexible*. The concept of routine is introduced later in the passage.

As is typical on the GRE, the correct answer choice avoids restating the passage. Instead, this choice uses synonyms (e.g. *rigid* instead of *inflexible*).

2. The author mentions the work of Darwin and Fabre in order to

(A) provide experimental evidence of the inflexibility of one kind of insect behavior
(B) contradict the conventional wisdom about "typical" wasp behavior
(C) illustrate the strength of the wasp's maternal affection
(D) explore the logical implications of the thesis articulated earlier
(E) highlight historical changes in the conduct of scientific research

Questions that ask about the purpose of a reference are SPECIFIC questions (subtype: Author's Purpose). We should go back to the passage to determine why this work was included, although we may be able to use our Headline List, since the question is asking about such a large component of the passage (the entire second half). In fact, we may even have jotted down in our Headline List something like the following:

> D: wasp won't drag g. w/o anten.
> F: similar evid

The sentences on Darwin and Fabre describe experiments that are used as examples of inflexible insect behavior. This concept is mirrored closely in answer choice (**A**), the correct answer.

We should always review all answer choices, as more than one may be promising.

We can eliminate answer choice (**B**). The passage does not mention any challenge to a conventional view; for all we know, the passage simply states the mainstream scientific position on insect behavior. [Out of Scope]

For answer choice (**C**) it might be tempting to infer that the wasp's persistence is caused by maternal affection. This inference is questionable, however, because the passage states that insect behavior is determined by mechanistic routines which appear to be unemotional in nature. Always avoid picking an answer choice that depends on a debatable inference, because the correct answer should not stray far from what is directly stated in the text. [Out of Scope]

Choice (**D**) is incorrect because Darwin's and Fabre's experiments do not explore the logical <u>implications</u> of the idea that insect behavior is inflexible. Rather, the experiments are presented as <u>evidence</u> of inflexibility. [Direct Contradiction]

Answer choice (**E**) goes beyond the scope of the passage. The paragraph mentions work by two scientists, but it does not tell us whether any differences in their methods were part of a historical change in the conduct of science. [Out of Scope]

3. Which of the following hypothetical variations in the experiments and results described in the passage would have most weakened the primary claim of the passage?

(A) Darwin removes the ovipositor, a small appendage, instead of the antennae; the wasp fails to deposit the grasshopper in the burrow.

(B) Darwin restrains the grasshopper while the wasp attempts to drag it by its antennae, which subsequently break off; although Darwin then releases the grasshopper, the wasp ignores it.

(C) Fabre moves the grasshopper several meters away during the wasp's inspection; the wasp takes significant time to retrieve the grasshopper, then re-inspects the burrow.

(D) Fabre repeatedly varies the exact position near the burrow to which he moves the grasshopper, causing the wasp to adjust its retrieval path slightly before re-inspecting the burrow.

(E) Fabre replaces the grasshopper with a paralyzed praying mantis, a rather different insect that the wasp inspects and then deposits in the burrow.

This is a SPECIFIC question (subtype: Weaken) that requires you to interpret the hypothetical effect of variations in the experiments and results described in the passage. The question cannot be answered with a simple lookup, but you should still ensure that the answer you choose is clearly justified by the exact contents of the passage.

Since the question asks "which variation would have most weakened the primary claim," we should articulate that primary claim again: insect behavior can be explained by unconscious, inflexible stimulus-response mechanisms. To weaken this claim most effectively, we need evidence that the insect can instead act in a flexible, even conscious way to achieve its goals. Armed with this template, we can now turn to the answer choices.

Answer choice (A) depicts a situation in which Darwin removes the small ovipositor appendage instead of the antennae. This removal disturbs the wasp enough to prevent it from using the grasshopper, although the slightness of the change is implied by the term "small appendage," and thus we can assume that the grasshopper would still be appropriate for the wasp's purpose (feed the larvae). This result actually strengthens the primary claim. [Direct Contradiction]

In answer choice (B), the wasp and Darwin get into a tug of war, during which the wasp winds up breaking off the antennae and then abandoning the grasshopper, even though the latter became available once Darwin released it. In essence, this choice is similar to the real experiment Darwin conducted, since in both cases, the wasp rejects a grasshopper lacking antennae; therefore, this choice also strengthens the primary claim. [Direct Contradiction]

In answer choice (C), the wasp re-inspects the burrow only after a long delay, because the grasshopper has been moved several meters away. Thus, the re-inspection might be seen as a result either of an inflexible stimulus-response mechanism ("inspect after bringing the grasshopper to the burrow") or of a flexible, conscious decision process ("since I have been absent from the burrow for a while, I'd better check it again"). This choice is tricky, since flexibility now enters the picture. However, choice (C) does not rule out the inflexible mechanism or create any preference one way or the other, so it does not attack the primary claim itself, which is still permitted. At most, we can say that this choice provides ambiguous evidence, and so does not really strengthen or weaken the primary claim. As such, this choice is "Out of Scope," because it does not provide definitive evidence one way or the other. [Out of Scope]

Answer choice (D) is attractive, because the insect is adapting in some way to changing circumstances while still pursuing its goal. However, a few particular words condemn this choice: "slightly," "exact position near the burrow." These words are not quite proof-positive that the choice is incorrect, but they indicate that the adjustments are small in nature. While we now see a degree of flexibility on the part of the wasp, this flexibility is minor. We might keep

this choice around, while we search for a better option, but we should be biased against accepting a choice that does its job so poorly. [One Word Wrong]

In answer choice (E), the wasp is confronted with a significantly changed situation (praying mantis instead of grasshopper). The wasp inspects the new insect, which is described as rather different, and then deposits it in the burrow. This indicates that the wasp is able to accept a significant difference and, after inspection, proceed with the original plan anyway; in other words, the wasp demonstrates substantial flexibility, especially in comparison to how it acts in the real experiments. The correct answer is **(E)**.

---

4. The passage supports which of the following statements about insect behavior?

(A) Reptiles such as snakes behave more flexibly than do insects.
(B) Insects such as honeybees can always be expected to behave inflexibly.
(C) Many species of insects leave eggs alongside living but paralyzed food sources.
(D) Stimulus-response mechanisms in insects have evolved because, under ordinary circumstances, they help insects to survive.
(E) More than one species of insect displays inflexible, routine behaviors.

This is a difficult SPECIFIC question (subtype: Lookup Detail). The key words *insect behavior* indicate the topic of the passage; they could plausibly refer to almost anything mentioned. Thus, we must change tactics and start with the answer choices. Each answer choice gives us additional key words; we use these to look up the reference for each answer choice and determine whether the choice is justified.

The key to finding the correct answer is to focus on what is explicitly stated in the passage, and to examine whether each answer choice goes beyond what can be supported by the passage. Again, justify every word in the answer choice that you select.

Answer choice **(A)** mentions reptiles and snakes. Since the passage never mentions either of these, you should eliminate this answer choice. This is the case even though one could argue that the passage draws an implicit contrast between insect inflexibility and the more flexible behavior of some other creatures. You should discard any answer choice that goes too far beyond the passage. [Out of Scope]

Answer choice **(B)** is a great example of a tempting GRE answer choice. Honeybees are insects, and the passage does claim that insect behavior tends to be inflexible. However, the passage does not say that every single species of insect behaves inflexibly; perhaps honeybees are an exception. Further, this answer choice states that honeybees *always* behave inflexibly, whereas the author states that insect behavior *often reveals a stereotyped, inflexible quality*. The extreme word *always* cannot be justified in this answer choice. [One Word Wrong]

Answer choice **(C)** seems plausible. The sphex wasp is probably not the only species of insect that provides its young with paralyzed prey. However, the word *Many* is not justified in the passage. We do not know the behavior of any other insect in this regard. Through the use of the word *Many*, answer choice **(C)** goes too far beyond the passage. [One Word Wrong]

The passage never explicitly mentions evolution, nor does it make any statement about why insects have stimulus-response mechanisms. Answer choice **(D)** also requires drawing inferences from beyond the text of the passage. [Out of Scope]

The first sentence of the passage tells us that *Insect behavior generally appears to be explicable in terms of unconscious stimulus-response mechanisms* and *often reveals a stereotyped, inflexible quality.* The passage goes on to describe the case of sphex wasps as a *classic example.* Thus, the passage clearly indicates that the case of sphex wasps is not completely unique; that is, there must be more than one species of insect that exhibits inflexible behavior. Note that *more than one* can be justified by the passage in a way that a more extreme term such as *most* or *all* cannot be. Answer choice **(E)** is correct.

---

5. Based on the passage, which of the following would prove a similar point to that promoted by the author? Select _all_ that apply.

A In a similar experiment, the paralyzed grasshopper was replaced with another, equally nutritive insect, and the wasp did not drag it into the burrow.

B In a similar experiment with a bird, the bird was shown to act in the exact same manner as the wasp.

C In a similar experiment with a different wasp, the wasp dragged the grasshopper into the burrow by its ovipositor.

This is another difficult specific question, presented in a select-all-that-apply multiple choice format. This means we need to deeply consider each answer choice on its own. We can start by reminding ourselves exactly what the point promoted by the author is. We can be quite sure by now it's that insects have inflexible stimulus-response mechanisms.

A. CORRECT. In this case, the wasp would have access to an insect that could provide just as much nutrition for her larvae as the grasshopper. This means that the rational, conscious response would be to drag the new insect into the burrow in place of the grasshopper. The decision not to drag the insect into the burrow would imply that the wasp is not being rational or logical, but obeying inflexible stimulus-response mechanisms, which require the insect at issue to be a grasshopper.

B. While at first glance this answer may seem tempting, as it describes an animal acting in the "exact same manner as the wasp," the passage is very specifically about insect behavior. Birds would not fit into that category. [One Word Wrong.]

C. We've read that the wasp only drags the grasshopper in by its antennae, and if those antennae are removed, it will not drag it into the burrow at all. If a wasp were to deviate from her typical process, dragging the grasshopper in by something other than its antennae, that would mean she was changing her response in reaction to circumstances, meaning her responses were NOT inflexible. This is actually the opposite of the point we want to make. [Direct Contradiction.]

The only correct answer is A.

---

6. Select the sentence that names the mechanism by which a seemingly conscious behavior can be proven autonomic?

This is a select-in-passage question, which by definition has to be specific. Don't be afraid of complex language on the GRE. Often the meaning of difficult words can be inferred from the context. In this case, even if you didn't know what the word "autonomic" meant, you could use context. It is being contrasted with "conscious behavior," so it likely means the opposite of that (unconscious behavior). So now we're looking for the sentence that names the mechanism used to prove that a seemingly conscious behavior was actually unconscious.

The fourth sentence says "As thoughtful as this behavior appears, it reveals its mechanistic character upon interference." The mechanism at issue has been named: "interference." While many of the following sentences give examples of interference, the mechanism is only NAMED in this sentence. Always be careful to read the question very carefully. It would be easy to pick one of the example sentences later in the paragraph if you didn't notice the use of the word "names" in the question.

Now reread the Model Long Passage, reproduced on the following page for your convenience. As you read, create a Skeletal Sketch. Do not try to reproduce the earlier version; simply make your own. On the pages that follow, try to answer each question in the appropriate amount of time (between 45 and 60 seconds) BEFORE you read the accompanying explanation.

Model Long Passage Revisited: *Electroconvulsive Therapy*

Electroconvulsive therapy (ECT) is a controversial psychiatric treatment involving the induction of a seizure in a patient via the passage of electricity through the brain. While beneficial effects of electrically induced seizures are evident and predictable in most patients, a unified mechanism of action has not yet been established and remains the subject of numerous investigations. According to most, though not all, published studies, ECT has been shown to be effective against several conditions, such as severe depression, mania, and some acute psychotic states, that are resistant to other treatments, although, like many other medical procedures, ECT has its risks.

Since the inception of ECT in 1938, the public has held a strongly negative conception of the procedure. Initially, doctors employed unmodified ECT. Patients were rendered instantly unconscious by the electrical current, but the strength of the muscle contractions from induced, uncontrolled motor seizures often led to compression fractures of the spine or damage to the teeth. In addition to the effect this physical trauma had on public sentiment, graphic examples of abuse were documented in nonfiction or loosely fictional books and movies, such as Ken Kesey's One Flew Over the Cuckoo's Nest, which portrayed ECT as punitive, cruel, overused, and violative of patients' legal rights. Indeed, the alternative term "electroshock" has a negative connotation, tainted by these depictions in the media.

In comparison with its earlier incarnation, modern ECT is virtually unrecognizable. The treatment is modified by the muscle relaxant succinylcholine, which renders muscle contractions virtually nonexistent. Additionally, patients are given a general anesthetic. Thus, the patient is asleep and fully unaware during the procedure, and the only outward sign of a seizure may be the rhythmic movement of the patient's hand or foot. ECT is generally used in severely depressed patients for whom psychotherapy and medication prove ineffective. It may also be considered when there is an imminent risk of suicide, since antidepressants often require several weeks to show results. Exactly how ECT exerts its influence on behavior is not known, but repeated applications affect several important neurotransmitters in the brain, including serotonin, norepinephrine, and dopamine.

The consensus view of the scientific and medical community is that ECT has been proven effective, but the procedure remains controversial. Though decades-old studies showing brain cell death have been refuted in recent research, many patients do report retrograde amnesia (of events prior to treatment) and/or anterograde amnesia (of events during or shortly after treatment). Patients have also reported that their short-term memories continue to be affected for months after ECT, though some doctors argue that this memory malfunction may reflect the type of amnesia sometimes associated with severe depression. A recent neuropsychological study at Duke University documents a significant decline in performance on memory tests, ironically accompanied at times by self-reports of improved memory function; however, the researchers recommended only that these potential detriments be weighed against the potential benefits of ECT in any particular case.

Your Skeletal Sketch:

1. The passage is primarily concerned with

(A) defending a provocative medical practice
(B) explaining a controversial medical treatment
(C) arguing for further testing of a certain medical approach
(D) summarizing recent research concerning a particular medical procedure
(E) relating the public concern toward a particular medical therapy

This is a GENERAL question (subtype: Main Idea). It asks for the primary purpose of the passage, although the question is worded slightly differently. We should be able to answer this question relying upon the comprehension of the passage that we gained through creating our Skeletal Sketch.

The answer to a question about the primary concern of a passage should reflect our understanding of the Point. As we noted before, the Point of this passage is the topic sentence of the fourth paragraph: *The consensus view… is that ECT has been proven effective, but it is not without controversy.* This Point is neutral and balanced; it is not advocating either the adoption or the elimination of ECT.

Answer choice (**A**) states that the passage explicitly *defends* ECT. The passage addresses ECT in an objective manner; the author neither defends nor argues against the continued use of ECT as a viable medical therapy. Answer choice (**A**) is incorrect. [One Word Wrong]

Answer choice (**B**) is correct. The primary purpose of the passage is to explain ECT. This includes briefly discussing both its purpose and the reasons why it has generated such controversy. This answer choice is reflected in our Skeletal Sketch and in our grasp of the Point.

We should continue to rule out other answer choices.

Answer choice (**C**) describes a need for further testing that is never mentioned in the passage. You might think that the passage implies this need, since we do not know *exactly how ECT exerts its effects,* for instance. However, the primary concern of the passage will not simply be implied; it will be asserted. Answer choice (**C**) is incorrect. [Out of Scope]

Although recent research concerning a particular side effect of ECT is mentioned in the final paragraph, this is not the primary purpose of the passage. This answer choice is too specific for a primary purpose question. It does not relate to the content of the passage as a whole. Using the scoring system strategy, you would give this answer choice only one point, since it relates to the final paragraph. In contrast, the correct answer choice (B) would be assigned 5 points since it relates to the first paragraph (2 points) and each of the subsequent 3 paragraphs (1 point each). Answer choice (**D**) is incorrect. [True But Irrelevant]

The passage does state that ECT is a controversial procedure that the public views in a negative manner; however, the passage only focuses on public concern over the procedure in the second paragraph. This answer choice is too specific for a primary purpose question, and does not encompass the majority of the passage. Using the point system strategy, this answer choice would receive only one point, since it relates to only the second paragraph (and perhaps the fourth). Thus, answer choice (**E**) is also incorrect. [True But Irrelevant]

2. Which of the following is NOT cited in the passage as a current or historical criticism of ECT?

(A) ECT causes the death of brain cells.
(B) ECT has been used to punish certain individuals.
(C) Seizures during ECT can cause bodily harm.
(D) Short-term memory loss results from ECT.
(E) Repeated applications of ECT affect several neurotransmitters in the brain.

This SPECIFIC question (subtype: Lookup Detail) asks us which criticism of ECT is NOT cited in the passage. A methodical process of elimination is the best approach to answer a "NOT" or "EXCEPT" question. Use your understanding of the passage to locate the important information in the passage. If necessary, refer to your Skeletal Sketch. Then eliminate each answer choice as soon as you prove that it *is* cited as a criticism of ECT.

The second sentence of the final paragraph indicates that the death of brain cells was the basis for a historical criticism of ECT. Although the research was recently refuted, brain cell death is still a side-effect that, at one time, caused criticism of the procedure. Answer choice (**A**) can be ruled out.

According to the second-to-last sentence of the second paragraph, one reason why the public has a negative perception of ECT is that certain uses (or abuses) of ECT have been *documented in nonfiction or loosely fictional books and movies*. The words *documented* and *nonfiction* mean that these abuses actually happened. Moreover, these abuses have been documented as *punitive;* in other words, ECT has been used to punish people. Thus, answer choice (**B**) can be eliminated.

The second paragraph explicitly and prominently mentions the bodily harm caused by seizures during unmodified ECT in its second and third sentences. Answer choice (**C**) is clearly incorrect.

The final paragraph also cites short-term memory loss as a major reason that ECT, in its current modified form, still generates controversy. Thus, answer choice (**D**) is incorrect.

The end of the third paragraph specifically states that *repeated applications [of ECT] affect several neurotransmitters in the brain.* However, this statement is offered in a neutral way, not as a criticism of ECT, but simply as additional information about the procedure. You might suppose that this effect is negative, but the text itself does not apply a judgment one way or the other. Answer choice (**E**) is the only answer choice that is not cited as a past or current criticism of ECT. Therefore answer choice (**E**) is the correct answer.

With a "NOT" or "EXCEPT" question, it is often easier to eliminate incorrect answer choices than to identify the correct answer choice directly. Also, the GRE has a slight but significant tendency to make the correct answer (D) or (E) on "EXCEPT" questions, to force you to read all of the answer choices. Thus, you may want to start with the last answer choice and work your way up, for this sort of question.

3. The passage suggests that the author regards ECT with

(A) conditional support
(B) academic objectivity
(C) mild advocacy
(D) unreserved criticism
(E) increasing acceptance

This is a GENERAL question (subtype: Infer About Opinions). Although you can often answer a Attitude question using only your general understanding of the passage, you should still closely examine the specific words the author uses to convey information. Here, the author presents evidence both for and against the efficacy and safety of ECT; he or she does not clearly lean toward or against more widespread adoption of the treatment. When presenting criticisms of ECT, the author does so in a manner that does not indicate a clear bias. The correct answer will reflect this balance.

Also, note that when answer choices are only two words long, the wrong answers will be wrong by just one or two words! Thus, all the incorrect answers below are One Word Wrong.

Answer choice **(A)** is incorrect, as the author's attitude does not indicate support for ECT. Moreover, there are no clear conditions placed upon any support by the author.

Answer choice **(B)** is the correct answer. The attitude of the author as expressed in the passage is impartial and objective. The passage explains the history and discussion of ECT in an unbiased, academic manner. We should still continue to examine all answer choices.

Answer choice **(C)** is incorrect, as the tone of the passage does not suggest even mild advocacy on the part of the author. Though the author admits the *proven* efficacy of ECT, this admission is counterbalanced by accounts of criticisms and controversy surrounding the treatment. The tone of the passage is not supportive overall.

Answer choice **(D)** is incorrect, as the language is too extreme. The tone of the passage is not unreserved, and the author is not clearly critical in his or her stance toward ECT.

Answer choice **(E)** is also not an accurate representation of the attitude of the author. It may be the case that ECT has achieved growing acceptance since its inception, but this reflects the popular or medical perception, not that of the author.

4. Which of the following statements can be inferred from the third paragraph?

(A) Greater amounts of the neurotransmitters serotonin, norepinephrine, and dopamine seem to reduce symptoms of depression.
(B) ECT is never used prior to attempting psychotherapy or medication.
(C) Succinylcholine completely immobilizes the patient's body.
(D) ECT generally works faster than antidepressants.
(E) One ECT treatment is often sufficient to reduce symptoms of depression significantly.

This is a SPECIFIC question (subtype: Infer About Facts). The answer to an inference question must be directly supported by evidence from the text. As always, be sure to pay particular attention to the precise words used in the answer choices and how they relate to the information presented in the passage.

For answer choice **(A)**, the third paragraph specifically states that ECT *affects* these particular neurotransmitters. However, no information is provided to suggest how these neurotransmitters are affected. Since the passage does not indicate an increase in these neurotransmitters, this cannot be the best answer. [Out of Scope]

The third paragraph states that *ECT is generally used in severely depressed patients for whom psychotherapy and medication prove ineffective.* This does not mean that ECT is *never* used before these other therapies. Answer choice **(B)** is too extreme to be the correct answer for this inference question. [One Word Wrong]

According to the third paragraph, succinylcholine renders muscle contractions *virtually nonexistent*, rather than *completely* nonexistent. Moreover, the passage states that a patient's hand or foot may rhythmically move during ECT. Thus the patient's body is not *completely* immobilized. Eliminate answer choice **(C)**. [One Word Wrong]

The paragraph also states that ECT may be used *when there is an imminent risk of suicide, since antidepressants often take several weeks to work effectively.* The conjunction *since* indicates that the length of time ECT takes to work is being contrasted with that of antidepressants. That is, it is implied that ECT works faster than antidepressants, at least in general. Answer choice **(D)** is correct. We see that this choice can be justified directly from proof sentences from the passage.

The final sentence of the third paragraph states that *repeated applications* of ECT affect several neurotransmitters. However, we are told nothing about how many treatments are needed to achieve results of any kind. Answer choice **(E)** is incorrect. [Out of Scope]

5. According to the passage, which of the following statements is true?

(A) Most severely depressed individuals have suicidal thoughts.
(B) The general public was unaware of the bodily harm caused by unmodified ECT.
(C) Research into the side effects of ECT has only recently begun.
(D) ECT does not benefit individuals with anxiety disorders.
(E) Severe depression can have symptoms unrelated to emotional mood.

This is a difficult SPECIFIC question (subtype: Lookup) that does not indicate a particular part of the passage in the question stem. Thus, you have to use key words from the answer choices, look up proof sentences, and eliminate choices one by one. Use your Skeletal sketch to quickly and accurately locate the important information in the passage, and then eliminate each answer choice as soon as you prove that it is not cited in the passage as true.

Answer choice (**A**) includes the key words *severely depressed* and *suicidal*, which lead us to the third paragraph of the passage. This paragraph indicates that ECT is considered as a treatment option *when there is an imminent risk of suicide*. However, nothing in the passage indicates the percentage (or number) of severely depressed individuals who have suicidal thoughts.
The use of the word *Most* is unjustified. Answer choice (**A**) can be eliminated. [One Word Wrong]

Answer choice (**B**) includes the key words *bodily harm* and *unmodified ECT*, which lead us to the second paragraph (which gives examples of the *bodily harm* caused by ECT in some cases). This paragraph describes ways in which the public was aware of the bodily harm caused by unmodified ECT. This knowledge influenced the general public's strongly negative conception of the procedure. Answer choice (**B**) is incorrect. [Direct Contradiction]

In answer choice (**C**), the key words *only recently* prompt us to look for time references. The second sentence of the final paragraph cites *decades-old studies* of ECT. Thus, research has not recently begun. Answer choice (**C**) should be ruled out. [Direct Contradiction]

The first paragraph states that *ECT is effective against severe depression, some acute psychotic states, and mania*. This does NOT necessarily mean that ECT is ineffective for *anxiety disorders*. With an "according to the passage" question, the correct answer must be provable by the passage text. Answer choice (**D**) is not shown by the passage to be true. [Out of Scope]

The final sentence of the passage states that a *memory malfunction* is a possible side effect of *severe depression*. A memory malfunction is clearly unrelated to emotional mood. Answer choice (**E**) is correct.

---

6. Which of the following statements represent of the general population's opinion of ECT? Select _all_ that apply.

[A] It has improved in the years since the treatment was first introduced.
[B] It has been affected by artistic representations of the treatment.
[C] It has likely had an effect on the terminology that proponents of ECT might use to describe the treatment.

This is a difficult SPECIFIC question presented in a select-all-that-apply format. The question is about the general population's opinion of ECT, which we know from our skeletal sketch is to be found primarily in the second paragraph. We should refer to that paragraph specifically when considering the three possible answer choices.

A. While we are told at the beginning of the fourth paragraph that "the consensus view of the scientific and medical community is that ECT has been proven effective," we are never told that the general public has come to the same conclusion. We are also told in the first sentence of the critical second paragraph that "since the inception of ECT in 1938, the public has held a strongly negative conception of the procedure." Nowhere does the passage state that this general opinion has improved, in spite of the fact that the process has grown far less violent and traumatic over the years. [Direct Contradiction]

B. CORRECT. In the second paragraph, we are told that Ken Kesey's One Flew Over the Cuckoo's Nest affected public sentiment by providing "graphic examples of abuse." This film can be described as an "artistic representation" of ECT, and so this answer is correct.

C. CORRECT. The final sentence of the second paragraph says that "the alternative term 'electroshock' has a negative connotation." This means that proponents of ECT would be unlikely to use the term, because it would summon up the negative feelings people have about the term. They would be more likely to call it ECT.

Both B and C are correct.

---

7. In the final two paragraphs, select a sentence that describes two possible causes of a given phenomenon.

This is a difficult SPECIFIC question of the select-in-passage variety. What makes it hard is that it fails to actively reference any individual detail of the passage. However, we are told that we should only look in the final two paragraphs. As the third paragraph is entirely taken up with explaining the factual science behind ECT, it is unlikely that we'll find what we're looking for there (though it would probably be safest to skim it again, just to be sure).

The third sentence of the final paragraph says "Patients have reported that their short-term memories continue to be affected for months after ECT, though some doctors argue that this memory malfunction may reflect the type of amnesia sometimes associated with severe depression." This sentence gives two possible explanations for the phenomenon of short-term amnesia: either ECT or the depression that the ECT was intended to cure.

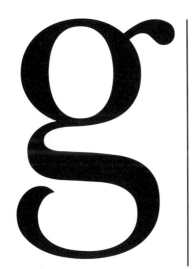

Chapter 8
of
READING COMPREHENSION & ESSAYS

PASSAGES & PROBLEM SETS

Problem Set

The following problem set consists of reading passages followed by a series of questions on each passage. Use the following guidelines as you complete this problem set:

1. Before you read each passage, identify whether it is long or short.

2. Preview the first question before reading, but do not attempt to answer any of the questions before you have read the whole passage.

3. As you read the passage, apply the 7 principles of active, efficient reading. Create a Headline List (for short passages) or a Skeletal Sketch (for long passages). Then, use your Headline List or Skeletal Sketch to assist you in answering all the questions that accompany the passage.

4. Before answering each question, identify it as either a General question or a Specific question. Use the 7 strategies for Reading Comprehension to assist you in answering the questions.

5. On the GRE, you will typically see one to three questions with short passages and about four questions with long passages. However, in this problem set, you will see six or seven questions associated with each passage. As such, use the following modified timing guidelines:

    For short passages: Spend approximately 1.5 minutes reading and creating your Headline List. Spend approximately 45 seconds answering General questions and between 45 and 60 seconds answering Specific questions. Select-all-that-apply questions and EXCEPT questions should be at the top end of this range, as they require you to seek out multiple specific items in the passage.

    For long passages: Spend approximately two to three minutes reading and creating your Skeletal Sketch. The time you should spend on each individual question is about the same as that listed for short passages.

Passage A: Japanese Swords

Historians have long recognized the traditional Japanese sword, or *nihonto*, as one of the finest cutting weapons ever produced, but it has even been considered a spiritual entity. The adage "The sword is the soul of the samurai" reflects the sword's psychic importance, not only to its wielder, but also to its creator, the master smith. Not classically regarded as artists, master smiths nevertheless exerted great care in the process of creating swords, no two of which were ever forged exactly the same way. Over hundreds of hours, two types of steel were repeatedly heated, hammered, and folded together into thousands of subtle layers, yielding both a razor-sharp, durable edge and a flexible, shock-absorbing blade. Commonly, though optionally, the smith physically signed the blade; moreover, each smith's secret forging techniques left an idiosyncratic structural signature. Each unique finished product reflected the smith's personal honor and devotion to craft, and today, the Japanese sword is valued as much for its artistic merit as for its historical significance.

1. **The primary purpose of the passage is to**

(A) challenge the observation that the Japanese sword is highly admired by historians
(B) introduce new information about the forging of Japanese swords
(C) identify the Japanese sword as an ephemeral work of art
(D) argue that Japanese sword makers were motivated by honor
(E) explain the value attributed to the Japanese sword

2. **Each of the following is mentioned in the passage EXCEPT**

(A) every Japanese sword has a unique structure that can be traced back to a special forging process
(B) master smiths kept their forging methodologies secret
(C) the Japanese sword was considered by some to have a spiritual quality
(D) master smiths are now considered artists by major historians
(E) the Japanese sword is considered both a work of art and a historical artifact

3. **The author is most likely to agree with which of the following observations?**

(A) The Japanese sword is the most important handheld weapon in history.
(B) The skill of the samurai is what made the Japanese sword so special.
(C) If a sword had a physical signature, other swords could be attributed to that sword's creator.
(D) Master smiths were more concerned about the artistic merit of their blades than about the blades' practical qualities.
(E) The Japanese sword has more historical importance than artistic importance.

4. **Which of the following can be inferred about the term "structural signature" in this passage?**

(A) It indicates the inscription that the smith places on the blade during the forging process.
(B) It implies the particular characteristics of a blade created by a smith's unique forging process.
(C) It suggests that each blade can be traced back to a known master smith.
(D) It reflects the soul of the samurai who wielded the sword.
(E) It refers to the unique curved shape of the blade.

5. **The author most likely describes the forging process in order to**

(A) present an explanation for a change in perception
(B) determine the historical significance of Japanese swords
(C) explain why each Japanese sword is unique
(D) compare Japanese master smiths to classical artists
(E) review the complete process of making a Japanese sword

6. **Select the sentence in the passage that describes the process master smiths could use to render their creations visually unique.**

7. **Which of the following statements about Japanese swords is supported by the passage? Select _all_ that apply.**

[A] There is a way to determine the creator of a given sword other than his signature on the blade.
[B] They have been viewed in terms other than the purely material.
[C] They have not always received the artistic recognition that they deserve.

Passage B: Television's Invention

In the early years of television, Vladimir Zworykin was considered its inventor, at least publicly. His loudest champion was his boss David Sarnoff, the president of RCA and the "father of television," as he was and is widely regarded. Modern historians agree that Philo Farnsworth, a self-educated prodigy who was the first to transmit live images, was television's technical inventor. But Farnsworth's contributions have gone relatively unnoticed, since it was Sarnoff, not Farnsworth, who put televisions into living rooms and, even more importantly, who successfully borrowed from the radio industry the paradigm of advertiser-funded programming, a paradigm still dominant today. In contrast, Farnsworth lacked business savvy and was unable to realize his dream of television as an educational tool.

Perhaps Sarnoff simply adapted his business ideas from other industries such as newspapers, for instance, replacing the revenue from subscriptions and newsstand purchases with that of television set sales, but Sarnoff promoted himself as a visionary. Some critics argue that Sarnoff's construct has damaged programming content. Others contend that it merely created a democratic platform allowing audiences to choose the programming they desire.

1.   **The primary purpose of the passage is to**

(A)   correct public misconception about Farnsworth's role in developing early television programs
(B)   debate the influence of television on popular culture
(C)   challenge the current public perception of Vladimir Zworykin
(D)   chronicle the events that led from the development of radio to the invention of the television
(E)   describe Sarnoff's influence on the public perception of television's inception, and debate the impact of Sarnoff's paradigm

2.   **It can be inferred from the second paragraph of the passage that**

(A)   television shows produced by David Sarnoff and Vladimir Zworykin tended to earn negative reviews
(B)   educational programs cannot draw as large an audience as sports programs
(C)   a number of critics feel that Sarnoff's initial decision to earn television revenue through advertising has had a positive or neutral impact on content
(D)   educational programs that are aired in prime time, the hours during which the greatest number of viewers are watching television, are less likely to earn a profit than those that are aired during the daytime hours
(E)   in matters of programming, the audience's preferences should be more influential than those of the advertisers

3. **According to the passage, the television industry, at its inception, earned revenue from**

(A) advertising only
(B) advertising and the sale of television sets
(C) advertising and subscriptions
(D) subscriptions and the sale of television sets
(E) advertising, subscriptions, and the sale of television sets

4. **The passage suggests that Farnsworth might have earned greater public notoriety for his invention if**

(A) Vladimir Zworykin had been less vocal about his own contributions to the television
(B) Farnsworth had been able to develop and air his own educational programs
(C) Farnsworth had adapted his business ideas from the radio today
(D) Sarnoff had involved Farnsworth in his plans to develop, manufacture, or distribute the television
(E) Farnsworth had a better understanding of the type of programming the audience wanted to watch most

5. **Select the sentence that provides factual evidence that Sarnoff's talents were more imitative than innovative.**

6. **Which of the following statements is supported by the passage? Select _all_ that apply.**

[A] The advertising-funded model of television has damaged programming content.
[B] The technical invention of television has been overshadowed by its popularization.
[C] There is no way to definitively prove who invented the first television.

Passage C: Life on Mars

Because of the proximity and likeness of Mars to Earth, scientists have long speculated about the possibility of life on Mars. Roughly three centuries ago, astronomers observed Martian polar ice caps, and later scientists discovered other similarities to Earth, including length of day and axial tilt. But in 1965, photos taken by the Mariner 4 probe revealed a Mars without rivers, oceans or signs of life. Moreover, in the 1990s, it was discovered that unlike Earth, Mars no longer possessed a substantial global magnetic field, allowing celestial radiation to reach the planet's surface and solar wind to eliminate much of Mars's atmosphere over the course of several billion years.

More recent probes have investigated whether there was once liquid water on Mars. Some scientists believe that the presence of certain geological landforms definitively resolves this question. Others posit that wind erosion or carbon dioxide oceans may be responsible for these formations. Mars rovers Opportunity and Spirit, which landed on Mars in 2004, have both discovered geological evidence of past water activity. These findings substantially bolster claims that there was once life on Mars.

1. **The author's stance on the possibility of life on Mars can best be described as**

(A) optimistic
(B) disinterested
(C) skeptical
(D) simplistic
(E) cynical

2. **The passage is primarily concerned with which of the following?**

(A) Disproving a widely accepted theory.
(B) Initiating a debate about the possibility of life on Mars.
(C) Presenting evidence in support of a controversial claim.
(D) Describing the various discoveries made concerning the possibility of life on Mars.
(E) Detailing the findings of the Mars rovers Opportunity and Spirit.

3. **Each of the following discoveries is mentioned in the passage EXCEPT**

(A) wind erosion and carbon dioxide oceans are responsible for certain geological landforms on Mars
(B) mars does not have a substantial global magnetic field
(C) mars does not currently have water activity
(D) the length of day on Mars is similar to that on Earth
(E) the axial tilt of Mars is similar to that of Earth

4. **In the first paragraph, the author most likely mentions the discovery of polar ice caps to suggest that**

(A) until recently Mars' polar ice caps were thought to consist largely of carbon dioxide
(B) Martian polar ice caps are made almost entirely of water ice
(C) Mars has many similarities to Earth, including the existence of polar ice caps
(D) Mars has only a small fraction of the carbon dioxide found on Earth and Venus
(E) conditions on the planet Mars were once very different than they are at present

5. **Each of the following can be inferred from the passage EXCEPT**

(A) the presence of certain geological landforms is not definitive proof that there was once life on Mars
(B) it is likely that there were few significant discoveries related to the possibility of life on Mars three centuries ago
(C) the absence of a substantial global magnetic field on Mars suggests that it would be difficult to sustain life on Mars
(D) the presence of water activity on Mars is related to the possibility of life on Mars
(E) the claim that there was once water on Mars has only limited and indirect support from recent discoveries

6. **It can be inferred from the passage that which of the following characteristics of a planet would imply that it might support life? Select _all_ that apply.**

[A] A significant global magnetic field
[B] Evidence of liquid carbon-dioxide on the planet's surface
[C] A size roughly approximating that of Earth

7. **Select the sentence in the passage that provides the best evidence that there has never been life on Mars.**

Passage D: Fossils

Archaeological discoveries frequently undermine accepted ideas, giving rise to new theories. Recently, a set of 3.3-million-year-old fossils, the remains of the earliest well-preserved child ever found, were discovered in Ethiopia. Estimated to be 3 years old at death, the female child was of the Australopithecus afarensis species, a human ancestor that lived in Africa over 3 million years ago. "Her completeness, antiquity and age at death make this find of unprecedented importance in the history of paleo-anthropology," said Zeresenay Alemseged, a noted paleo-anthropologist, opining that the discovery could reconfigure conceptions about early humans' capacities.

Previously, afarensis was believed to have abandoned arboreal habitats. However, while the new fossil's lower limbs support the view of an upright stance, its gorilla-like arms suggest that afarensis was still able to swing through trees, initiating a reexamination of long-held theories of early human development. Also, the presence of a hyoid bone, a rarely preserved larynx bone that supports throat muscles, has dramatically affected concepts of the origin of speech. Although primitive and more ape-like than human-like, this fossil hyoid is the first found in such an early human-related species.

1. **The organization of the passage could best be described as**

(A) discussing a controversial scientific discovery
(B) contrasting previous theories of development with current findings
(C) illustrating a contention with a specific example
(D) arguing for the importance of a particular field of study
(E) refuting a popular misconception

2. **The passage quotes Zeresenay Alemseged in order to**

(A) provide evidence to qualify the main idea of the first paragraph
(B) question the claims of other scientists
(C) provide evidence to support the linguistic abilities of the afarensis species
(D) provide evidence that supports the significance of the find
(E) provide a subjective opinion that is refuted in the second paragraph

3. **Each of the following is cited as a factor in the importance of the discovery of the fossils EXCEPT**

(A) the fact that the remains were those of a child
(B) the age of the fossils
(C) the location of the discovery
(D) the species of the fossils
(E) the intact nature of the fossils

4. **It can be inferred from the passage's description of the discovered fossil hyoid bone that**

(A) Australopithecus afarensis were capable of speech
(B) the discovered hyoid bone is less primitive than the hyoid bone of apes
(C) the hyoid bone is necessary for speech
(D) the discovery of the hyoid bone necessitated the reexamination of prior theories
(E) the hyoid bone was the most important fossil found at the site

5. **According to the passage, the impact of the discovery of the hyoid bone in the field of archaeology could best be compared to which one of the following examples in another field?**

(A) The discovery and analysis of cosmic rays lend support to a widely accepted theory of the origin of the universe.
(B) The original manuscript of a deceased 19th century author confirms ideas of the development of an important work of literature.
(C) The continued prosperity of a state-run economy stirs debate in the discipline of macroeconomics.
(D) Newly revealed journal entries by a prominent Civil War era politician lead to a questioning of certain accepted historical interpretations about the conflict.
(E) Research into the mapping of the human genome gives rise to nascent applications of individually tailored medicines.

6. **Select the sentence that most distinctly undermines an accepted paleo-anthropological theory.**

7. **The author of the passage suggests that which of the following is exemplified by the recent discovery? Select _all_ that apply.**

[A] Scientists' eagerness to embrace new discoveries
[B] The constantly evolving nature of paleo-anthropology
[C] The way in which new information can necessitate new theories

Passage E: Polygamy

Polygamy in Africa has been a popular topic for social research over the past several decades; it has been analyzed by many distinguished minds and in various well-publicized works. In 1961, when Remi Clignet published his book "Many Wives, Many Powers," he was not alone in sharing the view that in Africa co-wives may be perceived as direct and indirect sources of increased income and prestige. For instance, some observers argued that polygamous marriages are more able than monogamous marriages to produce many children, who can legitimately be seen as a form of wealth, as well as of "this-world" immortality connected to the transmission of family names (as opposed to "other-world" immortality in an afterlife). Moreover, polygamy is rooted in and sanctioned by many ancient traditions, both cultural and religious; therefore, some assert that polygamy can provide a stabilizing function within societies frequently under stress from both internal and external forces.

By the 1970s, such arguments had become crystallized and popular. Many other African scholars who wrote on the subject became the new champions of this philosophy. For example, in 1983, John Mbiti proclaimed that polygamy is an accepted and respectable institution serving many useful social purposes. Similarly, G.K. Nukunya, in his paper "Polygamy as a Symbol of Status," reiterated Mbiti's idea that a plurality of wives is a legitimate sign of affluence and power in African society.

However, the colonial missionary voice provided consistent opposition to polygamy by viewing the practice as unethical and destructive of family life. While they propagated this view with the authority of the Bible, they were convinced that Africans had to be coerced into partaking in the vision of monogamy understood by the Western culture. The missionary viewpoint even included, in some instances, dictating immediate divorce in the case of newly converted men who had already contracted polygamous marriages. Unfortunately, both the missionary voice and the scholarly voice did not consider the views of African women on the matter important. Although there was some awareness that women regarded polygamy as both a curse and a blessing, the distanced, albeit scientific, perspective of an outside observer predominated both on the pulpit and in scholarly writings.

Contemporary research in the social sciences has begun to focus on the protagonist's voice in the study of culture, recognizing that the views and experiences of those who take part in a given reality ought to receive close examination. This privileging of the protagonist seems appropriate, particularly given that women in Africa have often used literary productions, which feature protagonists and other "actors" undergoing ordeals and otherwise taking active part in real life, to comment on marriage, family and gender relations.

1. **Which of the following best describes the main purpose of the passage above?**

(A) To discuss scholarly works that view polygamy as a sign of prestige, respect, and affluence in the African society.
(B) To trace the origins of the missionary opposition to African polygamy.
(C) To argue for imposing restrictions on polygamy in the African society.
(D) To explore the reasons for women's acceptance of polygamy.
(E) To discuss multiple perspectives on African polygamy and contrast them with contemporary research.

2. **The third paragraph of the passage plays which of the following roles?**

(A) Discusses the rationale for viewing polygamy as an indication of prestige and affluence in the African society.
(B) Supports the author's view that polygamy is unethical and destructive of family life.
(C) Contrasts the views of the colonial missionary with the position of the most recent contemporary research.
(D) Describes the views on polygamy held by the colonial missionary and indicates a flaw in this vision.
(E) Demonstrates that the colonial missionary was ignorant of the scholarly research on monogamy.

3. **The passage provides each of the following, EXCEPT**

(A) the year of publication of Remi Clignet's book "Many Wives, Many Powers"
(B) the year in which John Mbiti made a claim that polygamy is an accepted institution
(C) examples of African women's literary productions devoted to family relations
(D) reasons for missionary opposition to polygamy
(E) current research perspectives on polygamy

4. **According to the passage, the colonial missionary and the early scholarly research shared which of the following traits in their views on polygamy?**

(A) Both considered polygamy a sign of social status and success.
(B) Neither accounted for the views of local women.
(C) Both attempted to limit the prevalence of polygamy.
(D) Both pointed out polygamy's destructive effects on family life.
(E) Both exhibited a somewhat negative attitude towards polygamy.

5. **Which of the following statements can most properly be inferred from the passage?**

(A) Nukunya's paper "Polygamy as a Symbol of Status" was not written in 1981.
(B) John Mbiti adjusted his initial view on polygamy, recognizing that the experiences of African women should receive closer attention.
(C) Remi Clignet's book "Many Wives, Many Powers" was the first well-known scholarly work to proclaim that polygamy can be viewed as a symbol or prestige and wealth.
(D) Under the influence of the missionary opposition, polygamy was proclaimed illegal in Africa as a practice "unethical and destructive of family life."
(E) A large proportion of the scholars writing on polygamy in the 1970s and 1980s were of African descent.

6. **Which of the following examples fit the model of cultural studies cited in the final paragraph of the passage? Select _all_ that apply.**

A A documentary about the modern-day slave trade that relied on interviews with those who had been enslaved
B A study of gorillas in confinement that made use of techniques for ascertaining the psychological state of each gorilla
C An experimental theater piece about blindness in which audience members were required to wear a blindfold

7. **Select the sentence in the first two paragraphs that cites a specific benefit of polygamy without mentioning the economic ramifications.**

Passage F: Sweet Spot

Though most tennis players generally strive to strike the ball on the racket's vibration node, more commonly known as the "sweet spot," many players are unaware of the existence of a second, lesser-known location on the racket face, the center of percussion, that will also greatly diminish the strain on a player's arm when the ball is struck.

In order to understand the physics of this second sweet spot, it is helpful to consider what would happen to a tennis racket in the moments after impact with the ball if the player's hand were to vanish at the moment of impact. The impact of the ball would cause the racket to bounce back-wards, experiencing a translational motion away from the ball. The tendency of this motion would be to jerk all parts of the racket, including the end of its handle, backward, or away from the ball. Unless the ball happened to hit the rack-et precisely at the racket's center of mass, the racket would additionally experience a rotational motion around its center of mass—much as a penny that has been struck near its edge will start to spin. Whenever the ball hits the racket face, the effect of this rotational motion will be to jerk the end of the handle forward, towards the ball. Depending on where the ball strikes the racket face, one or the other of these motions will predominate.

However, there is one point of impact, known as the center of percussion, which causes neither motion to pre-dominate; if a ball were to strike this point, the impact would not impart any motion to the end of the handle. The reason for this lack of motion is that the force on the upper part of the hand would be equal and opposite to the force on the lower part of the hand, resulting in no net force on the tennis players' hand or forearm. The center of percussion consti-tutes a second sweet spot because a tennis player's wrist typically is placed next to the end of the racket's handle. When the player strikes the ball at the center of percussion, her wrist is jerked neither forward nor backward, and she experiences a relatively smooth, comfortable tennis stroke.

The manner in which a tennis player can detect the center of percussion on a given tennis racket follows from the nature of this second sweet spot. The center of percussion can be located via simple trial and error by holding the end of a tennis racket between your finger and thumb and throwing a ball onto the strings. If the handle jumps out of your hand, then the ball has missed the center of percussion.

1.   **What is the primary message the author is trying to convey?**

(A)   A proposal for an improvement to the design of tennis rackets.
(B)   An examination of the differences between the two types of sweet spot.
(C)   A definition of the translational and rotational forces acting on a tennis racket.
(D)   A description of the ideal area in which to strike every ball.
(E)   An explanation of a lesser-known area on a tennis racket that dampens unwanted vibration.

2. **According to the passage, all of the following are true of the forces acting upon a tennis racket striking a ball EXCEPT**

(A) the only way to eliminate the jolt that accompanies most strokes is to hit the ball on the center of percussion
(B) the impact of the ball striking the racket can strain a tennis player's arm
(C) there are at least two different forces acting upon the racket
(D) the end of the handle of the racket will jerk forward after striking the ball unless the ball strikes the racket's center of mass
(E) the racket will rebound after it strikes the ball

3. **What is the primary function served by paragraph two in the context of the entire passage?**

(A) To establish the main idea of the passage.
(B) To provide an explanation of the mechanics of the phenomenon discussed in the passage.
(C) To introduce a counterargument that elucidates the main idea of the passage.
(D) To provide an example of the primary subject described in the passage.
(E) To explain why the main idea of the passage would be useful for tennis players.

4. **The author mentions "a penny that has been struck near its edge" in order to**

(A) show how the center of mass causes the racket to spin
(B) argue that a penny spins in the exact way that a tennis racket spins
(C) explain how translational motion works
(D) provide an illustration of a concept
(E) demonstrate that pennies and tennis rackets do not spin in the same way

5. **Which of the following can be inferred from the passage?**

(A) If a player holds the tennis racket anywhere other than the end of the handle, the player will experience a jolting sensation.
(B) The primary sweet spot is more effective at damping vibration than the secondary sweet spot.
(C) Striking a tennis ball at a spot other than the center of percussion can result in a jarring feeling.
(D) Striking a tennis ball repeatedly at spots other than a sweet spot leads to "tennis elbow."
(E) If a player lets go of the racket at the moment of impact, the simultaneous forward and backward impetus causes the racket to drop straight to the ground.

6. **Select the sentence in the second or third paragraph that describes the physics of the center of percussion's perceived "sweetness."**

7. **It can be inferred that a tennis ball that strikes a racket's center of percussion will do which of the following. Select _all_ that apply.**

A Cause at least some strain on the arm of the player swinging the racket
B Not cause the wrist to jerk
C Allow for a cleaner stroke than a ball striking a racket's primary sweet spot

Passage G: Chaos Theory

Around 1960, mathematician Edward Lorenz found unexpected behavior in apparently simple equations representing atmospheric air flows. Whenever he reran his model with the same inputs, different outputs resulted—although the model lacked any random elements. Lorenz realized that tiny rounding errors in his analog computer mushroomed over time, leading to erratic results. His findings marked a seminal moment in the development of chaos theory, which, despite its name, has little to do with randomness.

To understand how unpredictability can arise from deterministic equations, which do not involve chance outcomes, consider the non-chaotic system of two poppy seeds placed in a round bowl. As the seeds roll to the bowl's center, a position known as a point attractor, the distance between the seeds shrinks. If, instead, the bowl is flipped over, two seeds placed on top will roll away from each other. Such a system, while still not technically chaotic, enlarges initial differences in position.

Chaotic systems, such as a machine mixing bread dough, are characterized by both attraction and repulsion. As the dough is stretched, folded and pressed back together, any poppy seeds sprinkled in are intermixed seemingly at random. But this randomness is illusory. In fact, the poppy seeds are captured by "strange attractors," staggeringly complex pathways whose tangles appear accidental but are in fact determined by the system's fundamental equations.

During the dough-kneading process, two poppy seeds positioned next to each other eventually go their separate ways. Any early divergence or measurement error is repeatedly amplified by the mixing until the position of any seed becomes effectively unpredictable. It is this "sensitive dependence on initial conditions" and not true randomness that generates unpredictability in chaotic systems, of which one example may be the Earth's weather. According to the popular interpretation of the "Butterfly Effect," a butterfly flapping its wings causes hurricanes. A better understanding is that the butterfly causes uncertainty about the precise state of the air. This microscopic uncertainty grows until it encompasses even hurricanes. Few meteorologists believe that we will ever be able to predict rain or shine for a particular day years in the future.

1. **The main purpose of this passage is to**

(A) explain complicated aspects of certain physical systems
(B) trace the historical development of a scientific theory
(C) distinguish a mathematical pattern from its opposite
(D) describe the spread of a technical model from one field of study to others
(E) contrast possible causes of weather phenomena

2. **In the example discussed in the passage, what is true about poppy seeds in bread dough, once the dough has been thoroughly mixed?**

(A) They have been individually stretched and folded over, like miniature versions of the entire dough.
(B) They are scattered in random clumps throughout the dough.
(C) They are accidentally caught in tangled objects called strange attractors.
(D) They are bound to regularly dispersed patterns of point attractors.
(E) They are in positions dictated by the underlying equations that govern the mixing process.

3. **According to the passage, the rounding errors in Lorenz's model**

(A) indicated that the model was programmed in a fundamentally faulty way
(B) were deliberately included to represent tiny fluctuations in atmospheric air currents
(C) were imperceptibly small at first, but tended to grow
(D) were at least partially expected, given the complexity of the actual atmosphere
(E) shrank to insignificant levels during each trial of the model

4. **The passage mentions each of the following as an example or potential example of a chaotic or non-chaotic system EXCEPT**

(A) a dough-mixing machine
(B) atmospheric weather patterns
(C) poppy seeds placed on top of an upside-down bowl
(D) poppy seeds placed in a right-side-up bowl
(E) fluctuating butterfly flight patterns

5. **It can be inferred from the passage that which of the following pairs of items would most likely follow typical pathways within a chaotic system?**

(A) Two particles ejected in random directions from the same decaying atomic nucleus.
(B) Two stickers affixed to a balloon that expands and contracts over and over again.
(C) Two avalanches sliding down opposite sides of the same mountain.
(D) Two baseballs placed into an active tumble dryer.
(E) Two coins flipped into a large bowl.

6. **The author implies which of the following about weather systems? Select _all_ that apply.**

[A] They illustrate the same fundamental phenomenon as Lorenz's rounding errors.
[B] They are too complicated to ever be predicted with total accuracy.
[C] They are governed mostly by seemingly trivial events, such as the flapping of a butterfly's wings.

7. **Select the sentence in the second or third paragraph that illustrates why "chaos theory" might be called a misnomer.**

Answers to Passage A: Japanese Swords

Historians have long recognized the traditional Japanese sword, or *nihonto*, as one of the finest cutting weapons ever produced, but it has even been considered a spiritual entity. The adage "The sword is the soul of the samurai" reflects the sword's psychic importance, not only to its wielder, but also to its creator, the master smith. Not classically regarded as artists, master smiths nevertheless exerted great care in the process of creating swords, no two of which were ever forged exactly the same way. Over hundreds of hours, two types of steel were repeatedly heated, hammered, and folded together into thousands of subtle layers, yielding both a razor-sharp, durable edge and a flexible, shock-absorbing blade. Commonly, though optionally, the smith physically signed the blade; moreover, each smith's secret forging techniques left an idiosyncratic structural signature. Each unique finished product reflected the smith's personal honor and devotion to craft, and today, the Japanese sword is valued as much for its artistic merit as for its historical significance.

This is a short passage. Here is a model Headline List:

---

1) H: J sword = 1 of best cutting weapons, but even spiritual   ← Point
   —Soul of Samurai
   —Impt to smith too

2) —Smiths careful, swords unique
   —Forging process complex
   —Physical + structural signat.

---

1. The primary purpose of the passage is to

    (A) challenge the observation that the Japanese sword is highly admired by historians
    (B) introduce new information about the forging of Japanese swords
    (C) identify the Japanese sword as an ephemeral work of art
    (D) argue that Japanese sword makers were motivated by honor
    (E) explain the value attributed to the Japanese sword

To identify the primary purpose of the passage, you should examine the passage as a whole. Avoid answer choices that address only limited sections of the passage. The Point of the passage (*the Japanese sword has been considered not just a fine weapon but a spiritual entity*) is clearly established in the first two sentences; the purpose of the passage is to explain and support that Point.

(A) The passage does not call into question the admiration that historians have for the Japanese sword.

(B) The middle of the passage discusses forging techniques, but none of the information is presented as new. Moreover, these forging techniques are not the focus of the passage.

(C) The Japanese sword is not identified as an ephemeral (passing) work of art in the passage.

(D) Japanese sword makers were indeed motivated by honor, at least in part, according to the last sentence, but this is not the purpose of the passage, much of which describes the Japanese sword's physical properties and reasons for its importance.

(E) CORRECT. The passage as a whole describes the immense value of the Japanese sword to both the samurai (the sword's owner) and the smith (its maker). The saying *The sword is the soul of the samurai* is referenced early to indicate this importance. Later portions of the passage detail the tremendous effort that is put into each sword, reflecting the importance of each one.

2. Each of the following is mentioned in the passage EXCEPT

(A) every Japanese sword has a unique structure that can be traced back to a special forging process
(B) master smiths kept their forging methodologies secret
(C) the Japanese sword was considered by some to have a spiritual quality
(D) master smiths are now considered artists by major historians
(E) the Japanese sword is considered both a work of art and a historical artifact

For an "EXCEPT" question (almost always a Specific question), you should use the process of elimination to identify and cross out those details mentioned in the passage.

(A) In the passage this *unique signature* is referred to as a *structural signature*.

(B) The fifth sentence mentions the *secret forging techniques* used by each smith.

(C) The first sentence indicates that *the traditional Japanese sword...has even been considered a spiritual entity.*

(D) CORRECT. The time and effort master smiths devote to making a sword is discussed, and the passage does indicate that the Japanese sword is valued for its artistic merit. However, the passage does not state that most major historians consider master smiths themselves to be artists. *Major* historians are not referenced in the passage. Moreover, who values the Japanese sword for its artistic merit is not mentioned.

(E) In the last sentence, the passage indicates that *the Japanese sword is valued as much for its artistic merit as for its historical significance.*

3. The author is most likely to agree with which of the following observations?

(A) The Japanese sword is the most important handheld weapon in history.
(B) The skill of the samurai is what made the Japanese sword so special.
(C) If a sword had a physical signature, other swords could likely be attributed to that sword's creator.
(D) Master smiths were more concerned about the artistic merit of their blades than about the blades' practical qualities.
(E) The Japanese sword has more historical importance than artistic importance.

When looking for statements with which the author could agree, be sure to avoid extreme words and positions that go beyond the author's statements in the passage. This question requires attention to both the general Point of the passage and specific details throughout.

(A) The opening sentence says that *historians have long recognized the traditional Japanese sword ... as one of the finest cutting weapons ever produced*; however, there is no indication that the Japanese sword is the most important handheld weapon in history. There could be many others (e.g. handguns).

(B) This passage does not discuss the skill of the samurai warrior.

(C) CORRECT. According to the passage, every master smith had a *structural signature* due to his own secret forging process. Therefore, if a physical signature is present on a blade, that blade's structural signature could then be associated with a master smith, whose *master* status implies the creation of numerous swords.

(D) The passage mentions that each sword *reflected the smith's personal honor and devotion to craft*; however, there is no claim that master smiths emphasized their swords' artistic merit at the expense of practical qualities.

(E) The passage acknowledges that the Japanese sword is important both historically and artistically, but the author does not stress the sword's historical importance over its artistry.

>
> 4. **Which of the following can be inferred about the term "structural signature" in this passage?**
>
>   (A) It indicates the inscription that the smith places on the blade during the forging process.
>   (B) It implies the particular characteristics of a blade created by a smith's unique forging process.
>   (C) It suggests that each blade can be traced back to a known master smith.
>   (D) It reflects the soul of the samurai who wielded the swords.
>   (E) It refers to the unique curved shape of the blade.

The author states that *each smith's secret forging techniques left an idiosyncratic structural signature*. The words *idiosyncratic* and *signature* imply the uniqueness of the smith's process. Be careful not to infer any additional information, particularly when the question refers to a specific sentence or phrase.

(A) In the passage, such an inscription is referred to as a *physical signature*, not a *structural signature*.

(B) CORRECT. Note that the proof sentence indicates that each smith had his own process, and so the *"structural signature"* was unique to each smith (not necessarily to each individual blade).

(C) This statement seems reasonable. However, the passage does not say whether all master smiths are currently *known*. Certain swords with a structural signature may be of unknown origin.

(D) The second sentence mentions the saying *The sword is the soul of the samurai*, but we are not told that the structural signature was the aspect of the sword reflecting the soul of the samurai who wielded it. The second paragraph explains that the sword *reflected the <u>smith's</u> personal honor and devotion to craft*. This statement, however, does not justify the claim that the *structural signature* itself *reflects the soul of the samurai who wielded it*.

(E) The passage does not discuss the shape of any Japanese blade.

5. The author most likely describes the forging process in order to

(A) present an explanation for a change in perception
(B) determine the historical significance of Japanese swords
(C) explain why each Japanese sword is unique
(D) compare Japanese master smiths to classical artists
(E) review the complete process of making a Japanese sword

To determine the function(s) of any part of a passage, pay attention to the emphasized content of the part, in particular any reiterated points, and to the relationship the part has to other portions of the passage. In this case, the description of the forging process extends the idea introduced earlier that the Japanese sword is revered.

(A) The final sentence mentions that Japanese swords are now appreciated more for their artistic merit, but no explanation is provided.

(B) The term *historical significance* closes the passage, but the description of the forging process fails to explain or outline that significance.

(C) **CORRECT.** The description of the forging process underscores the uniqueness of individual Japanese swords. One sentence mentions that *no two [swords] were ever forged in exactly the same way.* Later, *structural signature* and *unique finished product* reinforce this point.

(D) The passage explains that master smiths were not considered artists in the classical sense, and then goes on to point out the painstaking creation of each sword. This implicitly draws a parallel between the creation of the sword and classical artistry. However, the passage does not actually describe or discuss classical artists, nor does it set forth criteria for classical artists. There is no actual comparison to classical artists, despite the mention of *artistic merit*. This answer choice goes too far beyond the passage; thus, it is incorrect.

(E) Elements of the forging process are discussed, but the whole or *complete* process of making a Japanese sword, such as making the handle, polishing the blade, etc. is not discussed in the paragraph.

6. Select the sentence in the passage that describes the process master smiths could use to render their creations visually unique.

This is a select-in-passage revolving around the notion of a sword's uniqueness. There are a number of sentences in the passage that discuss the concept of uniqueness, but only a couple describe any kind of process. The first is the fourth sentence, which describes the process that master smiths used to forge their blades. The sentence after that one states that "the smith physically signed the blade." While we are later told that the forging process created an "idiosyncratic structural signature," this wouldn't render the sword visually unique, as one would have to look at the underlying structure in order to locate the sword's uniqueness. The signature itself would be the most direct way of rendering a sword VISUALLY unique. The correct answer is the fifth sentence, beginning "Commonly, though optionally…"

7. Which of the following statements about Japanese swords is supported by the passage? Select _all_ that apply.

[A] There is a way to determine the creator of a given sword other than his signature on the blade.
[B] They have been viewed in terms other than the purely material.
[C] They have not always received the artistic recognition that they deserve.

A, B, and C: This is a GENERAL question of the select-all-that-apply variety. Make sure you take on each answer choice as if it were its own question.

(A) CORRECT. We are told in the second-to-last sentence that "each smith's secret forging techniques left an idiosyncratic structural signature." This would imply that this structural signature could be used to determine the creator of a given sword, even in the absence of a physical signature.

(B) CORRECT. The first sentence tells us that the Japanese sword "has even been considered a spiritual entity." This means that it has been viewed in terms other than the strictly material.

(C) CORRECT. The last sentence tells us that "today, the Japanese sword is valued as much for its artistic merit as for its historical significance." Earlier in the passage, however, we were told that master smiths were "not classically regarded as artists." This means that those smiths viewed as artists today did not always receive the recognition that they deserve, and neither did the swords they made.

Answers to Passage B: Television's Invention

In the early years of television, Vladimir Zworykin was considered its inventor, at least publicly. His loudest champion was his boss David Sarnoff, the president of RCA and the "father of television," as he was and is widely regarded. Modern historians agree that Philo Farnsworth, a self-educated prodigy who was the first to transmit live images, was television's technical inventor. But Farnsworth's contributions have gone relatively unnoticed, since it was Sarnoff, not Farnsworth, who put televisions into living rooms and, even more importantly, who successfully borrowed from the radio industry the paradigm of advertiser-funded programming, a paradigm still dominant today. In contrast, Farnsworth lacked business savvy and was unable to realize his dream of television as an educational tool.

Perhaps Sarnoff simply adapted his business ideas from other industries such as newspapers, for instance, replacing the revenue from subscriptions and newsstand purchases with that of television set sales, but Sarnoff promoted himself as a visionary. Some critics argue that Sarnoff's construct has damaged programming content. Others contend that it merely created a democratic platform allowing audiences to choose the programming they desire.

This is a short passage. Here is a model Headline List:

---

1) Early TV yrs, Z seen = TV invntr
   —champ by RCA pres Sarn (father of TV!)
    BUT now hist agree: F = TRUE invntr, tho unnoticed
   —S intro'd, resp for domin paradigm: advrs pay   ← Point
   —F: failed at TV = educ

2) Maybe S just adapted newsppr model
   —bad for content vs. democ platform?

---

1. The primary purpose of the passage is to

(A) correct public misconception about Farnsworth's role in developing early television programs
(B) debate the influence of television on popular culture
(C) challenge the current public perception of Vladimir Zworykin
(D) chronicle the events that led from the development of radio to the invention of the television
(E) describe Sarnoff's influence on the public perception of television's inception, and debate the impact of Sarnoff's paradigm

The answer to a primary purpose question should incorporate elements of the entire passage. Avoid answer choices that address limited sections of the passage. The Point that the author wants to convey is that Sarnoff was responsible for introducing television to the public and creating a dominant paradigm. This is foreshadowed when Sarnoff is called *the father of television*. The purpose of the passage should reflect the Point.

(A) Farnsworth's influence on the development of the television itself is only mentioned in the first paragraph. Farnsworth's role in developing programs is never mentioned, nor is the correction of a public misconception the focus of the passage.

(B) The impact of television is not discussed until the second paragraph. Although this paragraph debates whether or not Sarnoff's influence was a positive one, it does not address the influence of television on popular culture.

(C) Vladimir Zworykin is only mentioned briefly in the first paragraph, so he is clearly not the primary subject of the passage. Furthermore, even though we know the initial public perception, we know nothing about the current public perception of Zworykin.

(D) The passage discusses events that occurred after the invention; there is no mention of the events that led up to the invention of the television.

(E) **CORRECT.** This answer includes the main elements of both paragraphs; it functions as a good summary of the entire passage.

2. It can be inferred from the second paragraph of the passage that

(A) television shows produced by David Sarnoff and Vladimir Zworykin tended to earn negative reviews
(B) educational programs cannot draw as large an audience as sports programs
(C) a number of critics feel that Sarnoff's initial decision to earn television revenue through advertising has had a positive or neutral impact on content
(D) educational programs that are aired in prime time, the hours during which the greatest number of viewers are watching television, are less likely to earn a profit than those that are aired during the daytime hours
(E) in matters of programming, the audience's preferences should be more influential than those of the advertisers

The second paragraph states that some critics viewed Sarnoff's paradigm negatively and others thought it embodied a democratic concept. The correct answer must follow from those statements.

(A) We have been given no information about the television programs Sarnoff and Zworykin produced; in fact, we have not been told that they produced television shows. The paragraph is about the advertising revenue construct Sarnoff implemented, not about the television shows he produced.

(B) It is implied that ratings for educational programs are, in general, not strong, but that does not mean that any one particular educational program cannot have higher ratings than one particular sports program. Beware of answer choices that contain absolutes such as *cannot*.

(C) **CORRECT.** We are told that *some critics argue that Sarnoff's paradigm has damaged programming content*. Since the word is *some*, it must be true that others either feel it has played a positive role, or a neutral role. A group of these critics is mentioned in the last sentence of the paragraph.

(D) The passage does not differentiate programming based on what time television shows air, nor does it mention profitability.

(E) The word "should" implies a moral judgment, and the answer is therefore out of the scope of the passage. Furthermore, the second paragraph does not indicate a belief as to who should properly influence programming choices.

3. According to the passage, the television industry, at its inception, earned revenue from

(A) advertising only
(B) advertising and the sale of television sets
(C) advertising and subscriptions
(D) subscriptions and the sale of television sets
(E) advertising, subscriptions, and the sale of television sets

In order to trick you on a specific question such as this, the GRE will offer incomplete answers that incorporate language from throughout the passage but do not directly bear on the question at hand. Two sections in the passage discuss ways in which the television industry brought in revenue. The first paragraph mentions *advertiser-funded pro-*

gramming. The second paragraph states that the television industry benefited by *replacing the revenue from subscriptions and newsstand purchases with that of television set sales.*

(A) This answer choice does not account for the revenue generated from selling television sets.

(B) CORRECT. Advertising and the sale of television sets are the two ways mentioned through which the industry could generate revenue.

(C) Subscriptions are mentioned as a method for newspapers to earn revenue; the last paragraph clearly states that television replaced this revenue with that earned by selling the sets themselves.

(D) This choice does not mention advertising revenue; moreover, it incorrectly mentions subscription revenue.

(E) This answer choice incorrectly mentions subscription revenue.

> **4.** **The passage suggests that Farnsworth might have earned greater public notoriety for his invention if**
>
> (A) Vladimir Zworykin had been less vocal about his own contributions to the television
> (B) Farnsworth had been able to develop and air his own educational programs
> (C) Farnsworth had adapted his business ideas from the radio today
> (D) Sarnoff had involved Farnsworth in his plans to develop, manufacture, or distribute the television
> (E) Farnsworth had a better understanding of the type of programming the audience wanted to watch most

Farnsworth's notoriety, or lack thereof, is discussed at the beginning of the second paragraph: *In his own time, Farnsworth's contributions went largely unnoticed, in large part because he was excluded from the process of introducing the invention to a national audience.* Thus, the passage clearly suggests that if he had been included in that process of introducing the invention, his contributions would have been noticed more widely.

(A) There is no mention made of Zworykin being vocal about his own contributions. Furthermore, the passage hints at no connection between Zworykin's self-promotion and Farnsworth's lack of notoriety.

(B) Though we have been told that Farnsworth wanted to use television as an educational tool, we have not been told that he wanted to develop television shows himself. Additionally, it is debatable whether the development of educational television programs would have significantly contributed to Farnsworth's public notoriety, since programs may not have been successful.

(C) Even if Farnsworth had adapted his business ideas from the radio industry, he may not have been successful in implementing them.

(D) CORRECT. The passage states that Farnsworth's contributions went unnoticed partly because *it was Sarnoff, not Farnsworth, who put televisions into living rooms.* If Farnsworth had been involved in the development, manufacture, or distribution of the television, he would have been involved in the introduction process, and it logically follows that this could have led to greater notoriety—especially since Sarnoff evidently garnered such notoriety himself as the *widely regarded* "father of television."

(E) The passage does not connect Farnsworth's lack of notoriety with a lack of understanding about the television audience, nor does it state in any way Farnsworth's opinions about the audience. He might have been more successful in achieving his dream of using the television as an educational too, but that outcome might not have led to notoriety for him personally.

5. Select the sentence that provides factual evidence that Sarnoff's talents were more imitative than innovative.

This is a select-in-passage question relating to Sarnoff's legacy as an imitator versus his legacy as an innovator. There are two plausible candidates. First, the second-to-last sentence of the first paragraph, which says that Sarnoff "successfully borrowed from the radio industry the paradigm of advertiser-funded programming." This sentence states a fact proving that Sarnoff took a business model from another medium, which would be imitative rather than innovative.

The second possible answer is the first sentence of the second paragraph, which says "Perhaps Sarnoff simply adapted his business ideas from other industries such as newspapers." However, the use of the word "perhaps" means that this is an idea of the author's, rather than a statement of fact. For this reason, this cannot be the answer.

The correct answer is the second-to-last sentence of the first paragraph.

6. Which of the following statements is supported by the passage? Select _all_ that apply.

- [A] The advertising-funded model of television has damaged programming content.
- [B] The technical invention of television has been overshadowed by its popularization.
- [C] There is no way to definitively prove who invented the first television.

B: This is a select-all-that-apply inference question of a very GENERAL nature. The answers could be drawn from anywhere in the two paragraphs.

(A) While the last sentence says that some critics "argue that Sarnoff's construct has damaged programming content," this is not stated as a fact, only a possible opinion. Always be careful to differentiate between opinions and facts on RC passages.

(B) CORRECT. In the middle of the second paragraph, we are told that "Farnsworth's contributions have gone relatively unnoticed, since it was Sarnoff, not Farnsworth, who put televisions into living rooms..." This means that while Farnsworth may have technically invented the TV, he was overshadowed by Sarnoff, who popularized it.

(C) Though the passage describes the ways in which both Zworykin and Farnsworth have been described as the progenitor of television, and though it makes a case that there remains a lively debate over who deserves the credit, this does not mean that there is "no way" of determining who invented the first television. Always be wary of EXTREME language like this when dealing with inference questions.

Answers to Passage C: Life on Mars

Because of the proximity and likeness of Mars to Earth, scientists have long speculated about the possibility of life on Mars. Roughly three centuries ago, astronomers observed Martian polar ice caps, and later scientists discovered other similarities to Earth, including length of day and axial tilt. But in 1965, photos taken by the Mariner 4 probe revealed a Mars without rivers, oceans or signs of life. Moreover, in the 1990s, it was discovered that unlike Earth, Mars no longer possessed a substantial global magnetic field, allowing celestial radiation to reach the planet's surface and solar wind to eliminate much of Mars's atmosphere over the course of several billion years.

More recent probes have investigated whether there was once liquid water on Mars. Some scientists believe that the presence of certain geological landforms definitively resolves this question. Others posit that wind erosion or carbon dioxide oceans may be responsible for these formations. Mars rovers Opportunity and Spirit, which landed on Mars in 2004, have both discovered geological evidence of past water activity. These findings substantially bolster claims that there was once life on Mars.

This is a short passage. Here is a model Headline List:

1) S: Mars close, simil to Earth → poss life on M!
   —Sims (polar ice, day, tilt)
   —Diffs (no water, no more mag field)

2) Rec focus: was there water?
   —Evid: yes/no, now <u>more</u> support for life on M   ← Point

1.   **The author's stance on the possibility of life on Mars can best be described as**

(A) optimistic
(B) disinterested
(C) skeptical
(D) simplistic
(E) cynical

This passage is concerned with the possibility of life on Mars. It details the various discoveries that have been made over centuries. The passage can best be described as factual and unbiased. When considering a tone question such as this, look for instances in which the author's opinion is revealed. You should also remember to be wary of extreme words in the answer choices.

(A) The author is neither optimistic nor pessimistic about the possibility of life on Mars.

(B) CORRECT. Note that the primary meaning of *disinterested* is "impartial" or "neutral," which accurately describes the tone of the argument.

(C) There is no indication that the author of the passage is skeptical. The passage simply puts forth facts and does not offer an opinion one way or the other.

(D) The author considers several different factors in the determination of life on Mars. The author's stance could not appropriately be described as simplistic.

(E) Again, the author is objective in tone and could not accurately be characterized as cynical.

2. The passage is primarily concerned with which of the following?

(A) Disproving a widely accepted theory.
(B) Initiating a debate about the possibility of life on Mars.
(C) Presenting evidence in support of a controversial claim.
(D) Describing the various discoveries made concerning the possibility of life on Mars.
(E) Detailing the findings of the Mars rovers Opportunity and Spirit.

This passage is primarily concerned with the possibility of life on Mars. The two paragraphs discuss various discoveries that have been made over the past few centuries. The passage concludes that recent findings substantiate claims that there was once life on Mars. However, scientists are still not certain. In determining the purpose or main idea of the passage, you should avoid extreme words and be able to defend every word.

(A) This passage does not set out to *disprove* the theory that there is life on Mars. It is also too extreme to suggest that this is a *widely accepted* theory.

(B) This answer choice is tempting because it is relatively neutral. However, the passage does not seek to *initiate* a debate; it is more concerned with documenting findings that pertain to life on Mars. In other words, the passage presents the findings that frame a debate, not initiating the debate itself.

(C) The passage presents evidence in support of and against the possibility of life on Mars. It is too limited to suggest that the passage is primarily concerned with presenting evidence *in support of* life of Mars.

(D) CORRECT. This answer choice avoids extreme words and best summarizes the purpose of the passage.

(E) This answer choice is too specific. The passage does mention the Mars rovers Opportunity and Spirit, but it is inaccurate to suggest that the passage is primarily concerned with these two rovers.

3. Each of the following discoveries is mentioned in the passage EXCEPT

(A) wind erosion and carbon dioxide oceans are responsible for certain geological landforms on Mars
(B) mars does not have a substantial global magnetic field
(C) mars does not currently have water activity
(D) the length of day on Mars is similar to that on Earth
(E) the axial tilt of Mars is similar to that of Earth

To address this Specific question, point out specific evidence in the text to defend your answer choice. The passage discusses several discoveries; to answer this question, find which of the answer choices is NOT a discovery specifically mentioned in the passage.

(A) **CORRECT.** The passage does make mention of wind erosion and carbon dioxide oceans, but the author states that these are other possible explanations for certain geological landforms on Mars. Wind erosion and carbon dioxide oceans are *possible* causes of the geological landforms rather than discoveries.

(B) At the end of the first paragraph, the passage states that *in the 1990s, it was discovered that Mars, unlike Earth, no longer possessed a substantial global magnetic field.*

(C) The Mariner 4 probe revealed in 1965 that there are no rivers or oceans (water activity) on Mars in the third sentence of the first paragraph.

(D) Certain similarities of Mars to Earth were discovered sometime between three centuries ago and 1965, including the length of day in the second sentence of the first paragraph.

(E) Certain similarities of Mars to Earth were discovered sometime between three centuries ago and 1965, including the axial tilt of Mars being similar to that of the Earth in the second sentence of the first paragraph.

> 4. **In the first paragraph, the author most likely mentions the discovery of polar ice caps to suggest that**
>
>   (A) until recently Mars' polar ice caps were thought to consist largely of carbon dioxide
>   (B) Martian polar ice caps are made almost entirely of water ice
>   (C) Mars has many similarities to Earth, including the existence of polar ice caps
>   (D) Mars has only a small fraction of the carbon dioxide found on Earth and Venus
>   (E) conditions on the planet Mars were once very different than they are at present

This is a Specific question that refers back to the second sentence in the first paragraph. The best approach is to reread this sentence and determine, using surrounding sentences, what the author's purpose is in mentioning Mars' polar ice caps. If we read the second part of the sentence, *later scientists discovered other similarities to Earth, including length of day and axial tilt*, we notice that polar ice caps are introduced as an example of the similarity of Mars to Earth (note the use of the word *other*).

(A) The passage does not mention the content of the polar ice caps, just that they were observed.

(B) Again, we do not know, from the passage, the composition of Mars' polar ice caps.

(C) **CORRECT.** As stated above, polar ice caps are introduced as one of several similarities of Mars to Earth.

(D) The passage does not indicate the carbon dioxide content or Mars or Earth. It also does not mention Venus.

(E) While we know from the rest of the passage that conditions on Mars were probably different than they are now, the author does not mention polar ice caps in order to indicate this.

5.   Each of the following can be inferred from the passage EXCEPT

(A) the presence of certain geological landforms is not definitive proof that there was once life on
   Mars
(B) it is likely that there were few significant discoveries related to the possibility of life on Mars
   prior to three centuries ago
(C) the absence of a substantial global magnetic field on Mars suggests that it would be difficult to
   sustain life on Mars
(D) the presence of water activity on Mars is related to the possibility of life on Mars
(E) the claim that there was once water on Mars has only limited and indirect support from recent
   discoveries

A question that asks for an inference from the passage is a specific question; it is helpful to find evidence for any inference in the text. Make sure each inference can be defended by going back to the text, and does not go far beyond the language in the passage.

(A) In the second paragraph, the author states that while the presence of geological landforms may indicate the presence of water, it is also possible that these landforms were caused by wind erosion or carbon dioxide oceans.

(B) The first discoveries mentioned were roughly three centuries ago. Therefore, it is reasonable to conclude that it is likely that there were not many significant discoveries before this time. Notice that this inference avoids extreme words: It does not say that there were no discoveries, just that it is not *likely* that many preceded this period.

(C) In the second paragraph, the absence of a substantial global magnetic field is presented as evidence of the lack of life on Mars. Again, note that this answer choice avoids extreme words by using the word *suggests*.

(D) The first sentence in the second paragraph states that *more recent probes have focused on whether or not there was once water on Mars.* Given this purpose, it is clear that the existence of water is important in order to establish whether or not there was life on Mars.

(E) **CORRECT.** According to the second paragraph, the Mars rovers Opportunity and Spirit *have both discovered geological evidence of past water activity.* This is both significant (as made clear by the subsequent sentence that *these findings substantially bolster claims...*) and direct evidence supporting the claim that there was once water on Mars. Thus, the passage contradicts the statement that this claim is supported by only limited and indirect evidence.

6. It can be inferred from the passage that which of the following characteristics of a planet would imply that it might support life? Select _all_ that apply.

A A significant global magnetic field
B Evidence of liquid carbon-dioxide on the planet's surface
C A size roughly approximating that of Earth

A and C. This is a select-all-that-apply question of a fairly general nature, as most of the passage is about what aspects of Mars might or might not imply that it once supported life. Make sure to seek out direct language in the passage to prove or disprove each possible answer choice.

(A) **CORRECT.** The passage says that "Mars no longer possessed a substantial global magnetic field," which led to the disappearance of "Mars's atmosphere." This disimilarity with Earth is used in the passage as evidence against life on Mars.

(B) While the passage tells us that the presence of liquid water provides strong evidence that a planet might have once supported life, we are never told anything about liquid carbon dioxide.

(C) CORRECT. The first sentence of the passage says "Because of the proximity and likeness of Mars to Earth, scientists have long speculated about the possibility of life on Mars." Some aspects of a planet that relate are "length of day" and "axial tilt." Thus, physical aspects of a planet that prove it similar to Earth imply that it could support life.

> **7. Select the sentence in the passage that provides the best evidence that there has never been life on Mars.**

This select-in-passage question asks for something very specific. We need the sentence that comes closest to saying that there was NEVER life on Mars. This is very different from a piece of evidence proving that there isn't life now, or couldn't ever be in the future.

We can feel pretty certain that the correct answer will not be found in the second paragraph, which mostly provides evidence that there WAS life on Mars at one point. In the first paragraph, the third sentence says that "photos... revealed a Mars without rivers, oceans, or signs of life." This implies that there might never have been any life. The next sentence is also a viable candidate, as it tells us that a lack of a magnetic field has allowed radiation and solar wind to "eliminate much of Mars's atmosphere over the course of several billion years." However, this process has occurred over many years, implying that at one time there WAS a magnetic field which PREVENTED celestial radiation and solar wind. This means there WAS an atmosphere that could have supported life.

The former sentence provides a more definitive example that there might not have ever been life on Mars.

Answers to Passage D: Fossils

Archaeological discoveries frequently undermine accepted ideas, giving rise to new theories. Recently, a set of 3.3-million-year-old fossils, the remains of the earliest well-preserved child ever found, were discovered in Ethiopia. Estimated to be 3 years old at death, the female child was of the Australopithecus afarensis species, a human ancestor that lived in Africa over 3 million years ago. "Her completeness, antiquity and age at death make this find of unprecedented importance in the history of paleo-anthropology," said Zeresenay Alemseged, a noted paleo-anthropologist, opining that the discovery could reconfigure conceptions about early humans' capacities.

Previously, afarensis was believed to have abandoned arboreal habitats. However, while the new fossil's lower limbs support the view of an upright stance, its gorilla-like arms suggest that afarensis was still able to swing through trees, initiating a reexamination of long-held theories of early human development. Also, the presence of a hyoid bone, a rarely preserved larynx bone that supports throat muscles, has dramatically affected concepts of the origin of speech. Although primitive and more ape-like than human-like, this fossil hyoid is the first found in such an early human-related species.

This is a short passage. Here is a model Headline List:

---

1) In Arch: disc → undermine old, lead to new thries   ← Point
   —Child fossils of af. species in Eth

2) Before: thought af. abandnd arb hab of apes
   BUT this disc → reexam old thry of hum dev
   Also hy bone → chg thries ab speech

---

1. The organization of the passage could best be described as

(A) discussing a controversial scientific discovery
(B) contrasting previous theories of human development with current theories
(C) illustrating a general contention with a specific example
(D) arguing for the importance of a particular field of study
(E) refuting a popular misconception

When assessing a passage's organization, consider the main idea of each paragraph. This passage begins by noting that *archaeological discoveries frequently undermine accepted ideas, giving rise to new theories.* It supports this statement by relating the impact of one discovery in the field. Thus, the best answer will reference both the contention and the use of the example.

(A) This choice omits the phenomenon that the discovery is meant to illustrate, which is that discoveries often give rise to new theories. Also, there is nothing controversial about the described discovery.

(B) The passage does not focus on the contrast between previous theories of human development and current theories. Rather, it discusses a singular discovery that affects previous theories. The passage would need to outline both previous and current theories of development and then contrast them. Instead, the passage focuses on how one example illustrates a way in which the field of archeology evolves.

(C) CORRECT. The passage makes a general claim and uses a specific example to support that claim, just as this choice states.

(D) One might feel that the evolution of theories of human development is a worthwhile object of contemplation, but the passage does not argue for the importance of archaeology as a field of study. This answer choice misstates the organization of the passage.

(E) The passage does not indicate how widely held earlier theories of human development were. Indeed, they are too esoteric to be properly classified as a *popular misconception.* Also, the passage is organized around the example of a single discovery and its importance. The language employed in the passage does not warrant describing the passage as a refutation of past theories.

2. The passage quotes Zeresenay Alemseged in order to

(A) provide evidence to qualify the main idea of the first paragraph
(B) question the claims of other scientists
(C) provide evidence to support the linguistic abilities of the afarensis species
(D) provide evidence that supports the significance of the find
(E) provide a subjective opinion that is refuted in the second paragraph

This quotation in the first paragraph highlights the importance of the discovery and is followed by another similar reference. The quotation is used to emphasize the exceptional importance of this find; the correct answer for this Inference question will reflect this emphasis.

(A) The main idea of the first paragraph is that a new finding can call accepted archaeological theories into question. The rest of the paragraph provides an example of this phenomenon. However, the quotation emphasizes the importance of the discovery itself. Moreover, even if you take a broad interpretation of the quotation's role, the quotation does not qualify or limit the main idea of the first paragraph.

(B) The passage does not discuss claims of other scientists. Thus, this answer choice is incorrect.

(C) The discussion of the linguistic ability of the afarensis species is in the second paragraph and is unrelated to this quotation.

(D) CORRECT. The point of this paragraph is to illustrate that in archaeology, important factual discoveries lead to theoretical changes. The quotation provides evidence that this discovery is in fact a significant one.

(E) The quotation is offered as evidence of the importance of the discovery, and is not refuted at any point in the passage.

3. **Each of the following is cited as a factor in the importance of the discovery of the fossils EXCEPT**

(A) the fact that the remains were those of a child
(B) the age of the fossils
(C) the location of the discovery
(D) the species of the fossils
(E) the intact nature of the fossils

With a question of this sort, instead of looking for the correct answer, it is often easier to eliminate incorrect answer choices based on the information provided in the passage.

(A) The fourth sentence of the first paragraph cites a quotation from a noted paleo-anthropologist that the find of the child fossils was of unprecedented importance due to the child's *age at death*. Therefore, the fact that the remains were those of a child was of substantial significance.

(B) The *antiquity* (a synonym for *age*) of the fossils is mentioned in the first paragraph as a reason why the fossils were an important discovery.

(C) CORRECT. The location of the fossil discovery is mentioned in the first paragraph of the passage. However, the location is not provided as a reason why the fossils are significant.

(D) The fossils are described in the second paragraph of the passage as impacting *long-held theories of early human development*. The fossils are also shown to be important to the development of speech. These implications would not be applicable if the fossils were not of a species of human ancestor (e.g. the fossils of an ancient elephant). Also, there were specific preconceptions of the afarensis species that were called into question by the discovery of the fossils. Thus, the species of the fossils is of particular significance to the discovery.

(E) The fourth sentence of the first paragraph notes that the find was important due its *completeness*. The intact nature of the fossils is another way of saying that the fossils are complete.

4. **It can be inferred from the passage's description of the discovered fossil hyoid bone that**

(A) Australopithecus afarensis were capable of speech
(B) the discovered hyoid bone is less primitive than the hyoid bone of apes
(C) the hyoid bone is necessary for speech
(D) the discovery of the hyoid bone necessitated the reexamination of prior theories
(E) the hyoid bone was the most important fossil found at the site

The passage provides the following information about the discovered hyoid bone: it is the oldest ever found, since the bone is rarely preserved, and it is *primitive and more ape-like than human-like*. The passage also states the discovery will impact theories about speech. A good inference is a point that must follow <u>directly</u> from one of these statements.

(A) The passage gives no information about the linguistic capacities of Australopithecus afarensis. The passage does not give enough information to infer that they were capable of speech.

(B) The passage indicates that the discovered hyoid bone more closely resembles those of apes than humans. However, while the passage does generally relate to evolution, the discovered bone is not necessarily less primitive than that of an ape. It could be slightly different in an equally primitive way; not all differences in structure would make a bone more advanced.

(C) While it can be inferred that this bone has an effect on speech, the passage does not indicate that it is *necessary* for speech. It is possible that a modern species could be capable of speech without a hyoid bone.

(D) CORRECT. The passage states that the discovery of the hyoid bone *has dramatically affected concepts of the origin of speech*. The passage goes on to say that it is the first hyoid found in such an early human-related species, suggesting that the timeline of human verbal development would be changed by the discovery. Thus, it can be inferred that the discovery made the reexamination of prior theories necessary.

(E) The passage does not rank the importance of the fossils found; as a result, this choice is not necessarily correct. It is possible that other fossils were of equal or greater importance.

5. According to the passage, the impact of the discovery of the hyoid bone in the field of archaeology could best be compared to which one of the following examples in another field?

(A) The discovery and analysis of cosmic rays lend support to a widely accepted theory of the origin of the universe.
(B) The original manuscript of a deceased 19th century author confirms ideas of the development of an important work of literature.
(C) The continued prosperity of a state-run economy stirs debate in the discipline of macroeconomics.
(D) Newly revealed journal entries by a prominent Civil War era politician lead to a questioning of certain accepted historical interpretations about the conflict.
(E) Research into the mapping of the human genome gives rise to nascent applications of individually tailored medicines.

When you are asked in an Inference question to choose which answer best parallels a part of a passage, be sure that you grasp the nature of the comparison on the passage side before considering the answer choices.

The passage indicates that the discovery of the hyoid bone *has dramatically affected concepts of the origin of speech.* The author also places this discovery in parallel to discoveries of other bones of this particular fossil, which have initiated *a reexamination of long-held theories of early human development.*

These sentences indicate that the discovery of the hyoid bone has either expanded or called into question certain previously held ideas in the field. The correct answer will reflect this sort of impact in another field.

(A) This answer choice discusses the impact of the discovery and analysis of cosmic rays on the field of physics. However, in this example the discovery serves to support a widely accepted theory, as opposed to causing a reexamination of earlier ideas.

(B) This answer choice describes the original manuscript of an author that confirms ideas of the development of an important work of literature. However, in this answer choice the discovery serves to confirm earlier held ideas, as opposed to causing a reexamination of accepted ideas.

(C) This answer choice describes a current phenomenon, the continued success of a state-run economy, that stirs debate in the discipline of macroeconomics. This example is dissimilar from the discovery of the hyoid bone in a number of ways. First, the success of a state-run economy is a contemporary phenomenon rather than a discovery. Also, the provocation of debate is not analogous to a *reexamination of accepted theories,* as there is no indication that an accepted macroeconomic theory is applicable and being called into question. Last, the state-run economy in question could be the latest example in a long line of successful controlled economies, as opposed to being a discovery of any importance.

(D) CORRECT. This answer choice correctly describes a discovery that causes a reexamination of earlier ideas in another field. In this case, newly uncovered journal entries by a politician spur a re-evaluation of certain historical ideas regarding an important conflict.

(E) This answer choice describes scientific advances in the field of biology as giving rise to new applications. It does not discuss a discovery that calls accepted ideas into question.

6. Select the sentence that most distinctly undermines an accepted paleo-anthropological theory.

This is a select-in-passage question that asks us for an example of what is described in the very first sentence of the passage. The first paragraph of this passage describes a set of newly-discovered fossils, but we aren't told the implications of this discovery until the second paragraph.

The first sentence of the second paragraph tells us a previously accepted theory about afarensis. The next sentence describes how this theory was undermined, and is the correct answer here: "…its gorilla-like arms suggest that afarensis was still able to swing through trees, initiating a reexamination of long-held theories of human development." The example of the hyoid bone mentioned later never describes exactly what theory was undermined by its discovery.

7. The author of the passage suggests that which of the following is exemplified by the recent discovery? Select _all_ that apply.

[A] Scientists' eagerness to embrace new discoveries
[B] The constantly evolving nature of paleo-anthropology
[C] The way in which new information can necessitate new theories

C: This is a select-all-that-apply question, and the answer choices are dangerously general. Be very careful on these not to move too far away from what's written in the passage.

(A) Though the passage describes a new discovery, and even cites a particular scientist describing how the new discovery "could reconfigure conceptions about early humans' capability," this is not cited as evidence that scientists, taken as a whole, are always eager to embrace new discoveries. We hear nothing about the response or backlash to the new theories resulting from the discovery.

(B) The first sentence of the passage says that "archaeological discoveries frequently undermine accepted ideas, giving rise to new theories." However, we cannot extrapolate out from the one example given that paleo-anthropology itself is constantly evolving. For all we know, the majority of paleo-anthropological theories have remained static for decades. The key here is that the answer choice specifies "paleo-anthropology," not "archaeology."

(C) **CORRECT.** In the second paragraph, we are told that new information on both the limbs and the hyoid bone of the newly discovered fossil has initiated "a reexamination of long-held theories of human development" and "dramatically affected concepts of the origins of speech." The new information provided by the afarensis fossils required that new theories be created.

Answers to Passage E: Polygamy

Polygamy in Africa has been a popular topic for social research over the past several decades; it has been analyzed by many distinguished minds and in various well-publicized works. In 1961, when Remi Clignet published his book "Many Wives, Many Powers," he was not alone in sharing the view that in Africa co-wives may be perceived as direct and indirect sources of increased income and prestige. For instance, some observers argued that polygamous marriages are more able than monogamous marriages to produce many children, who can legitimately be seen as a form of wealth, as well as of "this-world" immortality connected to the transmission of family names (as opposed to "other-world" immortality in an afterlife). Moreover, polygamy is rooted in and sanctioned by many ancient traditions, both cultural and religious; therefore, some assert that polygamy can provide a stabilizing function within societies frequently under stress from both internal and external forces.

By the 1970s, such arguments had become crystallized and popular. Many other African scholars who wrote on the subject became the new champions of this philosophy. For example, in 1983, John Mbiti proclaimed that polygamy is an accepted and respectable institution serving many useful social purposes. Similarly, G.K. Nukunya, in his paper "Polygamy as a Symbol of Status," reiterated Mbiti's idea that a plurality of wives is a legitimate sign of affluence and power in African society.

However, the colonial missionary voice provided consistent opposition to polygamy by viewing the practice as unethical and destructive of family life. While they propagated this view with the authority of the Bible, they were convinced that Africans had to be coerced into partaking in the vision of monogamy understood by the Western culture. The missionary viewpoint even included, in some instances, dictating immediate divorce in the case of newly converted men who had already contracted polygamous marriages. Unfortunately, both the missionary voice and the scholarly voice did not consider the views of African women on the matter important. Although there was some awareness that women regarded polygamy as both a curse and a blessing, the distanced, albeit scientific, perspective of an outside observer predominated both on the pulpit and in scholarly writings.

Contemporary research in the social sciences has begun to focus on the protagonist's voice in the study of culture, recognizing that the views and experiences of those who take part in a given reality ought to receive close examination. This privileging of the protagonist seems appropriate, particularly given that women in Africa have often used literary productions, which feature protagonists and other "actors" undergoing ordeals and otherwise taking active part in real life, to comment on marriage, family and gender relations.

This is a long passage. Here is a model Skeletal Sketch:

---

1) <u>Past 4 decs: Polygamy in Afr = pop topic soc rsch</u>
 —'61 Clig: co-wives = income, prestige
 —Children = wealth, immort
 —polyg = tradition, stable

2) By 70s others agree
 —Many other Afr scholars

3) BUT missnry opp polygamy
 —Unfortly — miss + scholars: view of Afr wmn NOT impt ← Point (part)

4) Curr rsch: exps of protagonists (Afr wmn) ← Point (part)

---

1. Which of the following best describes the main purpose of the passage above?

(A) To discuss scholarly works that view polygamy as a sign of prestige, respect, and affluence in the African society.
(B) To trace the origins of the missionary opposition to African polygamy.
(C) To argue for imposing restrictions on polygamy in the African society.
(D) To explore the reasons for women's acceptance of polygamy.
(E) To discuss multiple perspectives on African polygamy and contrast them with contemporary research.

On questions asking about the main idea of the passage, be sure to avoid extreme answer choices and those answers that refer to only a part of the passage rather than the whole text. Typically, test writers will include several incorrect answers that will be factually true but will describe the purpose of just one paragraph. The Point of this passage is arguably split in at least two pieces. The author wants to convey not only that two views of polygamy in Africa (those of the early scholars and of the missionaries) were *unfortunately* limited, but also that current research is addressing this limitation by bringing in the perspectives of the women protagonists.

(A) Scholarly works that view polygamy as a sign of prestige and affluence are discussed only in the first two paragraphs of the passage. This answer is too narrow to capture the purpose of the entire text.

(B) While the third paragraph discusses the missionary opposition and traces its sources to the Bible, this analysis is not central to the entire passage and is thus too narrow to capture the scope of the entire text.

(C) While the text discusses multiple perspectives on polygamy, it does not argue in favor or against restricting polygamy.

(D) The passage provides no information about the reasons that women accept polygamy, other than mentioning that they view it as both *a curse and a blessing*.

(E) **CORRECT.** The entire passage is devoted to the discussion of multiple perspectives on polygamy. The first two paragraphs review scholarly works that view polygamy as a sign of prestige and respect, while the third paragraph offers an opposing view. Finally, the concluding paragraph contrasts both of these perspectives with contemporary research.

*Manhattan*GRE*Prep

2. The third paragraph of the passage plays which of the following roles?

(A) Discusses the rationales for viewing polygamy as an indication of prestige and affluence in the African society.
(B) Supports the author's view that polygamy is unethical and destructive of family life.
(C) Contrasts the views of the colonial missionary with the position of the most recent contemporary research.
(D) Describes the views on polygamy held by the colonial missionary and indicates a flaw in this vision.
(E) Demonstrates that the colonial missionary was ignorant of the scholarly research on monogamy.

This question asks us to summarize the role of the third paragraph. On this type of question, it is helpful to reread the topic sentence of the paragraph at issue. The topic sentence is typically in the first or second sentence of the paragraph. Furthermore, look for the answer that effectively captures the entire paragraph and avoids making unjustified statements.

(A) These rationales are discussed in the first and second rather than the third paragraph.

(B) While the third paragraph discusses the views of the colonial missionary, nothing in the passage suggests that the author shares this vision.

(C) While the third paragraph presents the position of the colonial missionary, the most recent contemporary research is discussed only in the concluding paragraph of the passage.

(D) CORRECT. The second paragraph describes the position of the colonial missionary and indicates a flaw in this perspective. Note that the missionary's position is described in the opening sentence of the paragraph: *However, the colonial missionary voice provided consistent opposition to polygamy by viewing the practice as unethical and destructive of family life.* Furthermore, after discussing this position, the author goes on to identify a deficiency in this reasoning: *Unfortunately, both the missionary voice and the scholarly voice did not consider the views of African women on the matter important.*

(E) While the third paragraph discusses the perspective of the colonial missionary, nothing is mentioned in the passage about the attitude of the missionary towards scholarly research on monogamy.

3. The passage provides each of the following, EXCEPT

(A) the year of publication of Remi Clignet's book "Many Wives, Many Powers"
(B) the year in which John Mbiti made a claim that polygamy is an accepted institution
(C) examples of African women's literary productions devoted to family relations
(D) reasons for missionary opposition to polygamy
(E) current research perspectives on polygamy

On detail questions, you can facilitate your decision process by looking for signal words. Since this is an "EXCEPT" question, we can answer it by findings the statements that were mentioned in the passage and eliminating them from our consideration set. In this process, make sure to use proper nouns (such as Remi Clignet) and dates (such as 1983) as your signals. Since dates and capitalized nouns stand out in the text, they can speed up the process of verifying the answer choices. (Of course, be aware that a wrong answer choice might include words from the passage but fail to include the idea behind the words.)

(A) The second sentence of the opening paragraph states that Remi Clignet published his book "Many Wives, Many Powers" in 1961.

(B) According to the second sentence of the second paragraph, John Mbiti proclaimed that polygamy is an accepted and respectable institution in 1983.

(C) CORRECT. The concluding paragraph mentions that *women in Africa have often used literary productions to comment on marriage* but provides no specific examples of such works.

(D) According to the third paragraph of the passage, the colonial missionary opposed polygamy because it considered this practice *as unethical and destructive of family life.*

(E) The opening sentence of the last paragraph provides a detailed description of the position of contemporary research towards polygamy.

> **4. According to the passage, the colonial missionary and the early scholarly research shared which of the following traits in their views on polygamy?**
>
> (A) Both considered polygamy a sign of social status and success.
> (B) Neither accounted for the views of local women.
> (C) Both attempted to limit the prevalence of polygamy.
> (D) Both pointed out polygamy's destructive effects on family life.
> (E) Both exhibited a somewhat negative attitude towards polygamy.

To answer this detail question, we need to refer to paragraph three, which offers a comparison of the views of the colonial missionary and those of early scholars. Note that the correct answer will outline the trait that was shared by both groups, while incorrect answers will typically restate characteristics that were true of only one rather than both groups.

(A) While the early scholarly researchers indeed viewed polygamy as a sign of prestige, this perspective was not shared by the colonial missionary, who declared it *unethical and destructive of family life.*

(B) CORRECT. This statement is explicitly supported by the penultimate sentence of the third paragraph: *Unfortunately, both the missionary voice and the scholarly voice did not consider the views of African women on the matter important.*

(C) While the passage suggests that the colonial missionary may have attempted to limit the prevalence of polygamy by coercing Africans *into partaking in the vision of monogamy,* nothing in the passage suggests that the scholarly research shared this perspective.

(D) This view was characteristic of the colonial missionary, as discussed in the third paragraph, but not of the early scholarly research.

(E) According to the third paragraph, the colonial missionary certainly maintained a negative attitude towards polygamy, considering this practice *unethical and destructive of family life.* By contrast, early scholarly research considered this phenomenon *a sign of affluence and power.* Nothing in the passage suggests that the early scholars had a negative attitude towards polygamy.

5.   **Which of the following statements can most properly be inferred from the passage?**

(A)   Nukunya's paper "Polygamy as a Symbol of Status" was not written in 1981.

(B)   John Mbiti adjusted his initial view on polygamy, recognizing that the experiences of African women should receive closer attention.

(C)   Remi Clignet's book "Many Wives, Many Powers" was the first well-known scholarly work to proclaim that polygamy can be viewed as a symbol or prestige and wealth.

(D)   Under the influence of the missionary opposition, polygamy was proclaimed illegal in Africa as a practice "unethical and destructive of family life."

(E)   A large proportion of the scholars writing on polygamy in the 1970s and 1980s were of African descent.

Since this is an inference question, we will be looking for an answer that can be inferred strictly based on the information given in the passage and without making any additional assumptions. Typically, the correct answer must be very closely connected to the actual text of the passage and directly supported by one or two sentences. Be sure to avoid inferences that may be seen as plausible but would require information not provided in the passage.

(A) CORRECT. The second paragraph states that Nukunya's work "Polygamy as a Symbol of Status" *reiterated Mbiti's idea that that plurality of wives is a sign of affluence and power....* Since Nukunya's work reiterated the views of Mbiti, "Polygamy as a Symbol of Status" must have been written <u>after</u> Mbiti expressed his perspective on polygamy. According to the text, it was not until 1983 that *John Mbiti proclaimed that polygamy is an accepted and respectable institution.* Therefore, Nukunya's "Polygamy as a Symbol of Status" must have been written after 1983; we can conclude that it was not written in 1981.

(B)   While the text mentions that contemporary research acknowledges that the perspective of African women should receive closer attention, nothing in the passage suggests that Mbiti subsequently embraced this view and changed his initial stance.

(C)   In the second sentence of the opening paragraph, the author states that *when Remi Clignet published his book "Many Wives, Many Powers," he was not alone in sharing the view...,* suggesting that at the time of publication, there were other scholarly works that viewed polygamy as a symbol or prestige and wealth. Therefore, Clignet's book was not the first to give this perspective.

(D)   While the passage mentions that the colonial missionary opposed polygamy, viewing it as *unethical and destructive,* nothing in the passage suggests that polygamy was declared illegal in Africa.

(E)   The passage provides no information regarding the background of the scholars who wrote about African polygamy. Moreover, even if this information were provided for the several examples of scholarly work mentioned in the passage, it would not be possible to make any conclusions about the scholars not mentioned in the passage.

6. Which of the following examples fit the model of cultural studies cited in the final paragraph of the passage? Select _all_ that apply.

[A] A documentary about the modern-day slave trade that relied on interviews with those who had been enslaved

[B] A study of gorillas in confinement that made use of techniques for ascertaining the psychological state of each gorilla

[C] An experimental theater piece about blindness in which audience members were required to wear a blindfold

A and B: This is a select-all-that-apply question that is specific to the last paragraph. It might be helpful to re-read that final paragraph before attempting to answer the question. The first sentence tells us that "contemporary research...has begun to to focus on the protagonist's voice...recognizing that the views and expereinces of those who take part in a given reality ought to receive close examination." So we're looking for examples in which those directly involved in something are the ones whose viewpoints are solicited.

(A) CORRECT. In this example, those actually involved in the slave trade are being interviewed about it. This would be a prime example of protagonist-centric research.

(B) CORRECT. In this example, researchers are attempting to figure out the psychological state of each gorilla, meaning that they are focusing on the experience of the protagonist, rather than what they themselves BELIEVE to be true about the protagonists' experience.

(C) In this example, audience members are being asked to step into the shoes of the blind. However, this does not represent a privileging of the protagonists (in this case, blind people), because no time is given to actual blind people describing their personal experience.

7. Select the sentence in the first two paragraphs that cites a specific benefit of polygamy without mentioning the economic ramifications.

This is a specific select-in-passage question. Notice the limiting factor "without mentioning economic ramifications." This eliminates a number of sentences, including the third sentence of the first paragraph ("a form of wealth") and the last sentence of the second paragraph ("a legitimate sign of affluence").

The second sentence of the second paragraph must be eliminated because it fails to cite a specific benefit; "many useful social purposes" is too general. The correct answer is the final sentence of the first paragraph, which says that "polygamy can provide a stabilizing function within socieities frequently under stress from both internal and external forces." This describes a specific benefit without mentioning any economic factors.

Answers to Passage F: Sweet Spot

Though most tennis players generally strive to strike the ball on the racket's vibration node, more commonly known as the "sweet spot," many players are unaware of the existence of a second, lesser-known location on the racket face, the center of percussion, that will also greatly diminish the strain on a player's arm when the ball is struck.

In order to understand the physics of this second sweet spot, it is helpful to consider what would happen to a tennis racket in the moments after impact with the ball if the player's hand were to vanish at the moment of impact. The impact of the ball would cause the racket to bounce back-wards, experiencing a translational motion away from the ball. The tendency of this motion would be to jerk all parts of the racket, including the end of its handle, backward, or away from the ball. Unless the ball happened to hit the racket precisely at the racket's center of mass, the racket would additionally experience a rotational motion around its center of mass—much as a penny that has been struck near its edge will start to spin. Whenever the ball hits the racket face, the effect of this rotational motion will be to jerk the end of the handle forward, towards the ball. Depending on where the ball strikes the racket face, one or the other of these motions will predominate.

However, there is one point of impact, known as the center of per-cussion, which causes neither motion to predominate; if a ball were to strike this point, the impact would not impart any motion to the end of the handle. The reason for this lack of motion is that the force on the upper part of the hand would be equal and opposite to the force on the lower part of the hand, resulting in no net force on the tennis players' hand or forearm. The center of percussion constitutes a second sweet spot because a tennis player's wrist typically is placed next to the end of the racket's handle. When the player strikes the ball at the center of percussion, her wrist is jerked neither forward nor backward, and she experiences a relatively smooth, comfortable tennis stroke.

The manner in which a tennis player can detect the center of per-cussion on a given tennis racket follows from the nature of this second sweet spot. The center of percussion can be located via simple trial and error by holding the end of a tennis racket between your finger and thumb and throwing a ball onto the strings. If the handle jumps out of your hand, then the ball has missed the center of percussion.

This is a long passage. Here is a model Skeletal Sketch:

---

1) Tennis plyrs try to hit ball on racket "sweet spot"
   <u>Many unaware: 2nd spot, CP, also dims arm strain</u>   ← Point

2) Assume no hand when ball hits, what happ?
   —Cd jerk handle back or fwd

3) If ball hits CP, no jerk—doesn't jerk wrist either

4) Can find CP w trial & error

---

1. What is the primary message the author is trying to convey?

(A) A proposal for an improvement to the design of tennis rackets.
(B) An examination of the differences between the two types of sweet spot.
(C) A definition of the translational and rotational forces acting on a tennis racket.
(D) A description of the ideal area in which to strike every ball.
(E) An explanation of a lesser-known area on a tennis racket that dampens unwanted vibration.

The primary message the author is trying to convey is the Point. If you have identified the Point as the second half of the first paragraph, then you are ready to answer this question. The first paragraph introduces the idea that there are two sweet spots on the face of a tennis racket: one well-known spot and another *lesser-known* spot. The second and third paragraphs detail how the mechanism of the second sweet spot, the center of percussion, works. The fourth paragraph describes a way to find the center of percussion.

(A) Nothing in the passage suggests that the author is trying to propose an improvement to the design of tennis rackets.
   The second sweet spot exists independent of the design of the racket.

(B) The passage does mention both types of sweet spot in the first paragraph, but it does not focus on the differences between the two.

(C) Paragraph two explains the types of forces acting on the racket, but this topic is too narrow to be the primary message of the overall passage. The passage as a whole focuses on the sweet spots as opposed to the forces acting on the racket.

(D) While the passage does mention one benefit of hitting the ball on a sweet spot, it does not claim that this is the *ideal* area to hit *every* ball. There may be other areas that convey other benefits. The word *every* is too extreme.

(E) CORRECT. This matches our initial summary, above: the passage introduces the notion of a *second, lesser-known* sweet spot which can also *diminish the strain* when a player strikes the ball.

2. According to the passage, all of the following are true of the forces acting upon a tennis racket striking a ball EXCEPT

(A) the only way to eliminate the jolt that accompanies most strokes is to hit the ball on the center of percussion
(B) the impact of the ball striking the racket can strain a tennis player's arm
(C) there are at least two different forces acting upon the racket
(D) the end of the handle of the racket will jerk forward after striking the ball unless the ball strikes the racket's center of mass
(E) the racket will rebound after it strikes the ball

"EXCEPT" questions require us to validate the answer choices. We must simply go through the choices one by one, labeling true answers with a T and the one false answer with an F.

(A) CORRECT. False. This choice contradicts information given in the first paragraph: the center of percussion is only one of two sweet spots which minimize vibration. The vibration node is the other sweet spot.

(B) True. The third sentence of the first paragraph introduces the concept that the impact can *strain* the player's arm.

(C) True. The second paragraph describes at least two different forces that act upon a tennis racket striking the ball: translational as described in the second and third sentences and rotational as described in the fourth and fifth sentences.

(D) True. The fourth sentence of the second paragraph states that *unless the ball happened to hit the racket precisely at the racket's center of mass, the racket would additionally experience a rotational motion.* The fifth sentence then reads *Whenever the ball hits the racket face, the effect of this rotational motion will be to jerk the end of the handle forward, towards the ball.*

(E) True. The second sentence of the second paragraph states that a racket will *bounce backward* after striking the ball; these words are synonyms for *rebound*.

3.   **What is the primary function served by paragraph two in the context of the entire passage?**

(A) To establish the main idea of the passage
(B) To provide an explanation of the mechanics of the phenomenon discussed in the passage
(C) To introduce a counterargument that elucidates the main idea of the passage
(D) To provide an example of the primary subject described in the passage
(E) To explain why the main idea of the passage would be useful for tennis players

Paragraph two introduces and explains, in great detail, the forces that act on a racket when striking a ball. It specifically explains the means by which the *lesser-known* sweet spot, the center of percussion, functions.

(A) The main idea is established in the first paragraph: there is a second sweet spot that results in minimal vibration when a tennis racket strikes a ball. The second paragraph explains the forces that affect how this second sweet spot functions; it does not itself establish the main idea of the passage.

(B) **CORRECT.** This matches the description of the second paragraph above: it explains the mechanics of the second sweet spot in great detail.

(C) The second paragraph introduces the forces that act on a racket when striking a ball, and the concept of a center of percussion is explained. The first paragraph indicates the existence of the center of percussion; therefore, it would be incorrect to refer to the second paragraph as a counterargument.

(D) While the second paragraph does provide an example, this is not an example of the center of percussion, which is the primary subject described in the passage. The example helps to explain the forces behind the center of percussion, but is not itself an example of a center of percussion.

(E) The first and third paragraphs, not the second paragraph, make reference to why tennis players would want to know about the sweet spot: to minimize strain on the arm.

4. **The author mentions "a penny that has been struck near its edge" in order to**

(A) show how the center of mass causes the racket to spin
(B) argue that a penny spins in the exact way that a tennis racket spins
(C) explain how translational motion works
(D) provide an illustration of a concept
(E) demonstrate that pennies and tennis rackets do not spin in the same way

The full sentence expressed in the passage is *the racket would additionally experience a rotational motion around its center of mass—much as a penny that has been struck near its edge will start to spin.* In other words, the motion of the penny is an example that closely mimics the situation with the tennis racket. The correct answer should match this characterization.

(A) The center of mass does not cause the racket to spin; rather, a ball striking the racket causes it to spin.

(B) The author does not present the information about the penny as an argument; rather, it is an example. In addition, the author implies, via the words *much as,* that the penny and the racket spin in similar ways; this is not the same as saying that they spin in the *exact* same way.

(C) This sentence is about rotational motion, not translational motion.

(D) CORRECT. The example of the penny is an analogy for the rotational motion experienced by the tennis racket.

(E) The example is intended to demonstrate a situation in which tennis rackets and pennies do spin in similar ways.

5. Which of the following can be inferred from the passage?

(A) If a player holds the tennis racket anywhere other than the end of the handle, the player will experience a jolting sensation.
(B) The primary sweet spot is more effective at damping vibration than the secondary sweet spot.
(C) Striking a tennis ball at a spot other than the center of percussion can result in a jarring feeling.
(D) Striking a tennis ball repeatedly at spots other than a sweet spot leads to "tennis elbow."
(E) If a player lets go of the racket at the moment of impact, the simultaneous forward and backward impetus causes the racket to drop straight to the ground.

Because the question applies to the whole passage, we must examine the answer choices first. It is useful to remember that when the GRE asks us to *infer*, we need to base our inference only on information presented in the passage.

(A) The passage does explain that holding the racket at the end of the handle and hitting the ball at a particular spot results in a comfortable stroke that reduces the strain on a player's arm. It does not address, however, what would happen if the player grasped the racket at a different point. It is possible that grasping the racket at another point would simply result in a different center of percussion.

(B) The passage states that there is one commonly known sweet spot and a second, lesser-known sweet spot. However, the passage says nothing about the relative efficacy of these two sweet spots.

(C) CORRECT. We are told that playing tennis can result in strain on a player's arm. We are also told that striking the ball at the center of percussion leads to a *smooth, comfortable stroke* or one which does not cause the same kind of damage as a *regular* stroke. Striking the ball at a spot other than the center of percussion then, could lead to a jarring stroke, or one that could cause damage to a player's arm.

(D) The passage mentions nothing about "tennis elbow" or what behavior can result in this injury; it merely talks about *strain.* Be careful not to add additional information beyond what is presented in the passage.

(E) The second paragraph obliquely addresses a situation in which a tennis player lets go of the racket at the moment of impact. However, this question does not specify the point at which the tennis ball struck the racket. If the ball did not strike a sweet spot, the racket may have some translational or rotational force transferred from the ball.

6. Select the sentence in the second or third paragraph that describes the physics of the center of percussion's perceived "sweetness".

This is a very specific select-in-passage question, asking us to find something in the highly complex second and third paragraphs. The second paragraph of the passage explores a hypothetical situation, but doesn't go into any detail about the sweet spot itself. The sentence we want will be in the third paragraph.

The correct sentence is the second sentence of the third paragraph: "The reason for this lack of motion is that the force on the upper part of the hand would be equal and opposite to the force on the lower part of the hand, resulting in no net force on the tennis players' hand or forearm." The final sentence of this paragraph describes the effects of hitting this second sweet spot, but it does not describe the actual physics of the "sweetness."

7. It can be inferred that a tennis ball that strikes a racket's center of percussion will do which of the following? Select _all_ that apply.

A | Cause at least some strain on the arm of the player swinging the racket
B | Not cause the wrist to jerk
C | Allow for a cleaner stroke than a ball striking a racket's primary sweet spot

A, B, and C: This is a select-all-that-apply question. The answers are likely to be found in the first or third paragraphs, as the second explores a hypothetical situation, and the fourth describes how to find the center of percussion.

(A) CORRECT. The last sentence of the first paragraph states that striking the center of percussion "will also greatly diminish the strain on a player's arm when the ball is struck." The word "diminish" implies that there will still be SOME amount of strain.

(B) CORRECT. The last sentence of the third paragraph says that a player who strikes the center of percussion will not have his or her wrist jerked "forward or backward."

(C) CORRECT. The same sentence cited in B goes on to say that the lack of a jerk will cause the player to experience "a relatively smooth, comfortable tennis stroke." Hitting the racket on its primary sweet spot will cause some amount of jerk (because only contact made on the center of percussion allows the player to avoid this jerk), so the stroke will necessarily be less clean.

Answers to Passage G: Chaos Theory

Around 1960, mathematician Edward Lorenz found unexpected behavior in apparently simple equations representing atmospheric air flows. Whenever he reran his model with the same inputs, different outputs resulted—although the model lacked any random elements. Lorenz realized that tiny rounding errors in his analog computer mushroomed over time, leading to erratic results. His findings marked a seminal moment in the development of chaos theory, which, despite its name, has little to do with randomness.

To understand how unpredictability can arise from deterministic equations, which do not involve chance outcomes, consider the non-chaotic system of two poppy seeds placed in a round bowl. As the seeds roll to the bowl's center, a position known as a point attractor, the distance between the seeds shrinks. If, instead, the bowl is flipped over, two seeds placed on top will roll away from each other. Such a system, while still not technically chaotic, enlarges initial differences in position.

Chaotic systems, such as a machine mixing bread dough, are characterized by both attraction and repulsion. As the dough is stretched, folded and pressed back together, any poppy seeds sprinkled in are intermixed seemingly at random. But this randomness is illusory. In fact, the poppy seeds are captured by "strange attractors," staggeringly complex pathways whose tangles appear accidental but are in fact determined by the system's fundamental equations.

During the dough-kneading process, two poppy seeds positioned next to each other eventually go their separate ways. Any early divergence or measurement error is repeatedly amplified by the mixing until the position of any seed becomes effectively unpredictable. It is this "sensitive dependence on initial conditions" and not true randomness that generates unpredictability in chaotic systems, of which one example may be the Earth's weather. According to the popular interpretation of the "Butterfly Effect," a butterfly flapping its wings causes hurricanes. A better understanding is that the butterfly causes uncertainty about the precise state of the air. This microscopic uncertainty grows until it encompasses even hurricanes. Few meteorologists believe that we will ever be able to predict rain or shine for a particular day years in the future.

This is a long passage (more than 35 lines on page). Here is a model Skeletal Sketch:

---

1) 1960 L: unexp behav in air flow eqs
   Reran model, diff results
   Cut detrm eq's: 2 + 2 = 4
   L: tiny rounding errors blew up → erratic results
   help dev <u>chaos thry</u>—<u>little to do with "randomness" (coin flip)</u> ← Point

2) Unpredict can come fr determ eqs
   —non-chaotic: 2 poppy seeds in or on bowl

3) Dough mixing (chaos): seed movmnt <u>seems</u> random but is NOT

4) Seeds go sep ways → unpredict, not truly random
   —weather, butterfly eff

---

1. The main purpose of this passage is to

(A) explain complicated aspects of certain physical systems
(B) trace the historical development of a scientific theory
(C) distinguish a mathematical pattern from its opposite
(D) describe the spread of a technical model from one field of study to others
(E) contrast possible causes of weather phenomena

The passage's main purpose can be determined by identifying the Point of the passage and then examining the role of each paragraph. The first paragraph introduces chaos theory by describing a historical moment in its development. The Point comes at the end of the first paragraph, i.e., *chaos theory has little to do with randomness*. The next three paragraphs focus on further explaining this mystery, namely, the way in which *unpredictability can arise from deterministic equations, that do not overtly involve chance outcomes*, as the first sentence of the second paragraph states. These paragraphs use analogies involving poppy seeds and bread dough to illustrate the explanations. Finally, as a minor addendum, the last paragraph mentions how this understanding of chaos theory might be applied to the weather, as a possible specific case of a chaotic system.

Taking all of these roles together, we see that the main purpose of the passage is to introduce chaos theory and explain how chaotic systems seem to be random but actually are governed by very complex equations.

(A) CORRECT. The *complicated aspects* are the characteristic features of chaotic systems, such as *sensitive dependence on initial conditions* and *staggeringly complex pathways*. The point of the passage is to explain such features.

(B) The first paragraph, as an introduction, describes a particular milestone in the historical development of chaos theory. However, the passage does not go on to describe other developments of this theory over time.

(C) Perhaps the behavior of chaotic systems could arguably be described as a *mathematical pattern*. However, the passage does not discuss any category of systems that are categorized clearly as the *opposite* of chaotic systems. Certain non-chaotic systems are described in the second paragraph, but it is not clear whether these systems would be the *opposite* of chaotic systems, or whether *random* systems would be the opposite.

(D) If chaos theory is the *technical model* mentioned in the answer choice, the passage never describes how that model spreads from one field of study to any other.

(E) In the fourth paragraph, the *"Butterfly Effect"* is mentioned as a popular explanation for at least some hurricanes. However, no other causes of weather phenomena are ever discussed.

2.   In the example discussed in the passage, what is true about poppy seeds in bread dough, once the dough has been thoroughly mixed?

(A) They have been individually stretched and folded over, like miniature versions of the entire dough.
(B) They are scattered in random clumps throughout the dough.
(C) They are accidentally caught in tangled objects called strange attractors.
(D) They are bound to regularly dispersed patterns of point attractors.
(E) They are in positions dictated by the underlying equations that govern the mixing process.

The question asks about the poppy seeds in mixed bread dough. The third paragraph describes what happens to these poppy seeds: they *are intermixed seemingly at random.* But the positions of the seeds are not random, as the next sentences emphasize. Rather, the seeds *are captured by "strange attractors," staggeringly complex pathways whose tangles… are in fact totally determined by the system's fundamental equations.* Thus, the positions of the seeds are themselves *determined by the system's fundamental equations.*

(A) The passage mentions nothing about any stretching or folding of the poppy seeds themselves.

(B) The poppy seeds are scattered throughout the dough, but not in random clumps.

(C) The poppy seeds are caught in strange attractors, but there is nothing *accidental* about their capture. Moreover, the strange attractors described in the passage are not physical objects but rather mathematical pathways.

(D) Point attractors are not mentioned in relation to the dough-mixing process. Also, the poppy seeds, which have been *intermixed seemingly at random,* are not placed at regular intervals.

(E) CORRECT. The poppy seeds may seem to be scattered at random, but they follow the pathways of the strange attractors. These pathways, and thus the seeds' positions, have been *determined by the system's fundamental equations.*

3. According to the passage, the rounding errors in Lorenz's model

(A) indicated that the model was programmed in a fundamentally faulty way
(B) were deliberately included to represent tiny fluctuations in atmospheric air currents
(C) were imperceptibly small at first, but tended to grow
(D) were at least partially expected, given the complexity of the actual atmosphere
(E) shrank to insignificant levels during each trial of the model

The question asks for specific details with the keywords *rounding errors* and *Lorenz's model.* The reference to Lorenz leads to the first paragraph, which contains the following sentence: *he realized that tiny rounding errors in his analog computer were mushrooming over time within each run of the model, leading to erratic results.* In other words, the rounding errors started out small but became larger.

Because the question uses the words *according to the passage,* we should not try to draw any kind of inference. Rather, we should look for an answer that matches as closely as possible to the statements in the passage.

(A) Although these rounding errors are in fact *errors*, nothing in the passage indicates or implies that the model over-all was built incorrectly.

(B) The errors were not deliberately included in the model. We know this from the passage's first sentence, which states that Lorenz found *unexpected behavior* in his model. It may be argued that the role of these errors is similar to the role of *tiny fluctuations in atmospheric air currents*—that is, they both introduce uncertainty that grows over time. However, this answer choice claims incorrectly that the errors were inserted on purpose.

(C) CORRECT. This answer choice corresponds very closely to the statement in the passage. Some synonyms have been used, but the meaning is the same: *were imperceptibly small at first* substitutes for *tiny*, and *tended to grow* substitutes for *mushroomed over time.*

(D) The passage indicates that the behavior of the model was unexpected. Nothing in the passage indicates that Lorenz expected the errors at all.

(E) The errors did not shrink but rather were *mushrooming over time.*

4. **The passage mentions each of the following as an example or potential example of a chaotic or non-chaotic system EXCEPT**

(A) a dough-mixing machine
(B) atmospheric weather patterns
(C) poppy seeds placed on top of an upside-down bowl
(D) poppy seeds placed in a right-side-up bowl
(E) fluctuating butterfly flight patterns

The passage mentions several examples of systems, both chaotic and non-chaotic, to illustrate the special characteristics of chaos. This question is an exercise in finding the references to the four wrong answers quickly.

(A) A dough-mixing machine is first mentioned at the beginning of the third paragraph as an example of chaos in action: *Chaotic systems, such as a machine mixing bread dough…*

(B) Atmospheric weather patterns as a system to be studied are mentioned in both the first and the last paragraphs. In the last paragraph, the passage states that the Earth's weather may be an example of a chaotic system.

(C) Poppy seeds placed on an upside-down bowl are described in the second paragraph as an example of a non-chaotic system that creates divergence.

(D) Poppy seeds placed in a bowl that is right-side-up are described in the second paragraph as an example of a non-chaotic system that creates convergence.

(E) CORRECT. Butterfly flight patterns are nowhere mentioned as a system. According to the last paragraph, the "Butterfly Effect" is caused by the flapping of a single butterfly's wings to potentially affect atmospheric systems.

5. **It can be inferred from the passage that which of the following pairs of items would most likely follow typical pathways within a chaotic system?**

(A) Two particles ejected in random directions from the same decaying atomic nucleus
(B) Two stickers affixed to a balloon that expands and contracts over and over again
(C) Two avalanches sliding down opposite sides of the same mountain
(D) Two baseballs placed into an active tumble dryer
(E) Two coins flipped into a large bowl

Stripped down to its essence, the question asks you to infer which of the five choices describes a system that is the most *chaotic,* according to the characteristics of chaos outlined in the passage. The most important proof sentence is at the beginning of the third paragraph: *Chaotic systems, such as a machine mixing bread dough, are characterized by both attraction and repulsion.* Thus, you should look for the system that is the most analogous to the dough-mixing machine. Moreover, the system should contain both attractive and repulsive elements: in other words, the two items embedded within the system should sometimes come near each other and then separate again.

At the beginning of the fourth paragraph, there is a "red herring" proof sentence: *During the dough-kneading process, two poppy seeds positioned next to each other eventually go their separate ways.* This sentence could lead you to think that the defining characteristic of chaotic systems is simply that two embedded items move away from each other. The question is asked in such a way as to focus your attention on the two items, so that you might then use this proof sentence alone and choose an incorrect answer.

(A) The two particles ejected from a nucleus do diverge, but they do not approach each other again. Moreover, there is no implication of any activity analogous to mixing bread dough.

(B) The stickers on the balloon separate and come together repeatedly. This behavior meets the criterion of *both attraction and repulsion.* However, there is no mixing, and as a result, the system cannot be said to be analogous to a machine mixing dough.

(C) As in answer choice (A), the two items in question (avalanches) separate but never draw near each other again. Likewise, there is no mixing in the system.

(D) CORRECT. Two baseballs placed into an active tumble dryer are analogous to two poppy seeds placed in bread dough being mixed by a machine: parts of the system are separated, intermingled and brought back together again in perfectly regular, though complex, ways, as determined by the laws of physics. The pathways of the two baseballs will diverge and converge repeatedly, as in any other chaotic system.

(E) The two coins flipped into a bowl is closely analogous to the example in the second paragraph of the passage of two poppy seeds placed in a bowl and allowed to fall; this system is presented as non-chaotic.

6. **The author implies which of the following about weather systems? Select *all* that apply.**

[A] They illustrate the same fundamental phenomenon as Lorenz's rounding errors.
[B] They are too complicated to ever be predicted with total accuracy.
[C] They are governed mostly by seemingly trivial events, such as the flapping of a butterfly's wings.

A: This is a select-all-that-apply question of a very specific variety. It is mostly relevant to the last paragraph of the passage, so we should make sure we have a solid understanding of the few sentences devoted to weather systems.

(A) CORRECT. Lorenz's rounding errors are actually found in the first paragraph, where we read that "Lorenz realized that tiny rounding errors…mushroomed over time." Similarly, in the final paragraph, we read that "this microscopic uncertainty grows until it encompasses even hurricanes." These are both examples of chaotic systems.

(B) The last sentence of the passage says that "few metereologists believe that we will ever be able to predict rain or shine for a particular day years in the future." This does not mean that weather systems, in general, are too complicated to be predicted with total accuracy. In fact, the sentence itself implies that SOME metereologists DO believe that we will be able to make predictions about the weather years in the future.

(C) While we are told that the wings of a butterfly can affect weather systems, we are never told that this is the most important contributing factor. Likely, major climatic events are more important than seemingly trivial events, such as a butterfly taking flight.

> **7. Select the sentence in the second or third paragraph that illustrates why "chaos theory" might be called a misnomer.**

"Misnomer" means that something has been given an incorrect or misleading name. We learned in the first paragraph that "despite its name," chaos theory "has little to do with randomness." So we want to find a sentence in the second or third paragraph that illustrates this point.

The final sentence of the third paragraph uses poppy seeds to show that even the bread-mixing machine, which appears to be mixing things at random (in a "chaotic" manner), is actually moving the seeds through "staggeringly complex pathways whose tangles appear accidental but are in fact determined by the system's fundamental equations." In other words, there's nothing chaotic at all, only a very complex organization. This is a perfect example of why "chaos theory" is a kind of misnomer.

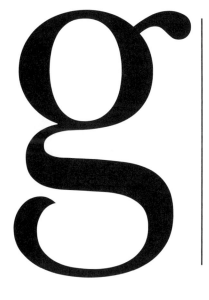

Chapter 9
of
READING COMPREHENSION & ESSAYS

ARGUMENT STRUCTURE PASSAGES

In This Chapter . . .

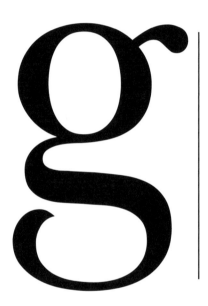

- Identifying Parts of an Argument
- Recognizing Argument Structure Passages
- Diagramming
- General Strategy
- Question Types

INTRODUCTION TO ARGUMENT STRUCTURE PASSAGES

Up until now, we've spoken almost exclusively about Short and Long Passages. But there is one more type of Reading Comprehension passage: Argument Structure Passages (ASPs).

You should expect to see about 3 ASPs on the test, and each passage will be accompanied by a single question. These individual questions shouldn't take any longer than a similar question on a Short or Long passage. Though there aren't multiple questions to preview, you absolutely must read the question before you read the passage, as it will tell you exactly what kind of ASP you're dealing with.

ASPs on the GRE involve reading brief arguments (each argument is generally one to three sentences long) and answering questions relating to those arguments. In order to analyze ASPs, it is important to understand that arguments are made up of premises, counter-premises, assumptions, and conclusions.

PREMISES are stated pieces of information or evidence that provide support for the conclusion. They may be facts, opinions, or claims. If they are opinions or claims, they will not be the overall claim the author is making; rather, they will be some intermediate claim the author is using to support the overall claim (conclusion).

COUNTERPREMISES are stated pieces of information or evidence that undermine or go against the conclusion. Occasionally an argument will present both sides of an argument, with evidence to support both. The passage will still come down one way or the other in terms of an overall conclusion, but some of the provided evidence will be used as premises, and some as counterpremises (supporting a kind of COUNTERCONCLUSION).

ASSUMPTIONS are unstated pieces of information that the argument requires to function.

The main point of the argument is the **CONCLUSION**, which is logically supported by the premises (and assumptions). Conclusions are in the form of an opinion or a claim. Facts will never be conclusions.

Here's a very simple example to illustrate:

> While the plot of the movie was compellling, the acting was atrocious. Thus, the movie will not win an Oscar.
>
> Conclusion: Thus, the movie will not win an Oscar.
>
> Supporting Premise: The acting was atrocious.
>
> Conterpremise: The plot of the movie was compelling.
>
> Assumption: Atrocious acting prevents a movie from winning an Oscar.

Identifying the Parts of an Argument

In order to do well on ASP questions, you must be able to identify the parts of an argument quickly as we did above. Consider the following argument, and see if you can find the different pieces on your own this time. Don't read on until you've tried.

> Studying regularly is one factor that has been shown to improve one's performance on the GRE. Melissa took the GRE and scored a 150. If she studies several times a week, Melissa can expect to improve her score.

In analyzing an argument, **you should first look for the conclusion**, which is the main point of the argument. The conclusion is often the last sentence of an argument, but not always. Sometimes the conclusion appears as the first sentence.

Where is the CONCLUSION? The main claim of this argument is the last sentence:

> If she studies several times a week, Melissa can expect to improve her score.

After finding the conclusion, look for the premises that lead to the conclusion. Premises include ALL the pieces of information written in the argument (except the conclusion). Premises provide evidence that usually supports, or leads to, the conclusion.

Where are the PREMISES? Each of the first two sentences is a premise.

> Premise: Studying regularly is one factor that has been shown to improve one's performance on the GRE.

> Premise: Melissa took the GRE and scored a 150.

What does this argument assume? It assumes that studying "several times per week" is the same as studying "regularly." Maybe "regularly" means every day!

Recognizing Argument Structure Passages

The Official Guide to the GRE Revised General Test does not differentiate between regular Reading Comprehension Passages and Argument Structure Passages (they also don't differentiate between Short and Long passages), but the difference is critical to your notetaking. Your first job on any passage will be to categorize it. Obviously, recognizing a long passage is easy, so the rest of this section will explain how to differentiate between short passages and ASPs. Here's a rundown of the major differences between these categories:

1) **Content.** Though subtle, this is probably the most fundamental difference between Short Passages and ASPs. Short Passages are similar to Long Passages, in that they discuss CONTENT. With a Short Passage, you could imagine multiple questions being asked about the relevant content (even if you're only given one question to answer), because there's a fair amount of detail. But ASPs present only a simple argument. On ASPs, the question you're asked is likely the only plausible, challenging question one could ask regarding the passage. The simplest way to think about this difference is that Short and Long Passages feature CONTENT (detail, simple stories, etc.), and ASPs feature only ARGUMENTS.

2) **Length.** ASPs are generally even shorter than Short Passages. One of the examples in the Official Guide is only one sentence long! If you see a passage this short, you know it's an ASP. ASPs will only be one paragraph, so any passage with two paragraphs must be a regular Short Passage. One paragraph passages of 3-4 sentences can be either Short Passages or ASPs.

3) **Question Types.** Neither select-in-passage nor select-all-that-apply questions ever appear on ASPs. So if you see a question of that type, you must be dealing with a Short Passage, not an ASP. ASP questions always ask you to choose exactly one answer choice.

Here's a breakdown of question types by passage type.

  a. Question types that only appear on Short/Long Passages:

   i. Tone/Attitude: ASPs are generally too short to get across any kind of overall tone.

   ii. Intention: Because ASPs only feature arguments, they won't ask you why the author made a certain point. If the question asks why a certain word, phrase or sentence is in the passage, the passage is not an ASP. ASPs break down into conclusions and premises. There's isn't enough complexity to warrant a question of intention.

  b. Question types that only appear on ASPs:

   i. Analyze Argument Structure: These questions provide passages with two bold statements, then ask you what purpose they're serving in the argument. Generally, when you see the word "argument," you should think ASP.

   ii. Resolve a Paradox/Explain a Discrepancy: Here, the passage presents a paradox and then asks you to explain it. This question type is an ASP classic.

   iii. Strengthen/Weaken: If a passage asks you to strengthen (support) or weaken (undermine) the argument given, it's an ASP.

  c. Question types that appear on both Short Passages and ASPs:

   i. Specific inference questions: When you're asked what can be inferred about a detail of the passage, there's no good way to know if it's a Short Passage or an ASP.

   ii. General inference questions: While technically both passage types ask general inference questions, the presentation should be markedly different. A question that asks you what the point of a passage was (particularly if it mentions the author) will be referring to a Short Passage. A question that asks you to "draw" the conclusion yourself will be referring to an ASP.

Don't worry. We'll look at plenty of examples in the pages to come.

Diagramming

The most effective way to improve your performance on ASPs is to DIAGRAM the arguments on paper. This is similar to the notetaking you've been learning for Short and Long Passages, but slightly more organized, and generally less time and ink-consuming. Remember that you should be writing something down for pretty much every RC passage. ASPs are particularly susceptible to good notetaking, because they present an argument, instead of a set of facts. ASPs should be EASIER to notate than Short Passages, because you're only writing down things that are structurally important, rather than trying to get your head around a complex set of facts.

How to Diagram an Argument: The T Diagram

Simply put, diagramming is a method of taking summary notes on the argument. Though we offer you one primary technique of diagramming, the form of the diagram is NOT essential. Rather, what matters is the act of analyzing the argument and taking summary notes.

The specific method of diagramming that we recommend is called the "T-Diagram." It will help you organize the different pieces of the argument (premises, counterpremises, conclusion).

First, draw a large T on your scratch paper. Make it asymmetrical, leaving more room on the left side, which will be the "pro" side. In most arguments, you will have very little on the "con" side (to the right).

Step 1.

Second, look for the conclusion. Once you find the conclusion, **write it above the top line of the T**, abbreviating heavily.

Step 2.

Conclusion

Third, read the argument sentence by sentence. As you do so, write anything that supports the conclusion on the left side of the T ("Pro" or "Premise"), and write anything that goes against the conclusion on the right side of the T ("Con" or "Counterpremise").

Step 3.

Conclusion

- Pro	- Con
- Pro	
- *[Assumption]*	

Finally, if you happened to think of any assumptions while reading, place them in brackets somewhere below the T. Make sure you can differentiate between stated premises and unstated assumptions when looking at your notes.

Let's look at a few examples:

Example 1:

1. Certain genetic diseases are more prevalent among certain ethnic populations. For example, Tay Sachs disease, a usually fatal genetic condition caused by the build-up of gangliocides in nerve cells, occurs more frequently among Ashkenazi Jews than among the general population.
    Which of the following assertions can most properly be drawn from the above information?

Did you notice that everything in this passage is a fact? There are no claims made! This argument doesn't have a conclusion; in fact, it's a Draw a Conclusion question (specific question types will be discussed in more detail later). But even though we won't be writing down a conclusion, that doesn't mean we shouldn't take notes. Scan the passage point by point and fill in the premises portion of your T-diagram,

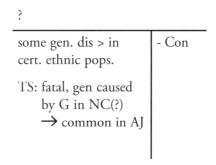

Notice that though the second sentence describes how Tay Sachs disease works, this information is represented only very simply in the diagram (and with the addition of a question mark, indicating that the reader did not quite understand that piece of information). ASPs revolve more often around logic than around how some technical fact works, so it is unlikely you would have to understand the phrase "the build-up of gangliocides in nerve cells." As such, it is not necessary to spend time detailing this sort of technical information. The most you need to understand is that the basic cause for this disease is given. If the question does ask about the cause, then you can take the time to re-read and try to understand that technical phrase.

2.   Environmentalist: The national energy commission's current plan calls for the construction of six new nuclear power plants during the next decade. The commission argues that these plants are extremely safe and will have minimal environmental impact on their surrounding communities. However, all six nuclear power plants will be located far from densely populated areas. Clearly, the government is tacitly admitting that these plants do pose a serious health risk to humans.

      Which of the following, if true, most seriously weakens the environmentalist's claim of an unspoken government admission?

The last sentence here is the conclusion of the argument. While the last sentence will not ALWAYS be the conclusion of an argument, the word "clearly" sets it up nicely. Notice that the second sentence of the argument is a kind of COUNTERCONCLUSION, providing the opinion of the commission, so we can put it on the right side of the T-diagram. Our main premise here is that the nuclear power plants will be located far away from densely populated areas. This supports the idea that the government suspects a possible health risk. This is in no way an ironclad argument. If it were, there'd be no way to weaken it, as the question demands. It might be helpful to think about assumptions. This argument is assuming there's no other good reason to keep nuclear plants away from people (such as their view of the plants, or just unfounded but ineradicable anxiety caused by the proximity of toxic waste).

Plnt – ↑ hlth rsk to ppl

All plnts far frm pop areas	Comm.: plnts safe, ↓ enviro impct
[No other reasons for distance: view, anxiety]	

3.   Two-dimensional bar codes are omni-directional, meaning that, unlike one-dimensional bar codes, they can be scanned from any direction. Additionally, two-dimensional bar codes are smaller and can store more data than their one-dimensional counterparts. Despite such advantages, two-dimensional bar codes account for a much smaller portion of total bar code usage than one-dimensional bar codes.

Which of the following, if true, would best explain the discrepancy above?

This is a Resolve a Paradox question. While there's no conclusion, there are plenty of premises to write down. Later, we'll discuss approaches for different question types. For now, it's enough to know that on some questions, you'll be able to write down both conclusions and premises, and on others, you won't be given any conclusion, and will have to stick to premises (and possibly counterpremises). For this question, just abbreviate the premises as best you can and put them in the bottom left portion of your T-diagram.

?

2D bar codes = scan
any dir. (unlike 1D BC)

2D smaller, store ↑ data

BUT 2D ↓↓ % of mkt
than 1D

By the way, how did we know that this passage has no conclusion? Reread the passage. After each sentence, ask yourself: "Was that a fact or an opinion?" If you get all facts, there is no conclusion.

General Strategy

The next piece of each ASP puzzle is the QUESTION that follows the argument. You can expect five different ASP question types on the GRE:

    (1) Strengthen the Conclusion
    (2) Weaken the Conclusion
    (3) Analyze the Argument Structure
    (4) Draw a Conclusion (Inference)
    (5) Resolve a Paradox.

Notice that all of these but Resolve a Paradox are entirely dependent on your understanding of the basic structure of the argument. Three of them are specifically about the conclusion!

Identifying the Question Type

In addition to giving you clues about the conclusion, the question stem will give you some indication as to the nature of the question. The vast majority of question stems will allow you to categorize a question, which will direct your notetaking and process of elimination, and for this reason the question stem should always be read first. However, some question stems may not be as helpful in determining the correct approach to the problem. If the question stem is not immediately helpful or the question type is difficult to identify, do not dwell on the issue. Simply go ahead and diagram the argument; afterwards, you can re-examine the question. In these cases, the process of diagramming will generally clarify the question stem.

"Fill in the Blank" Questions

The GRE may make a question a bit more complex by structuring it as a "Fill in the Blank" question. Once again, this is not a new type of question. "Fill in the Blank" is simply a disguised version of one of the question types listed above. These questions are sometimes harder to categorize than the more typical examples. Once you recognize that a "Fill in the Blank" question is of a certain type, you can use the standard strategies associated with that type.

Boundary Words in the Argument

For any question, it is helpful to focus your attention on the BOUNDARY words and phrases provided in the argument. These words and phrases narrow the scope of a premise. For example:

Premise: The percentage of literate adults has increased.

The boundary word "percentage" limits the scope of the premise. It restricts the meaning to percentage only, as opposed to the actual number of literate adults. For all we know, the actual number went down! The boundary word "adults" also limits the scope of the premise. It restricts the meaning to adults only, as opposed to the total population, or children. Finally, the word "literate" obviously restricts the category of adults that has increased.

Here is another example:

Conclusion: Controversial speech should be allowed, provided it does not incite major violence.

The boundary phrase "provided it does not incite major violence" limits the scope of the conclusion. It restricts the meaning to some types of controversial speech, as opposed to all types of controversial speech. The boundary word "major" limits the exception—controversial speech should not be allowed when it incites major violence, as opposed to any violence.

Boundary words and phrases are vital because they provide nuances to the argument. These nuances will often be manipulated in the answer choices of ASP questions. In other words, these nuances can single-handedly make some answer choices correct or incorrect. Therefore, in your diagram, be sure to include boundary words and underline them or capitalize them for emphasis. This will help you identify answer choices that try to trick you on the argument boundaries.

Extreme Words in the Argument

Another general strategy for all ASP questions involves EXTREME words and phrases in the body of the argument. Extreme words, such as "always," "never," "all," and "none," are the opposite of boundary words—they make the argument very broad or far-reaching.

Using extreme words opens up an argument unreasonably, making it very susceptible to strengthening or weakening. For example:

Conclusion: Sugar is never healthy for anyone trying to lose weight.

The extreme word "never" unreasonably opens up this argument, placing no limitation on the claim that sugar is unhealthy. A more moderate conclusion would argue that sugar is usually unhealthy, or that excessive sugar is unhealthy. The extreme word "anyone" further opens up this argument. A more moderate conclusion might be that this claim applies to most people trying to lose weight. You should note any extreme language used in premises or conclusions. Since good Argument Structure Passages rarely contain extreme words, any such words that you find will likely be very useful in responding to the question.

Boundary and Extreme Words in the Answer Choices

Boundary and extreme words also appear in the answer choices. They are just as important as boundary and extreme words in the body of the argument, though for a different reason. Extreme words in the answer choices usually make those answer choices incorrect (unless, of course, the argument justifies the use of extreme words). A correct answer choice must be 100% correct. As long as we interpret the words legitimately, such a choice must be valid no matter which way we interpret it. This principle gives us an approach to evaluating answer choices. When you see boundary or extreme words in an answer choice, ask yourself, "What is the most extreme example I can think of that would still fit the wording of this answer choice?" Then, using the conclusion and the question asked, see whether your extreme example allows you to eliminate that answer choice.

For example, an answer choice might say:

> (D) Some teachers leave the profession entirely within three years of beginning their teaching careers.

You might choose to address one of two different boundaries here. The word "some" refers to some number of teachers but does not specify the size of the group. The phrase "within three years" refers to a period of time but does not specify the exact length of time.

If you choose to address the word "some," you could say that 1% of teachers leave within three years, or that 99% of teachers do so. Either way, the statistics still fit the criterion that some teachers do this. Suppose the conclusion asserted that new teacher turnover is having a major impact on the industry. If only 1% of new teachers leave within three years, then new teacher turnover will probably not have much of an impact.

Alternatively, you could interpret "within three years" to mean that many teachers in this category leave after 1 day of teaching. You could also imagine that many teachers in this category leave after 2 years and 364 days of teaching. Again, either way, the statistics still fit the criterion that new teachers leave the profession within 3 years of beginning their careers. Depending upon the conclusion and the question, you would then try to disprove answer choices by using these extreme interpretations.

Extreme words, such as "only" or "never," can appear in correct answers. However, those same extreme words, or their equivalents, must be in the original argument. If the answer choice uses an extreme word that is not explicitly supported by the text of the argument, you should eliminate that choice.

General Answer Choice Strategy: Process of Elimination

For any ASP question, it is important to practice the process of elimination using your scratch paper. DO NOT simply eliminate answer choices in your head! As you go through many different questions during the test, it is very difficult to keep straight which answer choices you have ruled out. You do not want to find yourself re-evaluating answers that you have already eliminated! By the end of the verbal section of the GRE, your scratch paper should be filled with columns or rows of "A–E" (and a bit of "A-C") with incorrect answer choices crossed out and correct answers circled. You should practice using your scratch paper in this way so that you are completely comfortable using the scratch booklet provided to you when taking the GRE. Even if you believe you have found the correct answer, always check all of the answer choices. You may find that another answer choice is potentially correct, and you will have to rethink your initial choice.

Question Types

(1) Strengthen the Conclusion

Strengthen the Conclusion questions ask you to provide additional support for a given conclusion. The question stem may appear in a number of forms: Which of the following, if true, most strengthens the argument above? Which of the following, if true, most strongly supports the scientists' hypothesis? Which of the following provides the strongest reason to expect that the plan will be successful?

A premise that strengthens the conclusion should do at least one of the following:

> (1) Fix a weakness of the conclusion
> (2) Introduce additional supporting evidence.

The correct answer choice for a Strengthen question will typically function as a new premise. This choice will be related to the argument but generally introduce new information supporting the conclusion. A correct answer might provide an explanation of or support for a keyword in the conclusion.

Begin each Strengthen the Conclusion question as described earlier. After reading the question stem, read the passage, create a T-diagram, and fill in the conclusion, premises, and counter-premises. Keep in mind that some passages contain both arguments and counter-arguments. To outline these more complex questions, make sure you find the conclusion from the point of view of the AUTHOR first, then the conclusion of the OPPOSING argument. You might want to modify your T-diagram, with the author's conclusion and premises on the left side of the T, and the counter-conclusion and counterpremises on the right side of the T. Make sure you know WHICH conclusion you're trying to strengthen.

Create an S-W-Slash Chart

The process of elimination in Strengthen the Conclusion questions takes on a very specific form. Write down A through E. Then, as you evaluate each answer choice, note whether each answer:

  1. Strengthens the conclusion (note with an "**S**"),
  2. Weakens the conclusion (note with a "**W**"),
  3. Or is irrelevant to the conclusion (note with a "**–**").

It is very easy to reverse your thinking and to get confused as you work with a difficult Strengthen problem. By keeping your assessments organized and on paper, you will save yourself time and effort, and you will be less likely to make a mistake.

At times it may not be entirely clear whether an answer choice strengthens or weakens the conclusion. For example, an answer choice may serve to strengthen the conclusion, but only in an indirect or arguable way. If that is the case, you might note the answer choice with a lowercase "**s**" in order to indicate that the answer choice may only marginally strengthen the conclusion. As you assess the other choices, determine whether you need to refine your categorization of that answer choice. Depending upon the other answer choices, it may be obvious that this answer choice is wrong or, alternatively, that it is the best answer.

Consider the following example:

> Compensation has not been the reason for the recent rash of employee departures at QuestCorp. Rather, the departures have been caused by employee dissatisfaction with poor working conditions and the absence of advancement opportunities.
>
> Which of the following, if true, would most support the claim made above as to the cause of departures from QuestCorp?
>
> (A) Many prospective hires at QuestCorp have expressed that their compensation is negotiable.
> (B) All employees at QuestCorp's main competitor recently received a large and well-publicized raise.
> (C) Many departing employees have cited abusive managers and unsafe factories as responsible for their decision to leave QuestCorp.
> (D) Studies indicate that compensation is one of several important factors regarding the decision to switch jobs.
> (E) QuestCorp has recently initiated a review of its internal policies, including those regarding working conditions and employee promotions.

The conclusion is that the departures have been caused by employee dissatisfaction with poor working conditions and the absence of advancement opportunities. The first sentence offers a counterconclusion. No premises for this argument.

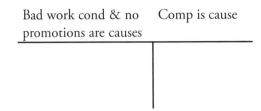

Bad work cond & no
promotions are causes   Comp is cause

Use an S-W-slash chart to categorize and eliminate answer choices.

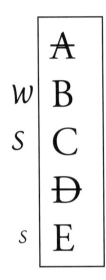

Answer choice (A) is irrelevant to the conclusion. The argument discusses recently departed employees, not prospective hires.

Answer choice (B), if anything, weakens the conclusion by suggesting that departing employees might have done so because they felt undercompensated.

Answer choice (C) strengthens the conclusion, providing examples of poor working conditions (abusive managers and unsafe factories) that were cited by departing employees. Notice that the choice does not need to make the conclusion definitively true; it just needs to make the conclusion more likely to be true. As always, we should continue to evaluate all answer choices.

Answer choice (D) is irrelevant. This answer choice refers to employees in general, not the particular employees that quit QuestCorp.

Answer choice (E) could be considered to strengthen the conclusion; perhaps the rash of departures has led to the review. However, "internal policies" is very broad, and this answer choice requires us to assume a particular motivation for the review. In fact, it is unclear from the answer choice what has motivated the reexamination of policies; it may simply be an annually scheduled review. Answer choices that require additional assumptions or logical leaps to strengthen the conclusion will generally be incorrect. Answer choice (E) should be labeled either irrelevant, or perhaps a very indirect strengthen with a lower-case "s."

Answer choice (C) is correct.

Wrong Answer Choice Types

A. No Tie to the Conclusion

Many wrong answers will be tied to a premise but not to the conclusion. The answer choice could simply provide unnecessary information about that premise (such as answer choice (A) in the previous example). Alternatively, a "No Tie to the Conclusion" answer choice could support that premise, but if the premise is already stated as a fact, it does not need support.

A few wrong answers with "No Tie to the Conclusion" do bring in language from the conclusion, but they do not meaningfully support the conclusion. Deceptive answers such as these seem relevant. Make sure that the answer you choose is not simply related to the conclusion, but in fact supports it.

Also, some wrong answers can be "Real-World Plausible." You are not assessing a choice's truth in the real world—only whether the choice strengthens the argument.

B. Wrong Direction

Many wrong answers on Strengthen questions in fact weaken the argument. Make sure that you note whether a particular question is a Strengthen the Conclusion or a Weaken the Conclusion question so that you do not mistakenly pick the wrong answer. In the compensation example provided above, answer choice (B) is an example of this deceptive answer type:

> (B) All employees at QuestCorp's main competitor recently received a large and well-publicized raise.

In fact, as noted above, this choice weakens the argument. The reason that ASPs use such answer choices is that they do have an effect on the argument (as opposed to being out of scope or irrelevant). Under exam pressure, you might get confused about which way such a choice affects the answer.

(2) Weaken the Conclusion

Weaken the Conclusion questions are exactly like Strengthen the Conclusion questions in every way except the obvious (they want you to weaken instead of strengthen!).

Weaken the Conclusion questions appear in a number of forms: Which of the following, if true, most seriously weakens the argument? Which of the following, if true, could present the most serious disadvantage of XYZ Corporation's new marketing initiative? Which of the following, if true, most strongly supports the view that the drug treatment program will NOT be successful?

Correct answers do not need to make the conclusion false or invalid. Correct answers merely need to make it less likely that the stated conclusion is valid.

Almost all correct answers to Weaken the Conclusion questions will introduce a new piece of evidence that undermines a faulty or tenuous assumption OR that negatively impacts the conclusion directly. Outline exactly as you would on Strengthen the Conclusion questions, keeping in mind that you may see both arguments and counterarguments in the passage.

Again, we will employ the S-W-slash chart to organize our process of elimination.

> The national infrastructure for airport runways and air traffic control requires immediate expansion to accommodate the proliferation of new private, smaller aircraft. The Federal Aviation Authority (the FAA) has proposed a fee for all air travelers to help fund this expansion. However, this fee would be unfair, as it would impose costs on all travelers to benefit only the few who utilize the new private planes.
>
> Which of the following, if true, would allow the FAA to counter the objection that the proposed fee would be unfair?
>
> (A) The existing national airport infrastructure benefits all air travelers.
> (B) The fee, if imposed, will have a negligible effect on the overall volume of air travel.
> (C) The expansion would reduce the number of delayed flights resulting from small private planes congesting runways.
> (D) Travelers who use small private planes are almost uniformly wealthy or traveling on business.
> (E) The Administrator of the FAA is appointed by the President, who is subject to national election.

In this argument, the conclusion is that this fee would be unfair, with the provided rationale that it would impose costs on all travelers to benefit only the few who utilize the new private planes.

Fee unfair	
Cost for all, benefits only for priv planes	

Evaluate each of the answer choices using an S-W-Slash chart.

A
B
C
D
E

W
S

Answer choice (A) suggests that the *existing* infrastructure benefits everyone who would be asked to pay the fee. This seems to speak to the question of fairness. However, the *fee itself* does not benefit the wide range of air travelers, and it is the fairness of the fee that is in question. This choice is best categorized as irrelevant.

Answer choice (B) indicates that the fee will not impact the volume of air travel, implying that the fee will not drive any travelers to stay home or switch to another mode of transportation. This is irrelevant to the conclusion, as a fee can still be unfair even if it does not change behavior.

Answer choice (C) weakens the conclusion. If the expansion would reduce delays for all travelers, then all travelers would stand to benefit from the new fee. The issue of fairness is mitigated, since all would benefit in some way from the fee, not only the few assumed by the author of the argument.

Answer choice (D), if anything, strengthens the conclusion by pointing out that those who use private planes are generally better able to pay a fee than the average traveler. It may be considered unfair to charge the less well-off to benefit those with more resources.

Answer choice (E) implies that the fee may be considered fair because the FAA is headed by an individual who is appointed by the President, who is elected. The implication is that any action that stems from the actions of an elected official must be fair. Alternatively, the choice suggests that nothing is unfair since people can elect a new President, who can appoint a new administrator, who can change the fee policy. Notice the large logical leaps required to argue that this answer choice weakens the conclusion. This choice is better classified as irrelevant.

Answer choice (C) is the correct answer.

Wrong Answer Choice Types

The common categories of wrong answers for Weaken the Conclusion questions are essentially the same as those for Strengthen the Conclusion questions.

A. No Tie to the Conclusion

Many wrong answers are tied to a premise but not to the conclusion. An incorrect answer choice can simply provide unnecessary information about that premise.

B. Wrong Direction

Some wrong answers on Weaken questions in fact strengthen the argument. Make sure that you note whether a particular question is a Weaken the Conclusion or a Strengthen the Conclusion question so that you do not mistakenly pick the wrong answer.

(3) Analyze the Argument Structure

Analyze the Argument Structure questions ask you to describe the role of a part or parts of the argument that have been rendered in boldface. Unfortunately, the arguments tend to be complex, often with an argument/counterargument structure. If you see this structure, use a modified T-diagram allowing for conclusions/premises on one side and counterconclusions/counterpremises on the other.

Your task is to determine the role that each boldface statement plays in the argument. At one level, there are three primary options for each statement:

(1) The statement in boldface is the author's CONCLUSION.
(2) The statement in boldface is a premise that SUPPORTS the author's conclusion.
(3) The statement in boldface is a premise that WEAKENS the author's conclusion.

Thus, you should classify each statement according to these categories. Make sure you outline BEFORE you attempt to do this, and that you've both outlined and categorized the boldfaced statements BEFORE you look to the answer choices.

Consider the following example:

Mathematician: Recently, Zubin Ghosh made headlines when he was recognized to have solved the Hilbert Conjecture, made a hundred years ago. Ghosh simply posted his work on the Internet, rather than submitting it to established journals. In fact, **he has no job, let alone a university position**; he lives alone and has refused all acclaim. In reporting on Ghosh, the press unfortunately has reinforced the popular view that mathematicians are antisocial loners. **But mathematicians clearly form a tightly knit community**, frequently collaborating on important efforts; indeed, teams of researchers are working together to extend Ghosh's findings.

In the argument above, the two portions in boldface play which of the following roles?

(A) The first is an observation the author makes to illustrate a social pattern; the second is a generalization of that pattern.
(B) The first is evidence in favor of the popular view expressed in the argument; the second is a brief restatement of that view.
(C) The first is a specific example of a generalization that the author contradicts; the second is a reiteration of that generalization.
(D) The first is a specific counterexample to a generalization that the author asserts; the second is that generalization.
(E) The first is a judgment that counters the primary assertion expressed in the argument; the second is a circumstance on which that judgment is based.

The author's conclusion is that mathematicians actually form a tightly knit community. The counterargument is that mathematicians are antisocial loners. Now, label each statement as either Conclusion, Premise For, or Premise Against. In the above argument, the first boldface represents an example that supports the counterargument. Thus, the first statement is Premise Against. The second boldface represents the author's conclusion. Now we can write down our assessment of the boldface statements:

#1 = Premise Against
#2 = Conclusion

Turning to the answer choices, we should assess each one methodically.

Evaluate the first half of choice (A) first. This says that the author uses this statement to illustrate a social pattern. In other words, this choice asserts that statement #1 is Premise For. We have labeled the first statement as Premise Against, so this choice is incorrect.

The first half of choice (B) says the first statement supports the popular view. The popular view is the counterargument, so this choice argues that #1 is Premise Against. The second half of choice (B), however, says that the second statement is the popular view. The second statement is the author's conclusion, not the counterargument. Eliminate this choice.

The first half of choice (C) says that the first statement is an example of the counterargument (in other words, Premise Against). The second half of choice (C) says that the second statement reiterates the counterargument, but the second statement is the author's own conclusion. Eliminate this choice.

The first half of choice (D) says that the first statement is a counterexample to the author's conclusion (in other words, Premise Against). The second half of choice (D) says that the second statement is the author's conclusion. We agree with these labels, so this is the correct answer. As always, you should read all the answer choices, but you may be at the two-minute mark already, in which case you should select (D) and move on.

The first half of choice (E) says that the first statement is a premise against the author's conclusion (in other words, Premise Against). The second half of this choice, however, says that the second statement is another Premise Against. Eliminate this choice.

Alternative Approach

If you have trouble with this approach, you can try an alternative method that may be quicker. Read the passage and label each boldface statement as one of the following:

- (a) Fact   (a verifiable statement)
- (b) Opinion   (a minor claim, or an opinion of someone other than the author)
- (c) Conclusion (the major claim of the author)

Nearby non-bolded words can help you classify the boldface statements. Then skim each answer choice, ONLY looking for terminology that matches Fact, Opinion, or Conclusion.

- (a) Fact   = "evidence" "circumstance" "finding"
- (b) Opinion   = "judgment" "claim" "position" (taken by someone else)
- (c) Conclusion = "position" (taken by the argument) "assertion" (of the author)

Do NOT interpret the content of the answer choices at this stage. Eliminate answer choices that do not match the Fact/Opinion/Conclusion classification. You can generally get rid of at least one incorrect answer choice—and in some cases, you can completely solve the problem.

The advantage of this method is speed. You can quickly classify the boldface statements as Fact/Opinion/Conclusion and scan the answer choices without getting bogged down. However, you might not be able to eliminate all the wrong answers. In the example above, for instance, we would classify the boldface statements as Fact and Conclusion. This pattern does not fit answer choice (E), which is Opinion and Fact, but every other answer choice could be Fact and Conclusion.

Analyze the Argument Structure is a very difficult question type. If you can only figure out how to categorize one of the two boldface statements, then assess the corresponding half of the answer choices. Eliminate whatever answer choices you can, pick intelligently from among the remaining answer choices, and move on.

(4) Draw a Conclusion (Inference)

Draw a Conclusion questions ask you to conclude something from a set of given premises. The question stem may take many different forms:

> If the statements above are true, which of the following must be true?
> Which of the following conclusions can best be drawn from the information above?
> The statements above, if true, best support which of the following assertions?
> Which of the following can properly be inferred from the statement above?

Any question mentioning something specific from the passage is likely a Draw a Conclusion question, for example: "The passage above emphasizes which of the following points about pyramids?"

You might also fill in a blank after a conclusion signal: "Therefore, _____"

When an ASP provides a conclusion in an argument, that conclusion is an arguable statement, or claim, that is partially supported by the premises of the argument. By contrast, if you are asked to DRAW a conclusion, that conclusion MUST be true as a result of only the given premises. The conclusion should not require you to make any additional assumptions at all, even tiny ones. The correct answer to a Draw a Conclusion question is NOT a claim or an arguable statement. Rather, it is a FACTUAL deduction based only upon information that you have been given.

Draw a Conclusion questions often use the word "infer." For example, a question may ask: Which of the following can be properly inferred from the passage?

The word inference is essentially a synonym for conclusion. As such, an inference should also follow directly from the premises; it should be unequivocally true according to those premises.

When outlining Draw a Conclusion ASPs, you should only fill in the "premises" portion of your T-diagram. If you can predict a possible conclusion, you might pencil it in, but don't let it keep you from considering all five of the answer choices.

Consider the following simplified example:

> Premises: Samantha and Isabel are the only two people in the dining room. They are both women.

What can be safely inferred from these facts? That is, what MUST be true as a result?

> Conclusion: There are no men in the dining room.

This conclusion may not seem very meaningful or important in a real-world sense, but you should avoid grand conclusions in Draw a Conclusion problems. A correct answer might simply restate one or more of the premises, using synonyms. Alternatively, a correct answer might be a mathematical or logical deduction.

Consider the following example:

> In certain congested urban areas, commuters who use public transportation options, such as trains and subways, spend approximately 25 percent less time in transit, on average, to reach their destinations than commuters who travel by car. Even individuals who drive their entire commute in carpool lanes, which are typically the least congested sections of roadways, still spend more time, on average, than commuters who use trains and subways.
>
> The statements above, if true, best support which of the following assertions about commuting in the congested urban areas mentioned above?

(A) Waiting in traffic accounts for approximately 25 percent of the commuting time for individuals who drive to their destinations.

(B) Walking between a subway or train station and one's final destination does not, on average, take longer than walking between one's car and one's final destination.

(C) Using carpool lanes does not, on average, reduce driving time by more than 25 percent.

(D) Individuals who commute via public buses spend approximately 25 percent more time in transit than those who commute using public trains or subways.

(E) Subways and trains are available in the majority of congested urban areas.

In Draw a Conclusion questions, the entire body of the argument represents premises. A T-diagram for the above argument might look like this:

$$T/S \overset{25\%}{<} car$$
$$T/S < Carpool\ lanes$$

We are looking for a conclusion that must be true according to this information.

Answer choice (A) states that waiting in traffic accounts for 25 percent of the commuting time for drivers. However, the passage never mentions "waiting in traffic." As a result, we cannot conclude anything about how much waiting in traffic contributes to the commute.

Answer choice (B) makes a claim about particular segments of the different commutes. However, the passage never mentions which segments of the commute provide the speed advantage to public transportation. It is certainly possible that walking to the subway takes longer than walking to one's car and that the speed advantage is realized from some other segment of the commute.

Answer choice (C) does not make much of a claim at all. It simply restates the information given in the passage. If taking subways or trains reduces one's commute time, on average, by 25 percent, and if using carpool lanes does not eliminate the speed advantage of public transportation, then it follows that carpool lanes do not reduce driving time by more than 25 percent. Thus, answer choice (C) is correct.

Answer choice (D) introduces a claim about public buses, which are never mentioned in the passage. While it is possible that public buses are similar to cars in terms of commuting time, it is certainly not necessary and does not follow from any information given.

Answer choice (E) makes a claim about the majority of congested urban areas. The premises, on the other hand, reference only certain congested urban areas. Thus, this answer choice uses an overly broad term that goes beyond the scope of the passage. It does not have to be true that a majority has these specific types of public transport.

Notice that the correct answer, (C), did NOT weave together all the premises into a grand plan. The correct conclusion that you can draw from a set of premises must always be a provable fact. Thus, it will generally restate a premise, sometimes in a mathematically equivalent way. The mathematical equivalence provides a slight disguise for the truth. For instance, the premise More precipitation falls on the Sahara than on Antarctica can be restated as Less precipitation falls on Antarctica than on the Sahara.

Wrong Answer Choice Types

Just as with Strengthen and Weaken questions, knowing common categories of wrong answers on Draw a Conclusion questions can help you with the process of elimination. You should make use of these classifications while studying/ reviewing questions, or if you get stuck between a couple answer choices. Don't think about them when you're doing questions on real tests, as it will take up more time than it's worth.

A. Out Of Scope

For Draw a Conclusion questions, "Out of Scope" answers require you to assume at least one piece of information not explicitly presented in the argument. For example, answer choice (D) in the above example goes beyond the scope of the argument by bringing up buses.

A subset of Out of Scope answers will contain information that seems "Real-World Plausible." In other words, this information is very plausible, or likely to be true in the real world. The answer may even contain what people would reasonably surmise to be true in an article or conversation about the general topic. The Draw a Conclusion question type, however, requires us to find something that *must* be true according to the given premises, not something that *could* be true or merely sounds reasonable. Often people are surprised at how simple the conclusions are—the correct answer will be very closely tied to the premises. Another choice may seem reasonable in the real world, but you are not allowed to go outside the premises given. If you cannot say that the premises prove an answer choice to be true, eliminate that answer choice. Do not bring external knowledge into the picture on Draw a Conclusion questions.

B. Wrong Direction

"Wrong Direction" answers might provide a conclusion that is the opposite of what the argument says. The reason why such a conclusion would be proposed is that under exam pressure, you might not notice the reversal. For example, a "Wrong Direction" answer choice for the argument above could just be the opposite of the correct answer:

> Using carpool lanes <u>does</u>, on average, reduce driving time by more than 25%.

This statement actually asserts the opposite of what the premises together imply, but because it brings up some of the issues one might expect to see, it would be easy to misread and then choose as the correct answer.

(5) Resolve a Paradox

This question type poses two seemingly contradictory premises and asks you to find the answer choice that best reconciles them. The question will often, though not always, indicate what the discrepancy is or provide a keyword pointing to the discrepancy in the argument. For example: Which of the following statements, if true, would best explain the sudden drop in temperature? Which of the following, if true, most helps to resolve the paradox described above?

Like Draw a Conclusion arguments, Resolve a Paradox passages will contain only premises, so your notetaking should be relatively easy.

To solve Resolve a Paradox problems, look for the answer choice that provides a new, fact-based premise that directly illustrates why the apparent discrepancy is not a discrepancy after all. The correct answer will often contain some very specific new piece of information that resolves the given discrepancy. You might not have anticipated this information ahead of time, but after you add it to the existing premises, the situation should make sense.

Consider the following example:

> In a recent poll, 71% of respondents reported that they cast votes in the most recent national election. Voting records show, however, that only 60% of eligible voters actually voted in that election.
>
> Which of the following pieces of evidence, if true, would provide the best explanation for the discrepancy?

(A) The margin of error for the survey was plus or minus five percentage points.

(B) Fifteen percent of the survey's respondents were living overseas at the time of the election.

(C) Prior research has shown that people who actually do vote are also more likely to respond to polls than those who do not vote.

(D) Some people who intend to vote are prevented from doing so by last-minute conflicts on election day or other complications.

(E) Polls about voting behavior typically have margins of error within plus or minus three percentage points.

The argument consists entirely of factual premises. The facts in the first sentence appear to contradict the facts in the second sentence. The correct answer will provide a new premise that resolves this apparent discrepancy.

Answer choice (A) begins promisingly by discussing a margin of error. The choice does not go far enough. A margin of error of 5 percentage points will not close the 11 percentage point gap between the two statistics in the argument.

Answer choice (B) mentions a percentage larger than the 11 point discrepancy in the argument. The percentage, however, applies to the percentage of respondents living overseas at the time of the election. This 15% could be part of the group that did not vote, or these people could have voted by absentee ballot, or we could have some mix of the two. In any event, this does not give us enough information to resolve the discrepancy.

Answer choice (C) provides a reason why a higher percentage of the poll respondents said that they voted than eligible voters actually voted. If those voters are also more likely to respond to polls, then they will be over-represented in the poll numbers.

While answer choice (D) may be true, it does not explain the discrepancy in the statistics presented in the argument. The poll asked about voters' actual actions during the last election, not what they intended to do.

Answer choice (E) may also be true, but it does not explain the discrepancy in the statistics presented in the argument. Even after adjusting for a three percent margin of error, the statistics are substantially different.

A common wrong answer type will typically discuss one of the premises but not actually address the discrepancy between conflicting premises. Choices (A), (B), and (D) fall into this category.

Another common wrong answer type is Wrong Direction. A choice of this type will support the fact that the discrepancy exists, rather than explaining why there is not actually a discrepancy after all. Choice (E), above, falls into this category. Be careful not to misread the question and think that we are supposed to explain why the apparent discrepancy exists. Remember that this is not what we are supposed to do on problems of this type. Rather, we must explain why the apparent discrepancy is not a real discrepancy.

ASP Practice Problems

The following practice set will test the skills taught in the previous chapter. All question types are represented, so make sure that your first step is always to read the question stem and determine the question type. Then, outline the passage, make use of any specific techniques recommended for that question type (i.e. the S-W-Slash Chart), and pick the correct answer. Be sure you read and consider all five answer choices before you make your final decision!

1. John was flying from San Francisco to New York with a connecting flight in Chicago on the same airline. Chicago's airport is one of the largest in the world, consisting of several small stand-alone terminals connected by trams. John's plane arrived on time. John was positive he would make his connecting flight thirty minutes later, because _____.

 Which of the following most logically completes the argument above?

 (A) John's airline is known for always being on time
 (B) a number of other passengers on John's first flight were also scheduled to take John's connecting flight
 (C) at the airport in Chicago, airlines always fly into and out of the same terminal
 (D) John knew there was another flight to New York scheduled for one hour after the connecting flight he was scheduled to take
 (E) the airline generally closes the doors of a particular flight ten minutes before it is scheduled to take off

2. Media Critic: Network executives have alleged that television viewership is decreasing due to the availability of television programs on other platforms, such as the internet, video-on-demand, and mobile devices. These executives claim that **declining viewership will cause advertising revenue to fall so far that networks will be unable to spend the large sums necessary to produce programs of the quality now available**. That development, in turn, will lead to a dearth of programming for the very devices which cannibalized television's audience. However, technology executives point to research which indicates that **users of these platforms increase the number of hours per week that they watch television** because they are exposed to new programs and promotional spots through these alternate platforms. This analysis demonstrates that networks can actually increase their revenue through higher advertising rates, due to larger audiences lured to television through other media.

 The portions in boldface play which of the following roles in the media critic's argument?

 (A) The first is an inevitable trend that weighs against the critic's claim; the second is that claim.
 (B) The first is a prediction that is challenged by the argument; the second is a finding upon which the argument depends.
 (C) The first clarifies the reasoning behind the critic's claim; the second demonstrates why that claim is flawed.
 (D) The first acknowledges a position that the technology executives accept as true; the second is a consequence of that position.
 (E) The first opposes the critic's claim through an analogy; the second outlines a scenario in which that claim will not hold.

3. In the last year, real estate prices, such as those for houses and condominiums, have gone up an average of 7% in the city of Galway but only 2% in the town of Tuam. On the other hand, average rents for apartments have risen 8% in Tuam over the last year, but only 4% in Galway.

Which of the following is an inference that can be reasonably drawn from the premises given above?

(A) In the last year, the ratio of average apartment rents to average real estate prices has increased in Tuam but fallen in Galway.
(B) Tuam has experienced a greater shift in demand toward the rental market than Galway has.
(C) It has become easier for Galway real estate to be bought and sold, whereas it has become easier for Tuam real estate to be rented.
(D) The supply of rental apartment units has decreased more in Tuam than in Galway.
(E) The average amount spent on housing is higher in Galway than it is in Tuam.

4.   Due to the increase in traffic accidents caused by deer in the state, the governor last year reintroduced a longer deer hunting season to encourage recreational hunting of the animals. The governor expected the longer hunting season to decrease the number of deer and therefore decrease the number of accidents. However, this year the number of accidents caused by deer has increased substantially since the reintroduction of the longer deer hunting season.

Which of the following, if true, would best explain the increase in traffic accidents caused by deer?

(A) Many recreational hunters hunt only once or twice per hunting season, regardless of the length of the season.
(B) The deer in the state have become accustomed to living in close proximity to humans and are often easy prey for hunters as a result.
(C) Most automobile accidents involving deer result from cars swerving to avoid deer, and leave the deer in question unharmed.
(D) The number of drivers in the state has been gradually increasing over the past several years.
(E) A heavily used new highway was recently built directly through the state's largest forest, which is the primary habitat of the state's deer population.

5.   Political Analyst: After the Soviet Union collapsed, some hoped that freedom would encourage Russians to multiply, but as a result of dislocation and insecurity, the Russian population continues to dwindle at the rate of 700,000 a year. The government proposes to address the problem with a wide range of financial incentives, along with investments in improved health care, road safety and the like. These are positive measures, but **they have been tried before, to little avail.** A better plan to reverse the population decline is to improve the country's governance in both the public and the private sphere. **If a greater part of the population participated in important decisions and shared in the country's wealth, then larger families would result.** In addition, if corruption and greed among the elite were curbed, public health would improve and average life expectancy would increase.

The two boldfaced statements serve what function in the argument above?

(A) The first is the main point of the analyst's argument; the second is a premise that supports the first.
(B) The first is a premise that undermines an alternative to the analyst's proposal; the second is a premise that supports the analyst's main claim.
(C) The first is a premise that contradicts the main point made by the analyst; the second is the main point of the argument.
(D) The first is a premise that supports a proposal; the second is that proposal.
(E) The first is a conclusion that the argument endorses; the second is a premise that opposes that conclusion.

6. Displayco is marketing a holographic display to supermarkets that shows three-dimensional images of certain packaged goods in the aisles. Displayco's marketing literature states that patrons at supermarkets will be strongly attracted to goods that are promoted in this way, resulting in higher profits for the supermarkets that purchase the displays. Consumer advocates, however, feel that the displays will be intrusive to supermarket patrons and may even increase minor accidents involving shopping carts.

   Which of the following, if true, most seriously weakens the position of the consumer advocates?

   (A) The holographic displays are expensive to install and maintain.
   (B) Many other venues, including shopping malls, are considering adopting holographic displays.
   (C) Accidents in supermarkets that are serious enough to cause injury are rare.
   (D) Supermarkets tend to be low-margin businesses that struggle to achieve profitability.
   (E) Studies in test markets have shown that supermarket patrons quickly become accustomed to holographic displays.

7. Brand X designs and builds custom sneakers, one sneaker at a time. It recently announced plans to sell "The Gold Standard," a sneaker that will cost five times more to manufacture than any other sneaker that has ever been created.

   Which of the following, if true, most supports the prediction that The Gold Standard shoe line will be profitable?

   (A) Because of its reputation as an original and exclusive sneaker, The Gold Standard will be favored by urban hipsters willing to pay exceptionally high prices in order to stand out.
   (B) Of the last four new sneakers that Brand X has released, three have sold at a rate that was higher than projected.
   (C) A rival brand recently declared bankruptcy and ceased manufacturing shoes.
   (D) The market for The Gold Standard will not be more limited than the market for other Brand X shoes.
   (E) The Gold Standard is made using canvas that is more than five times the cost of the canvas used in most sneakers.

8. With information readily available on the Internet, consumers now often enter the automobile retail environment with certain models and detailed specifications in mind. In response to this trend, CarStore has decided to move toward a less aggressive sales approach. Despite the fact that members of its sales personnel have an average of ten years of experience each, CarStore has implemented a mandatory training program for all sales personnel, because _____.

   (A) the sales personnel in CarStore have historically specialized in aggressively selling automobiles and add-on features
   (B) the sales personnel in CarStore do not themselves use the Internet often for their own purposes
   (C) CarStore has found that most consumers do not mind negotiating over price
   (D) information found on the Internet often does not reflect sales promotions at individual retail locations
   (E) several retailers that compete directly with CarStore have adopted "customer-centered" sales approaches.

9. Government restrictions have severely limited the amount of stem cell research American companies can conduct. Because of these restrictions, many American scientists who specialize in the field of stem cell research have signed long term contracts to work for foreign companies. Recently, Congress has proposed lifting all restrictions on stem cell research.

Which of the following statements can most properly be inferred from the information above?

(A) Some foreign companies that conduct stem cell research work under fewer restrictions than some American companies do.
(B) Because American scientists are under long-term contracts to foreign companies, there will be a significant influx of foreign professionals into the United States.
(C) In all parts of the world, stem cell research is dependent on the financial backing of local government.
(D) In the near future, American companies will no longer be at the forefront of stem cell research.
(E) If restrictions on stem cell research are lifted, many of the American scientists will break their contracts to return to American companies.

10. Traditionally, public school instructors have been compensated according to seniority. Recently, the existing salary system has been increasingly criticized as an approach to compensation that rewards lackadaisical teaching and punishes motivated, highly-qualified instruction. Instead, educational experts argue that, to retain exceptional teachers and maintain quality instruction, teachers should receive salaries or bonuses based on performance rather than seniority.

Which of the following, if true, most weakens the conclusion of the educational experts?

(A) Some teachers express that financial compensation is not the only factor contributing to job satisfaction and teaching performance.
(B) School districts will develop their own unique compensation structures that may differ greatly from those of other school districts.
(C) Upon leaving the teaching profession, many young, effective teachers cite a lack of opportunity for more rapid financial advancement as a primary factor in the decision to change careers.
(D) A merit-based system that bases compensation on teacher performance reduces collaboration, which is an integral component of quality instruction.
(E) In school districts that have implemented pay for performance compensation structures, standardized test scores have dramatically increased.

SOLUTIONS:

1.   John was flying from San Francisco to New York with a connecting flight in Chicago on the same airline. Chicago's airport is one of the largest in the world, consisting of several small stand-alone terminals connected by trams. John's plane arrived on time. John was positive he would make his connecting flight thirty minutes later, because _____ .

Which of the following most logically completes the argument above?

(A) John's airline is known for always being on time
(B) a number of other passengers on John's first flight were also scheduled to take John's connecting flight
(C) at the airport in Chicago, airlines always fly into and out of the same terminal
(D) John knew there was another flight to New York scheduled for one hour after the connecting flight he was scheduled to take
(E) the airline generally closes the doors of a particular flight ten minutes before it is scheduled to take off

This is a fill-in-the-blank question, but remember that MANY question categories can be presented this way. In this case, we're dealing with a Strengthen question. The argument addresses John's concern about making a connecting flight. The airport with the connecting flight is very large, consisting of several small stand-alone terminals. The correct answer choice will support (strengthen) John's conclusion that he can likely make his connecting flight thirty minutes later despite the size of the airport.

(A) Irrelevant. This is a general observation about the timeliness of John's airline, but it does not provide any new information—it is already established in the premises that John's particular flight arrived on time. The fact that his connecting flight will likely depart on time may even weaken the argument.

(B) Irrelevant. Airlines have been known to delay flights in order to ensure that a large number of passengers can make the connection, but we should not have to make an additional assumption in order to say that this choice strengthens the given conclusion.

(C) CORRECT. Strengthen. This answer choice provides information that John will not have to leave his terminal in order to reach his connecting flight. The premises describe the terminals as "small." This information provides us with the strongest piece of information that suggests John will be able to make his flight within thirty minutes.

(D) Irrelevant. The following flight has no bearing on John's ability to catch the flight on which he is currently booked.

(E) Irrelevant / weaken. If anything, this choice weakens the idea that John will catch the connecting flight by shortening the length of time he has to get to the second flight's gate.

2.   Media Critic: Network executives have alleged that television viewership is decreasing due to the availability of television programs on other platforms, such as the internet, video-on-demand, and mobile devices. These executives claim that **declining viewership will cause advertising revenue to fall so far that networks will be unable to spend the large sums necessary to produce programs of the quality now available**. That development, in turn, will lead to a dearth of programming for the very devices which cannibalized television's audience. However, technology executives point to research which indicates that **users of these platforms increase the number of hours per week that they watch television** because they are exposed to new programs and promotional spots through these alternate platforms. This analysis demonstrates that networks can actually increase their revenue through higher advertising rates, due to larger audiences lured to television through other media.

The portions in boldface play which of the following roles in the media critic's argument?

(A) The first is an inevitable trend that weighs against the critic's claim; the second is that claim.

(B) The first is a prediction that is challenged by the argument; the second is a finding upon which the argument depends.

(C) The first clarifies the reasoning behind the critic's claim; the second demonstrates why that claim is flawed.

(D) The first acknowledges a position that the technology executives accept as true; the second is a consequence of that position.

(E) The first opposes the critic's claim through an analogy; the second outlines a scenario in which that claim will not hold.

This problem is an Analyze the Argument Structure question. In order to properly evaluate the role of the two boldface portions, we must first identify the critic's conclusion: Networks can actually increase their revenue through higher advertising rates, due to larger audiences lured to television through other media. The first boldface portion opposes this position by predicting smaller audiences; the second lends support to it by citing evidence that alternate media platforms lead their users to watch more television. More simply, the first boldface statement is a Premise Against, and the second boldface statement is a Premise For. The correct answer choice will reflect this pattern.

(A) The first boldface statement does weigh against the critic's claim, but it is a prediction, rather than an inevitable trend. The second boldface statement supports the claim; it is not the conclusion itself.

(B) CORRECT. The critic's conclusion about a potential increase in network revenue is contrary to the first boldface statement's prediction about shrinking audiences and falling revenue. Also, the argument in fact depends upon the second boldface statement's assertion that users of alternate devices will actually watch more hours of television.

(C) The first boldface statement opposes the critic's claim, rather than clarifies it. The second boldface statement is used to support the critic's claim; it does not indicate that the critic's claim is flawed.

(D) The description of the first boldface statement is incorrect in that the technology executives neither accept nor deny the prediction of the network executives. The second boldface statement contradicts, rather than follows as a consequence of, that prediction.

(E) The first boldface statement is incorrect as described, because it does not use an analogy. The second boldface statement is in agreement with, not in opposition to, the critic's claim.

3.   In the last year, real estate prices, such as those for houses and condominiums, have gone up an average of 7% in the city of Galway but only 2% in the town of Tuam. On the other hand, average rents for apartments have risen 8% in Tuam over the last year, but only 4% in Galway.

Which of the following is an inference that can be reasonably drawn from the premises given above?

(A) In the last year, the ratio of average apartment rents to average real estate prices has increased in Tuam but fallen in Galway.

(B) Tuam has experienced a greater shift in demand toward the rental market than Galway has.

(C) It has become easier for Galway real estate to be bought and sold, whereas it has become easier for Tuam real estate to be rented.

(D) The supply of rental apartment units has decreased more in Tuam than in Galway.

(E) The average amount spent on housing is higher in Galway than it is in Tuam.

(A) CORRECT. In Tuam, rents have gone up at a faster rate (8%) than real estate prices (2%). Thus, the ratio of average rents to average real estate prices must have grown in that city—the numerator has grown faster than the denominator. In contrast, Galway rents have gone up at a slower rate (4%) than real estate prices (7%). Thus, the ratio of average rents to average real estate prices has actually decreased.

(B) It is not necessarily true that Tuam has experienced a greater shift in demand toward the rental market. For instance, the larger increase in Tuam rents could be explained by a reduction in the supply of rental units in Tuam.

(C) The premises do not indicate whether Galway real estate is easier or harder to be bought and sold, or whether Tuam real estate is easier or harder to be rented. The premises simply indicate the growth in prices and rents.

(D) It is not necessarily true that the supply of rental units has decreased more in Tuam than in Galway. For instance, there could be a sudden growth in demand in Tuam for rental units (e.g. because of an influx of young singles who are eager to rent), causing rents to increase more rapidly.

(E) The premises indicate nothing about the actual amounts of money spent in the two towns. We are given only percentage growth rates.

4.   Due to the increase in traffic accidents caused by deer in the state, the governor last year reintroduced a longer deer hunting season to encourage recreational hunting of the animals. The governor expected the longer hunting season to decrease the number of deer and therefore decrease the number of accidents. However, this year the number of accidents caused by deer has increased substantially since the reintroduction of the longer deer hunting season.

Which of the following, if true, would best explain the increase in traffic accidents caused by deer?

(A) Many recreational hunters hunt only once or twice per hunting season, regardless of the length of the season.
(B) The deer in the state have become accustomed to living in close proximity to humans and are often easy prey for hunters as a result.
(C) Most automobile accidents involving deer result from cars swerving to avoid deer, and leave the deer in question unharmed.
(D) The number of drivers in the state has been gradually increasing over the past several years.
(E) A heavily used new highway was recently built directly through the state's largest forest, which is the primary habitat of the state's deer population.

This Resolve a Paradox question presents us with a problem. Attempting to decrease the number of deer in his state, a governor extended the recreational hunting season. However, since the reintroduction of the longer hunting season, the number of accidents caused by deer has not declined—it has in fact substantially increased. We are asked to resolve this contradiction.

(A) The fact that many hunters only hunt once or twice per hunting season regardless of the length of the season may help to explain the inefficacy of the governor's measure. However, this would not explain the observed increase in accidents.

(B) This answer choice, if anything, indicates that the governor's extension of the hunting season would be *effective* in reducing the deer overpopulation. It does not explain the increase in traffic accidents.

(C) The fact that deer often are left unharmed by traffic accidents does not explain any increase in accidents.

(D) This answer choice would contribute to an explanation of a gradual increase in traffic accidents involving deer over the last several years. However, it does not explain a substantial increase in accidents from last year to this year. Both the extent of the increase and the time frame serve to make this answer choice an unsatisfactory explanation of the observed rise in accidents.

(E) CORRECT. A new highway system recently built directly through the primary habitat of the state's deer population would provide a specific explanation as to why the number of accidents involving deer has increased. It also explains the time frame of the increase.

5.   Political Analyst: After the Soviet Union collapsed, some hoped that freedom would encourage Russians to multiply, but as a result of dislocation and insecurity, the Russian population continues to dwindle at the rate of 700,000 a year. The government proposes to address the problem with a wide range of financial incentives, along with investments in improved health care, road safety and the like. These are positive measures, but **they have been tried before, to little avail.** A better plan to reverse the population decline is to improve the country's governance in both the public and the private sphere. **If a greater part of the population participated in important decisions and shared in the country's wealth, then larger families would result.** In addition, if corruption and greed among the elite were curbed, public health would improve and average life expectancy would increase.

The two boldfaced statements serve what function in the argument above?

(A) The first is the main point of the analyst's argument; the second is a premise that supports the first.
(B) The first is a premise that undermines an alternative to the analyst's proposal; the second is a premise that supports the analyst's main claim.
(C) The first is a premise that contradicts the main point made by the analyst; the second is the main point of the argument.
(D) The first is a premise that supports a proposal; the second is that proposal.
(E) The first is a conclusion that the argument endorses; the second is a premise that opposes that conclusion.

In this Analyze the Argument Structure passage, the analyst recounts a proposal by the Russian government to increase the Russian population. The analyst then dismisses that proposal and makes a counterproposal that he or she then supports with hypothetical scenarios. The claim that the counterproposal (to try good governance) is preferable is the conclusion of the argument.

(A) This choice is incorrect. The first boldface is a fact that indicates the government plan has failed before; it is not the conclusion of the argument. The second is a premise in support of the argument's proposal, not in support of the first bold.

(B) CORRECT. The first is the fact that the government plan has "been tried before, to no avail," a fact that undermines the alternative proposal made by the government. The author's proposal is to improve the country's governance, and the second boldface supports that plan by showing one way in which better governance might lead to a population increase.

(C) The first does not contradict the argument's conclusion that improved governance will reverse the decline in population. Rather, it undermines the other proposal presented by the government, which is a claim that the argument does not support. The second is not the argument's main point, but an assertion that supports the conclusion of the argument by showing one way in which better governance might lead to a population increase.

(D) The first is a premise that the government plan has "been tried before, to an avail," which weighs against the preceding proposal. The second is not the proposal that the first directly supports, but an assertion that supports the conclusion of the argument by showing one way in which better governance might lead to a population increase.

(E) The first is not a conclusion at all, rather a factual premise that these measures "have been tried before, to little avail." The second boldface does not oppose the first boldface, rather it is an assertion that supports the conclusion of the argument by showing one way in which better governance might lead to a population increase.

6.   Displayco is marketing a holographic display to supermarkets that shows three-dimensional images of certain packaged goods in the aisles. Displayco's marketing literature states that patrons at supermarkets will be strongly attracted to goods that are promoted in this way, resulting in higher profits for the supermarkets that purchase the displays. Consumer advocates, however, feel that the displays will be intrusive to supermarket patrons and may even increase minor accidents involving shopping carts.

Which of the following, if true, most seriously weakens the position of the consumer advocates?

(A) The holographic displays are expensive to install and maintain.
(B) Many other venues, including shopping malls, are considering adopting holographic displays.
(C) Accidents in supermarkets that are serious enough to cause injury are rare.
(D) Supermarkets tend to be low-margin businesses that struggle to achieve profitability.
(E) Studies in test markets have shown that supermarket patrons quickly become accustomed to holographic displays.

This passage contains both an argument and a counter-argument. The first argument is articulated by Displayco, which argues that holographic displays will attract supermarket patrons and increase supermarket profits. The counter-argument is voiced by consumer advocates, who hold that the holographic displays will be intrusive to customers and may even increase minor accidents. This Weaken question relates to the second argument; thus, the correct answer choice will suggest that the concerns presented by the consumer advocates are not problematic.

(A) Irrelevant. This answer choice may weaken the argument of Displayco, but we were asked to weaken the consumer advocates' argument. This choice does not influence whether patrons will find the displays intrusive and distracting.

(B) Irrelevant. The potential adoption of holographic displays by other venues does not impact the concerns of consumer advocates that the displays will be intrusive and distracting. It could be the case that holographic displays will be intrusive and distracting in all of these other venues as well.

(C) Irrelevant. One might think that this answer choice would weaken the consumer advocates' argument. However, the consumer advocates' argument did not use the standard of "causing injury" as a threshold for minor accidents. Minor accidents can be bothersome to patrons without causing injury.

(D) Irrelevant. While this choice might help Displayco to convince supermarkets to use its product, we were asked to weaken the consumer advocates' concerns. The struggles of supermarkets to achieve profitability is not relevant to the consumer advocates' concerns.

(E) CORRECT. If studies in test markets have shown that patrons quickly become accustomed to holographic displays, then patrons are much less likely to find the displays intrusive after an initial adjustment period. Further, if patrons become used to the displays, the displays are unlikely to increase the frequency of minor accidents involving shopping carts.

7.   Brand X designs and builds custom sneakers, one sneaker at a time. It recently announced plans to sell "The Gold Standard," a sneaker that will cost five times more to manufacture than any other sneaker that has ever been created.

Which of the following, if true, most supports the prediction that The Gold Standard shoe line will be profitable?

(A) Because of its reputation as an original and exclusive sneaker, The Gold Standard will be favored by urban hipsters willing to pay exceptionally high prices in order to stand out.

(B) Of the last four new sneakers that Brand X has released, three have sold at a rate that was higher than projected.

(C) A rival brand recently declared bankruptcy and ceased manufacturing shoes.

(D) The market for The Gold Standard will not be more limited than the market for other Brand X shoes.

(E) The Gold Standard is made using canvas that is more than five times the cost of the canvas used in most sneakers.

The conclusion is located in the question: the prediction that The Gold Standard shoe line will be profitable. In the passage, we have been given information that seems to run counter to this conclusion—the costs of manufacturing this shoe are exceptionally high. We can think of profit as revenue minus cost. If costs are exceptionally high, the only way a profit can be made is if revenue is also exceptionally high. We want to strengthen the conclusion by supporting that assumption about revenue.

(A) CORRECT. Strengthen. If urban hipsters are willing to pay exceptionally high prices, the exceptionally high costs might be offset enough for the shoe line to be profitable.

(B) Irrelevant. A higher sales rate than projected does not actually give us any information about profitability. In any case, the results of past releases are not necessarily indicative of the case at hand.

(C) Irrelevant. One can argue that this is good for Brand X, in that it will mean that there is one less competitor, or that this is bad for Brand X, in that it is indicative of a sagging sneaker market. In any case, there is no direct connection between this rival brand and the potential profitability of The Gold Standard.

(D) Irrelevant. We have been told nothing that connects the market to profitability. We also lack information about the profitability of past sneakers.

(E) Irrelevant. This is perhaps one reason why manufacturing costs are so high, but we already knew the costs were high from the argument. This choice does not in any way support the conclusion that the new sneaker will be profitable.

8.   With information readily available on the Internet, consumers now often enter the automobile retail environment with certain models and detailed specifications in mind. In response to this trend, CarStore has decided to move toward a less aggressive sales approach. Despite the fact that members of its sales personnel have an average of ten years of experience each, CarStore has implemented a mandatory training program for all sales personnel, because _____.

    (A) the sales personnel in CarStore have historically specialized in aggressively selling automobiles and add-on features

    (B) the sales personnel in CarStore do not themselves use the Internet often for their own purposes

    (C) CarStore has found that most consumers do not mind negotiating over price

    (D) information found on the Internet often does not reflect sales promotions at individual retail locations

    (E) several retailers that compete directly with CarStore have adopted "customer-centered" sales approaches.

This is a Resolve a Paradox question presented with a fill-in-the-blank. The argument describes CarStore's decision to move toward a less aggressive sales approach in response to consumers now entering the retail environment with automobile models and specifications in mind. This is presented implicitly in contrast to how consumers entered the retail environment prior to the Internet. The passage then states that, despite the fact that its sales personnel are very experienced, CarStore is implementing a mandatory training program. We are asked to complete the passage; the explanation for the training program should resolve the apparent discrepancy between the extensive experience of CarStore's employees and the company's new mandatory training program.

(A) CORRECT. If the sales personnel at CarStore have historically specialized in aggressive sales tactics and promoting add-on features, they will need to learn new sales tactics. This explains the need for a mandatory retraining program. This answer choice also ties directly to the first and second premises provided, as aggressive selling is less appropriate if consumers already know what model and features they would like to purchase.

(B) Though it may be helpful for the sales personnel of CarStore to use the Internet themselves so that they can relate to many of their customers, this is irrelevant to the argument. The argument describes CarStore's new policy as promoting a less aggressive sales approach; there is no indication that the training should involve edifying salespeople about how to use the Internet.

(C) The fact that consumers do not mind negotiating over price, if true, suggests that a less aggressive sales approach may not be necessary. This does not fit logically with the overall argument abut CarStore adopting a new, less aggressive sales approach.

(D) The fact that information gained from the Internet may not be exhaustive or up-to-date is irrelevant to the argument, which centers on the need for training salespeople in a less aggressive sales approach. Also, experienced salespeople would presumably know about location-specific sales promotions and be able to describe them to consumers without any additional training.

(E) That several competitors to CarStore have adopted "customer-centered" sales approaches may help explain why CarStore has also decided on a less aggressive sales approach. However, the actions of CarStore's competitors are outside the scope of the argument. Also, this answer choice does not satisfactorily explain the need to retrain veteran salespeople.

9.   Government restrictions have severely limited the amount of stem cell research American companies can conduct. Because of these restrictions, many American scientists who specialize in the field of stem cell research have signed long term contracts to work for foreign companies. Recently, Congress has proposed lifting all restrictions on stem cell research.

      Which of the following statements can most properly be inferred from the information above?

      (A) Some foreign companies that conduct stem cell research work under fewer restrictions than some American companies do.

      (B) Because American scientists are under long-term contracts to foreign companies, there will be a significant influx of foreign professionals into the United States.

      (C) In all parts of the world, stem cell research is dependent on the financial backing of local government.

      (D) In the near future, American companies will no longer be at the forefront of stem cell research.

      (E) If restrictions on stem cell research are lifted, many of the American scientists will break their contracts to return to American companies.

In this argument, a cause-and-effect relationship is presented between American scientists signing long-term contracts with foreign companies and the U.S. government's restrictions on stem cell research. This cause-and-effect relationship is the key to finding the correct answer to this Draw a Conclusion question.

(A) CORRECT. If American scientists signed contracts with foreign companies specifically because of U.S. restrictions, we can infer that the new companies they signed with operate under fewer restrictions. Therefore, at least some foreign companies must work under fewer restrictions than some American companies do.

(B) While it is possible that once the restrictions are banned American companies will want to hire more scientists and will seek them overseas, there are too many unknowns to draw this conclusion using the given premises.

(C) This passage is about government restrictions; we are given no information about financial backing.

(D) We are not given any information regarding America's current or future position in terms of stem cell research. Though government restrictions and scientists switching companies could be issues related to a company's prosperity, we are given no information about how these directly affect America's position.

(E) Though this might happen, we cannot conclude for certain that it will happen.

10. Traditionally, public school instructors have been compensated according to seniority. Recently, the existing salary system has been increasingly criticized as an approach to compensation that rewards lackadaisical teaching and punishes motivated, highly-qualified instruction. Instead, educational experts argue that, to retain exceptional teachers and maintain quality instruction, teachers should receive salaries or bonuses based on performance rather than seniority.

Which of the following, if true, most weakens the conclusion of the educational experts?

(A) Some teachers express that financial compensation is not the only factor contributing to job satisfaction and teaching performance.
(B) School districts will develop their own unique compensation structures that may differ greatly from those of other school districts.
(C) Upon leaving the teaching profession, many young, effective teachers cite a lack of opportunity for more rapid financial advancement as a primary factor in the decision to change careers.
(D) A merit-based system that bases compensation on teacher performance reduces collaboration, which is an integral component of quality instruction.
(E) In school districts that have implemented pay for performance compensation structures, standardized test scores have dramatically increased.

The argument is concerned with how public school teachers are compensated. It suggests that educational experts believe that a system of teacher compensation based on performance rather than seniority would help to retain exceptional teachers and maintain quality instruction. The correct answer to this Weaken question will be the one that most undermines the contention of the educational experts.

(A) Irrelevant. The fact that other factors also contribute to job satisfaction and teaching performance neither weakens nor strengthens the argument for a performance-based pay structure for public school teachers.

(B) Irrelevant. Nothing in the argument indicates that one universal system of compensation must be adopted in order to implement this plan. It is very possible that several effective models of performance-based pay could be developed and implemented successfully.

(C) Strengthen. This choice indicates that many young, effective teachers are extremely frustrated by the traditional pay structure, in which financial advancement is directly tied to seniority. Thus, these teachers would likely welcome a change that allows them more rapid opportunity for financial advancement.

(D) CORRECT. Weaken. This choice indicates that collaboration among teachers is integral to high-quality instruction and that a system of compensation based on teacher performance reduces collaboration. Thus, the effect of a merit-based system of pay would be to undermine quality instruction, which is one of the two stated goals of the educational experts.

(E) Strengthen. The educational experts' argument in favor of performance-based compensation is bolstered if standardized tests scores have dramatically risen in school districts that have instituted such pay structures.

Chapter 10
of
READING COMPREHENSION & ESSAYS

ESSAYS
STRATEGY

In This Chapter . . .

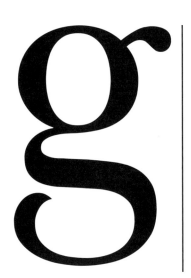

- The GRE Essay

- Analysis of an Issue

- Analysis of an Argument

- GRE Issue Essay Quotes

The GRE Essay

When you arrive to take the GRE, the first part of the exam will consist of two essays to be completed in 60 minutes:

Analyze an Issue (30 minutes) – Discuss a general interest topic.
Analyze an Argument (30 minutes) – Analyze the argument presented.

These essay assignments can occur in either order, but the essay section will always come first. The essays do not factor into your main GRE score; they are scored on a separate 6-point scale in increments of 0.5 (0 is lowest, 6 is highest).

In a Nutshell

For those who consider themselves already very good at essay writing and have limited study time, here's the skinny:

The Issue essay is very much **like every other 5-or-so paragraph academic essay** you've ever written. Some people have trouble thinking of examples for abstract topics ("Is justice more important in a society than compassion?"), but if you feel confident about that, little preparation is probably required.

The Argument essay requires you to analyze a flawed argument. You're not being asked to bring in outside information or give your own opinion. If you've taken philosophy or logic classes, been on a debate team, or studied for GMAT Critical Reasoning or LSAT Logical Reasoning questions, you shouldn't have much trouble here. However, if none of the above applies to you, you'll probably want to read the Analysis of an Argument portion of this chapter. You don't need tons of preparation, but you want to **go in with a gameplan** and a box of tools, so you can calmly get to work.

Write a lot. No matter what the official rules say, longer essays get higher scores.

Pay attention to the specific instructions. On the new GRE, ETS has gone out of its way to write a dozen or so different specific instructions for both Analyze an Issue and Analyze an Argument essays. In the *Official Guide to the GRE Revised General Test*, test takers are warned that even if they write an otherwise perfect essay, they will not score higher than a 4 without addressing the specific instructions provided in the question prompt.

You can actually read all of the essay prompts in advance at:

http://www.ets.org/gre/revised_general/prepare/analytical_writing/issue/pool
http://www.ets.org/gre/revised_general/prepare/analytical_writing/argument/pool

Certainly don't spend the time to write practice essays for each of the prompts on these lists, but do scan through them so that you can get a sense for the types of prompts you could receive on your exam.

How Essays are Used by Graduate Schools

ETS, the maker of the GRE, tells us: "Validity research has shown that the Analytical Writing essay score is correlated with academic writing more highly than is the personal statement." That is, the essay you write under controlled conditions in a testing environment is guaranteed to be your own work, whereas your actual application essays might have benefited from the assistance of others (as well as a spell-check program!).

In the "Guide to the Use of Scores" that ETS offers to university admissions departments, ETS writes, "A GRE essay response should be considered a rough first draft since examinees do not have sufficient time to revise their essays during the test. Examinees also do not have dictionaries or spell-checking or grammar-checking software available to them."

It is impossible to say how much (or even whether) the essay "counts" in graduate school admissions: there are simply too many programs and too many schools. Some math and science programs may take little or no account of the essay, and some more writing-intensive graduate programs may consider the essays more carefully. Graduate schools may use the essays as a screening device (so a very low essay score might keep the rest of your application from being given a serious review). It's also reasonable to presume that your essays are more likely to be taken into account if your first language is not English, or if you are applying from a country outside the United States.

In sum, the admissions department at the particular university to which you are applying is the best source of information about how the GRE essay will be used. If the admissions department is not forthcoming (many schools will simply say "We look at each student's entire application holistically," or something like that), you'll just have to do your best (a good policy anyway).

Graduate schools to which you send your GRE scores will be able to read your actual essays. Don't write anything you wouldn't want the admissions committee to read (avoid writing anything offensive or anything with a very political or self-exposing slant).

The Physical Mechanics of Essay Writing

Assuming that you are taking a computer-based GRE (this will be the vast majority of you), you will be typing your essays into a text box. There is no limit to how much text you can enter, but you can only see about 10 lines of what you've written before you have to scroll. The system feels like a clunky, old-fashioned word processing program. You will have "cut" and "paste" buttons, and an "undo" button. There is no bold, italic, or underline. There is no tab/indent. The program does not offer any type of spell-check or grammar check.

In addition to "Cut," "Paste," and "Undo," you will also have the following basic functions:

> **Arrow Keys** move the cursor up, down, left, or right
> **Enter** inserts a paragraph break (no indent—simply moves down to a new line)
> **Page Up** moves the cursor up one screen
> **Page Down** moves the cursor down one screen
>
> **Backspace** removes the character to the left of the cursor
> **Delete** removes the character to the right of the cursor
>
> **Home** moves the cursor to the beginning of the line
> **End** moves the cursor to the end of the line

You will have scratch paper (the same stapled paper booklet you use for the rest of the exam) on which to plan your essay, but you can also outline in the text box (though be sure to delete any notes or outlines before submitting your essay).

Once you've completed an essay and clicked on "submit," you cannot go back. If you complete an essay before the time expires, you can go immediately to the next section. If you finish before the time is up, you do NOT get to use that time on other sections.

You do not get a break between the two essay assignments, but you do get a 10-minute break after both essays have been completed.

Essay Length

For each essay, think of a five-paragraph structure as a baseline. Sometimes you'll write four paragraphs, sometimes you'll write 6–7 (many high-scoring essays contain 6–7 paragraphs, actually), but the basic structure is an intro and a conclusion "sandwiching" three or more main examples or reasons, each in its own body paragraph.

Interestingly, Manhattan GRE's analysis of published GRE essays written by actual students and given real scores shows a very strong correlation between length and score. This is also consistent with ETS's grading on other tests, such as the SAT.

Let's be very clear: *Even when ETS says that essay length doesn't matter, it does. A lot.*

To ensure your essay is long enough, you will have to brainstorm and plan your essay very efficiently (3–4 minutes for the Issue, 2–3 minutes for the Argument) so you can get started writing as soon as possible.

Write as much as you can in the time allotted!

Spelling and Grammar

Many other GRE books have long chapters on essay writing containing exercises on how to use the semicolon and other such feats of literary mechanics (we suspect these publishers have simply recycled essay-writing chapters from other textbooks, with little concern for how the GRE essay is scored).

However, while of course good spelling and grammar are better than poor spelling and grammar, the ideas you present (and the length of your essay) are far more important.

According to ETS, "scorers are trained to focus on the analytical logic of the essays more than on spelling, grammar, or syntax. The mechanics of writing are weighed in their ratings only to the extent that these impede clarity of meaning." In other words, as long as the grader can understand you, he or she is not supposed to count off for spelling and grammar.

The ETS report also says, "The ability of ESL students to write in English may be affected not only by their language capacity but also by their prior experience with the kinds of critical writing tasks in the test. Where educational systems do not stress these skills, performance may not reflect the applicant's ability to learn these skills in a graduate setting." In other words, ETS is of the opinion that students from educational systems focused more on memorization than on critical reasoning may have particular trouble writing high-scoring essays. (But don't worry! The strategies in this chapter will help!)

Scoring

As mentioned earlier, essays are scored from 0–6, and the essay score does not count as part of your main GRE score. According to ETS, an essay that scores a 6 addresses the specific instructions while:

- presenting an insightful position on the issue
- developing the position with compelling reasons and/or persuasive examples
- sustaining a well-focused, well-organized analysis, connecting ideas logically
- expressing ideas fluently and precisely, using effective vocabulary and sentence variety
- demonstrating facility with the conventions (i.e., grammar, usage, and mechanics) of standard written English, with possibly a few minor errors

Essays are scored by specially trained college and university faculty who will not see your name, gender, geographical location, or any other identifying information. Each of your essays will be read by two graders, giving a total of four essay scores (two for each essay). These scores are averaged, and then the averaged score is rounded up to the nearest half point. (Thus, it is possible to get a score such as 4.5.) The two graders for any one essay will always grade within one point of each other; if they were to grade further apart, a third grader would be brought in to adjudicate.

It goes without saying that any evidence of cheating, which includes using anyone else's work without citation, will get your GRE score (the entire thing, not just the essays) canceled and your fee forfeited.

ANALYZE AN ISSUE

For the Analyze an Issue assignment, you will be presented with a statement or a claim. Your job is to agree or disagree with the statement, and then write a compelling essay to support the position you've taken.

The topic that you are given on the real test will be chosen from a list of topics available on the ETS website:

http://www.ets.org/gre/revised_general/prepare/analytical_writing/issue/pool

Yes, that's right! You can view all of the possible topics ahead of time. The topic you end up writing about will be on the list at the page above, possibly with minor wording changes.

In the issue essay, you are generally expected to TAKE A SIDE, which means it will not be enough to simply deconstruct the particular issue. When arguing one side or another of an argument, be sure to acknowledge the issue's complexity. That is, acknowledge that the other side has some merit (in a way that doesn't hurt your own argument).

That being said, it is critical that you pay attention to the specific instructions given along with the essay, which may affect how much or little you have to write about the side of the argument you are NOT in support of. ETS lists six different possible ways you might be prompted to respond to a topic. Here they are, from page 13 of *The Official Guide for the GRE Revised General Test:*

1. Write a response in which you discuss the extent to which you agree or disagree with the statement and explain your reasoning for the position you take. In developing and supporting your position, you should consider ways in which the statement might or might not hold true and explain how these considerations shape your position.

2. Write a response in which you discuss the extent to which you agree or disagree with the recommendation and explain your reasoning for the position you take. In developing and supporting your position, describe specific circumstances in which adopting the recommendation would or would not be advantageous and explain how these examples shape your position.

Manhattan **GRE** ® Prep
the new standard

3. Write a response in which you discuss the extent to which you agree or disagree with the claim. In developing and supporting your position, be sure to address the most compelling reasons or examples that could be used to challenge your position.

4. Write a response in which you discuss which view more closely aligns with your own position and explain your reasoning for the position you take. In developing and supporting your position, you should address both of the views presented above.

5. Write a response in which you discuss the extent to which you agree or disagree with the claim **AND** the reason on which that claim is based. (NOTE: For this prompt, the claim will be accompanied by a reason why the claim has been made. You'll need to give your opinion on both.)

6. Write a response in which you discuss your views on the policy above and explain your reasoning for the position you take. In developing and supporting your position, you should consider the possible consequences of implementing the policy and explain how these consequences shape your position.

These instructions may seem quite different, but they really fall into three general categories:

1) Pick a side of the prompt and defend it, but explain when the other side might be true or more logical (#1, #2, #3 and #4 from above).

2) Pick a side of the prompt, and also make sure to discuss the reason given in defense of that prompt (#5 from above).

3) Pick a side and discuss the consequences of your opinion (#6 from above).

There is not yet enough data to determine how much weight ETS will put on these specific instructions. While they claim that no essay that fails to address them will score above a 4, the top-scoring essay examples given in *The Official Guide to the GRE Revised General Test* do not seem to do a very good job of addressing the specific instructions. What seems most likely is that if you write an essay that intelligently supports your own position while also fairly describing and responding to the other side of an argument, you will do well whatever the specific instructions. As it turns out, because the instructions are tailored to the prompt itself, it can be difficult to write intelligently on the subject and NOT address the specific instructions.

In the end, you will ALWAYS want to do the following, regardless of the Issue prompt you're given:

(1) Take a point of view on the given issue.
(2) Support your point-of-view using relevant and SPECIFIC examples.
(3) Acknowledge both sides of the issue and the specific instructions in the question.

Brainstorming

Spend 3–4 minutes brainstorming specific, real-world examples for each side. Why brainstorm both sides of an issue? It is often true that the side you don't believe is the easier side to write—perhaps because, when we believe something strongly, it seems obvious to us, and it's harder to come up with concrete reasons or examples. Another good reason to brainstorm both sides is…

You don't always have to agree.

Some people just have a habit of being agreeable. That is, some students just automatically assume they should agree with the topic. However, some GRE topics are actually phrased in a pretty extreme way, such that they would be difficult to defend.

For instance, one example from the GRE's topic pool reads, "Societies should try to save every plant and animal species, regardless of the expense to humans in effort, time, and financial well-being." While most people are in favor of saving endangered species, the phrase "regardless of the expense to humans" makes it sound as though we would have to do things such as shut down an entire city in order to save a threatened form of bacteria. You're welcome to argue in favor, of course, but this is a topic it would be much easier to argue against. (An argument against this topic can still certainly be in favor of saving *some* or *most* endangered species—in fact, such a view would definitely be encouraged as part of "acknowledging both sides of the issue.")

That said, here's how you get started brainstorming. Let's try it with this topic:

> **"The better a new idea is, the greater the opposition to that idea when it is first presented. Only later, usually once the person who had the idea is no longer around to enjoy its success, do we consider the thinker a genius."**

First, make a T-chart, like this:

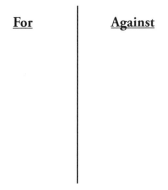

For | **Against**

By writing down "For" and "Against," you are setting yourself up to think in each direction. This is especially useful when you are trying to come up with counter examples. When we say "brainstorm," we really just want you to write down one-word tags for each possible reason or example. For instance, Galileo might pop to mind, because he was persecuted for saying that the Earth moved around the sun, and in fact had to spend the rest of his life under house arrest; after his death, his ideas were vindicated and he was considered a scientific hero. On the other hand, there are plenty of geniuses who are renowned during their own lifetimes (Einstein was quite famous in his own time). Jot these down on your T-chart—Galileo on the left, and Einstein on the right.

A good way to get your brainstorming done quickly is to "piggyback" off examples you already have. Once you've thought of Galileo, can you think of other people like him, who were persecuted for their ideas—ideas we now consider correct? You might think of someone like Nelson Mandela, who spent 27 years in prison. But wait! He's still alive, and everyone considers him a hero! He was the first democratically elected president of South Africa! This is actually a pretty good example for the other side. (This is why it's good to brainstorm both sides!)

Also on the "against" side—once you've thought of Einstein, can you think of other famous geniuses? How about Stephen Hawking? If you run out of steam, think to yourself, "Hmmn, Einstein and Stephen Hawking are both scientists. Can I think of the 'Einstein' of some other field?" Perhaps someone like W. E. B. DuBois, who was considered a radical in his own time; however, after his death, his ideas were vindicated by the civil rights movement of the 1960s. Is there someone else who was a social activist whose ideas were later vindicated? How about the early feminists, such as Elizabeth Cady Stanton and Lucretia Mott? See, we're on a roll!

Here, for the sake of demonstrating the brainstorming process, we've gone a little further than we needed to. You probably could have stopped after Nelson Mandela above—stop as soon as you have 2–3 good ideas for one side.

<u>**For**</u>	<u>**Against**</u>
Galileo	**Einstein**
	Stephen Hawking
	Mandela
	DuBois
	E.C. Stanton/ "suffragettes"

You may have noticed that our examples above were drawn from history and current events. While personal examples are allowable, we find that they don't tend to make for the most rigorous and persuasive essays. Personal examples should be considered a backup plan for when you get stuck in your brainstorming.

Of course, you are NOT required to use example after example in your essay. You are also perfectly welcome to use well-considered reasoning. However, some topics lend themselves better to examples, while other topics lend themselves better to argumentation. Here's another example topic:

> **"Every nation should require students to study at least one foreign language from the elementary school level through the university level."**

This topic seems to lend itself better to reasoning than to concrete examples, although you might be able to come up with enough examples—the U.S. doesn't typically require foreign language study, and most European countries do. You could use these examples on either side—for instance, you could argue that the U.S. doesn't need foreign language study because, in being a world power, the U.S. prompts everyone else to follow its lead; or you could argue that Europeans are, by and large, much more educated than Americans and therefore run more peaceful societies and have more appreciation for culture. Many examples are really quite flexible.

In any case, let's try an argument-based brainstorming. Again, make a T-chart:

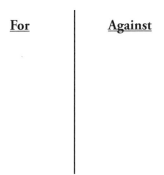

Your challenge here is to "divide up" your reasoning into discrete (that means separate!) arguments, so that your essay doesn't just ramble on without structure.

You might just start with the first thing that comes to mind. For instance, people in large countries, such as the U.S. and China, don't seem to need foreign languages as much as people in smaller countries do. Many people in the U.S. and China never leave their own countries. Jot this down in the right column.

On the other hand, our world is becoming more connected. Most people who end up conducting international business, or emigrating to new lands, don't know from childhood that they're going to do so. As children, they're not in a position to decide whether to take foreign languages. It would be best to require foreign languages so that they're prepared for whatever happens in their adult lives. This would go in the left column.

One possible thesis might be, "While foreign language study has many benefits, both practical and intellectual, it is going too far to say that such study should be mandatory for every citizen of every nation. Other factors, such as whether the nation's primary language is already an 'international' language, whether the nation's primary language is in danger of dying out, and whether the nation has more pressing, survival-related concerns should be taken into account." This thesis certainly isn't arguing that foreign language study is bad—it is taking a very reasonable, balanced approach.

When a topic is phrased in an extreme way ("everyone should do X"), **don't ignore practical issues**. In some nations, it would be difficult to even find foreign language teachers. Some nations barely have schools of any kind, so foreign language instruction hardly seems like a main priority. And who decides which languages are mandatory? Not all students are the same—maybe most students could be required to take foreign languages, but the few who are having trouble with basic skills that they will need for adult life ought to be waived from foreign language requirements so they can focus on things they will really need.

Let's see a sample T-chart containing some of the ideas above:

For	Against
World is more int'l—students don't know what they'll need as adults, so prep them now	**Some nations need F.L. more than others**
	Some nations not practical— schools very basic, no F.L. teachers
	Which F.L.? Who decides?
	Preserve culture, some nations' languages might die out
	ALL PEOPLE EVERYWHERE? Some students can't, some nations must focus on survival! Too Extreme.

It's totally okay to have an "unbalanced" T-chart. We WANT to use this to pick which side to write on. It looks like we have our answer! (Of course there is no "right" answer to an Issue question, and your T-chart might have led you to argue in favor.)

The chart above shows five arguments against. We probably won't have time to write an entire body paragraph about each one, and some ideas are really building off of other ones (for instance, it might be hard to write an entire paragraph on the idea "Who decides which foreign languages to take?"). So we want to either pick our 3 or so strongest arguments, or else GROUP our arguments into 3 or so groups.

Here is what a test-taker might jot on paper next to the chart above:

FL good but shouldn't be mandatory for all

    I.   diff countries, diff needs
    II.   some nations must focus on survival—priorities!
    III.   not practical—some nations can't, what lang?, some want to preserve culture
    IV.   individual students are diff

We also want to make sure to **acknowledge the other side** (usually in the introduction, although sometimes in the course of the body paragraphs). This is very easy to do, since you have brainstormed both sides! Just take a point or two from the side you *didn't* pick, and say something like, "While a reasonable person might think X, actually Y is more important," or "While a reasonable person might think X, this is not the case *all of the time*." For instance, on the foreign language topic:

> *While a reasonable person might suggest that because children don't know whether they'll move to other nations or engage in international business as adults, we should prepare them for such experiences now.*

However, children also don't know whether they'll do manual labor, become a doctor, or run for President. There's no way to prepare young people for everything that might happen, so it makes sense to leave decisions about education in the hands of each nation and its school systems.

Acknowledging the other side is a great way to fill out your introduction, or, if you have a lot to say, you can write a body paragraph of the form "objection → your response → your argument."

In other words, *anticipate counterarguments and respond to them.* This is especially important if you have decided on what you know to be an unusual viewpoint. If your argument is that governments should not provide public schools, you absolutely must address the first thing that pops into everyone's mind: "But what about children whose parents can't afford to pay private school fees?"

A brief mention of specific instructions. While the specific instructions may ask you to add something into your essay that you wouldn't necessarily have included otherwise, there shouldn't be any need to radically change an essay from the standard format described here in order to obey the specific instructions. Generally, adding a single sentence to each paragraph, or even a few words, will suffice. For example, one set of instructions, taken from *The Official Guide for the GRE Revised General Test,* says this:

"Write a response in which you discuss the extent to which you agree or disagree with the statement and explain your reasoning for the position you take. In developing and supporting your position, you should consider ways in which the statement might or might not hold true and explain how these considerations shape your position."

Notice that the instructions don't really recommend anything that a well-written essay wouldn't do anyway. Therefore, feel free to write your outline without even worrying about the instructions, then simply check to be sure there will be space to include whatever little details the specific instructions requested (in this case, instances when the statement might or might not hold true). If we've done a good job in our brainstorming, adding sentences to address these instructions shouldn't be very difficult.

Finally, a word about your thesis or main idea. While sometimes it makes sense to simply agree or disagree with the topic, feel free to take a balanced, "in-between" approach. The graders enjoy nuance. Just be very clear about what you mean. When we say "in-between," we don't mean vague or wishy-washy. For instance, if you want to say that foreign language instruction should be mandatory in some countries and not others, say exactly what should be the deciding factor. A good thesis (for someone who is more on the "for" side of the foreign language topic) might be:

Because foreign language instruction is increasingly important in our interconnected world, it should be a priority in school curricula. However, in some nations, foreign language instruction is simply not practical or even possible. Thus, foreign language instruction should be mandatory at all levels of schooling except in nations where such a requirement is impracticable, or for individual students whose learning difficulties make the requirement unreasonable.

Note that this person isn't exactly arguing for the topic as written. But there's no question what the writer's position is. This is a detailed, balanced, and reasonable thesis.

Your thesis or main idea might be simpler, but make sure it's clear. It's fine to modify the argument, as in the example above, to meet what it is you want to prove. A good standard we like to use is the **dinner table test**. Imagine yourself presenting your thesis at the dinner table. Would you really want to defend the idea that every student everywhere must study a foreign language? Even students in severely distressed nations where it might be more important to learn something else? Even students with severe learning disabilities? Literally everyone? This is starting to sound a bit ridiculous, right?

the new standard

Now imagine yourself at the dinner table presenting the thesis above—foreign languages should be mandatory, excepting countries where that isn't practical and individual students with learning difficulties. Now, you're still saying something someone could disagree with (you are, after all, arguing that most Americans should have been better educated!), but you sound like a pretty reasonable person starting an interesting discussion.

Now imagine that you took your thesis too far in the *other* direction—saying something no one could ever disagree with. Like, "Foreign language instruction should be made available to students who want it, when the school system has enough money and teachers to offer it." Umm… so what? Your dinner companions are dozing off in their seats. You are boring everyone. Someone will probably shrug and change the subject. You went a little *too* far in making your main idea non-extreme. Here are six **sample main ideas**, divided into three groups:

TOO EXTREME:

All human beings should be forced to study a foreign language.

Foreign languages should not be made mandatory for any students, because students should never have to study something they don't want to. Children should always make their own decisions.

TOO MUSHY:

Students who want to should be able to study a foreign language if it's available.

Foreign languages can be valuable in certain pursuits. For example, foreign language study can help students become translators, foreign language teachers, or travel writers. (Note: not only is this so mushy no one could argue with it, it also fails to address the question!)

JUST RIGHT:

Foreign languages should be mandatory for most students in nations where it is practicable to offer such instruction on a national basis.

Foreign language instruction is important and should be encouraged, but for every subject one learns, there's another subject one will not have time to learn. Foreign language study should not be made mandatory, thus allowing students free choice in how to best engage and nurture their individual interests and talents.

In sum, your thesis or main idea shouldn't be something so extreme you can't defend it, but it also shouldn't be something so humdrum and obvious that a reasonable person couldn't take an opposite view. Don't oversimplify the topic. Pick a thesis you would use to start an interesting, intelligent discussion among reasonable people. Mentally trying the dinner table test is a good start.

About Timing: Note that the brainstorming and planning process above might sound as though it would take a person MUCH longer than the 3–4 minutes we recommended at the beginning of the chapter. Keep in mind that we've written a bit more in our sample T-charts than you would have to, since you'll only be writing for yourself. If you write "SH" for "Stephen Hawking," you only have to remember what your abbreviation means for a couple of minutes, so feel free to be brief. You also don't have to write a separate outline—that might be more of a mental process, or you might just write "I," "II," "III" next to various arguments on the T-chart.

About Brainstorming Practice: Some practice with brainstorming will also speed up the process. You may find that the same examples seem to pop up for you over and over. There's nothing wrong with that! We find that many topics lend themselves to discussing global warming, for instance—the issue of whether technology/progress/new ideas can have a

downside seems to be a common underlying theme. And, of course, write about what you know. If you were a philosophy major, or an environmental science major, etc., feel free to draw disproportionately on those types of examples.

Again, you can practice brainstorming by visiting this link and exploring the pool:

http://www.ets.org/gre/revised_general/prepare/analytical_writing/issue/pool

Try making T-charts, picking a side, and making a rough outline, as described above, for some of the topics listed.

Don't just pick out the topics that you most want to write about! Force yourself to start at the beginning, or scroll down a bit and do the first topic you see.

When you practice brainstorming, give yourself plenty of time the first time through—maybe 10 minutes. The next time, cut it down to 8 minutes, then 6, 5, 4…. With practice, you should be able to reliably brainstorm in 3–4 minutes, or even less.

How to Avoid Getting Stuck: As one GRE student told us, lamentably: "It seems, since I graduated from college, I've forgotten everything I used to know!"

If you suffer from this problem, be assured that it is only temporary! One good suggestion is to simply jog your memory regarding what you once knew quite well—how about reading your old college papers? If you majored in a humanities field, you might have dozens of your own essays saved on your computer, ready to mine for ideas. Similarly, your old college textbooks might be fruitful (more so if you majored in history or sociology than if you majored in chemistry, though).

Also keep in mind that you are not limited to talking about things the grader will have heard of. If you attended school in a non-English speaking country, you can still use examples from your own education.

If you still feel like you need new information to draw from, we have several good suggestions.

The book *The Intellectual Devotional Modern Culture: Revive Your Mind, Complete Your Education, and Converse Confidently with the Culturati*, by David S. Kidder and Noah D. Oppenheim, provides interesting single-page summaries of 365 topics from civil disobedience to Walt Disney to the European Union. There is actually an entire series of *Intellectual Devotional* books, so you might also check out the original book, or the American history one, as per your interests. All are available at Amazon.com.

The website **www.aldaily.com** (Arts and Letters Daily) is an excellent source of articles with high intellectual content. In addition, magazines such as *The New Yorker, The Economist,* and *The Atlantic* are good sources of generally well-reasoned, in-depth articles on topics that may be of use to you in brainstorming.

Of course, it's too late for all of this once you get to the real test, so expand your reading list as soon as possible!

Okay. We've done a bunch of planning. Now let's talk about how to actually write this thing.

Writing the Issue Essay

Structure

Here is a basic structure for the Issue Essay:

I. **Introduction:** Briefly restate the issue *with the goal of demonstrating to the grader that you understand the topic.* Do not simply repeat the prompt (the grader knows what topic you are writing about). Then define terms (if needed), acknowledge complexity, and establish your "take" or thesis on the issue.

II. **Body:** Write 2–6 paragraphs, each illustrating one of your main points.

> ### DON'T SPEND TOO MUCH TIME MAKING A SINGLE POINT OR YOU WILL RUN OUT OF TIME!

III. **Conclusion:** Re-summarize your position, acknowledging the other side. An exemplary conclusion adds some final extra insight—a new window to the main idea you've been discussing all along.

Three sentences is a good benchmark for a conclusion, although sentences can vary widely in length and content. A relevant quote would be a good way to fill out a conclusion.

A conclusion often ends with a final sentence that either generalizes the situation and makes it more universal, or looks toward the future. For instance:

> *As our world becomes more interconnected through technology and increasingly global outlooks, we must look for every possible way to prepare the next generation for a more international world —a world replete with possibilities, if we are willing to look beyond our already blurring national boundaries and engage with humanity at large.*

Of course, many of us are right near the end of our 30 minutes when we get around to writing a conclusion. So while a "new insight" would be nice, it may not realistically happen. Don't stress. In general, if you are running out of time or stuck for a final concluding sentence, try something along the lines of "In order to have a better world in the future, we must do X."

Style Points

Tone: There's no rule against saying "I," but don't be too informal. Avoid conversational asides, and don't try to be funny. Keep the tone serious and academic.

Varied Diction: Throughout the essay, you will say the same thing several times. Don't use the exact same words! That is, paraphrase yourself. If in the introduction, you wrote, "The most important virtue in a leader is a strong sense of ethics," in your conclusion, you might write, "A strong moral framework is paramount for a leader."

However, don't get excessive about it—if you're writing an essay about the environment, you're definitely going to have to use the word "environment" numerous times. It would be great if you could switch up "environment" every now and then with something like "global ecosystem," but don't get too distractingly creative (Mother Earth, Gaia, the rotating blue orb we call home…).

Varied Sentence Structure: Aim for a mix of long and short sentences. Throw in an occasional semicolon, hyphen, colon, or rhetorical question. Example:

Is it the case that sacrifice is the noblest of all virtues? Even a cursory analysis ought to indicate that it is not; the greatest of all virtues can hardly be said to be the one with, typically, the least utilitarian value.

Make sure you know how to correctly use any punctuation you decide to include, of course!

Vocabulary: Use GRE-type words in your writing (but only if you're sure you can use them correctly!). Some good vocab words to think about are those about arguments themselves, since those will work in nearly any essay. Some examples:

aver, extrapolate, contend, underpin, claim, hypothesize, rebuttal, postulate, propound, concur…

Transitions: A top-scoring essay has body paragraphs that lead logically into one another. You can create this chain of logic by arranging your examples or reasons in a progressive way, and by using transition phrases and similar signals. The simplest transitions involve phrases such as "On the other hand…" or "Finally…" A more sophisticated transition might take the form:

The obstacles towards international cooperation include not only [the stuff I discussed in my last paragraph], but also [the stuff I'm about to discuss in this paragraph].

Transitions are usually located in the first sentence of a new body paragraph.

Million Dollar Quotes: This is by no means mandatory, but it looks great if you can throw in a relevant quote you've memorized. Example:

As Winston Churchill famously said upon assuming control of Parliament and the British war effort: "I have nothing to offer but blood, toil, tears, and sweat." Similarly, great leaders are those who get in the trenches with their people.

As an appendix to this chapter, we've included a sample list of quotes that we felt would be relevant to a variety of topics. Memorize a few that appeal to you.

Finally, as a reminder: *length* on the GRE essay is highly correlated with scores. If you had a choice between checking your spelling and punctuation and writing another paragraph, it would probably be best to write another paragraph (provided that the paragraph contained an additional idea that contributed to the essay as a whole).

Trouble Getting Started?

Remember, you're writing on a computer. If you "freeze" when trying to start your introduction, write something else first! Just pick whichever example seems easiest to write and dive in! You can certainly cut and paste as needed. In the worst case, use a starter sentence to turn the engine over in your mind: "This is a dumb idea because…" or "This is a great idea because…" Just keep an eye on the clock and make sure you leave enough time for both an intro and a conclusion.

A Note on Proofreading

Very few test takers will have time for significant proofreading. Keep in mind that the graders are aware of your time con-straints. They are not judging your spelling or punctuation, except where it muddies your meaning. In fact, the most important part of proofreading on the revised GRE is to check that you responded to the specific instructions that were presented in the prompt. Beyond that, just try to put yourself in the shoes of the grader, and check that all of your points are stated clearly. Let the commas fall where they may.

*Manhattan*GRE Prep
the new standard

Sample Essays

> **Every nation should require students to study at least one foreign language from the elementary school level through the university level.**
>
> Write a response in which you discuss the extent to which you agree or disagree with the recom-mendation and explain your reasoning for the position you take. In developing and supporting your position, describe specific circumstances in which adopting the recommendation would or would not be advantageous and explain how these examples shape your position.

Foreign language study can be a valuable component of a balanced education. So, too, can poetry, economics, or public speaking. But students are individuals, and live in a wide variety of circumstances around the world. It is going too far to say that every nation should require its students to study foreign languages.

Different countries have different needs and circumstances. While many bemoan the lack of international outlook in the U.S., it is reasonable to note that most Americans do just fine speaking only one language. Of course, universities, prep schools, and other institutions are still free to make foreign language instruction mandatory, as many do now. In Sweden, however, it is a sound policy to make foreign language mandatory for nearly everyone; Sweden has an excellent school system, free through the university level, and it is clear that Swedish is a minority language, while English is the language of international business throughout Europe. Sweden currently mandates the teaching of English, as it should. If the government did not compel students to learn English, they would struggle to compete in the global job market.

While Sweden has one of the highest standards of living in the world, many nations simply have no ability to provide foreign language instruction, nor does it seem as though such instruction should be the top priority. In many countries, primary schools cost money, and many girls don't get to go to school at all, or must drop out due to lack of funds, early marriage, or their families' needing them to work. If female students in Afghanistan are to receive only a few years of education in their entire lives, it seems absurd to mandate that they learn foreign languages, as this would be a waste of their time and effort. Individual schools and teachers should be free to decide how to best use the limited time available.

Finally, not only are nations different from one another, but so are students. Many students have learning disabilities that make foreign language learning virtually impossible. Even those who don't have such disabilities have in-dividual differences and interests that should be respected. A scientific prodigy who may go on to cure cancer or AIDS ought to be permitted to focus solely on science at least at certain levels of his or her education. For every hour spent learning a foreign language there is an opportunity cost, something else not being mastered.

Of course, virtually everyone is in favor of a more global outlook, and virtually no one thinks that foreign language study is bad. However, making foreign language instruction mandatory in every nation, at every level of schooling, is unjustifiable. Different nations have different needs, and different individuals have their own capacities and goals. Foreign language study can truly open the world to those who partake, but there are many reasons not to mandate it.

Comments:

This is a moderately lengthy, argument-based essay that takes the somewhat obvious tack of disagreeing with an extreme topic.

The essay contains good transitions at the top of the third and fourth paragraphs, linking a discussion of Sweden to a discussion of poorer nations, and then linking differences among nations to differences among individuals. The examples progress in a logical way.

The language and ideas are clear, and the essay persuades by acknowledging common beliefs on the topic ("virtually everyone is in favor of a more global outlook, and virtually no one thinks that foreign language study is bad") and addressing them ("there are many reasons not to mandate it"). Also, the essay responds to the specific instruction to describe how the mandate would be advantageous (as in Sweden's case) or not advantageous (as in the case of the U.S, learning-disabled children, etc.).

This essay is not perfect, but would likely receive a 6.

Strong beliefs prevent people from thinking clearly about issues.

Write a response in which you discuss the extent to which you agree or disagree with the claim. In developing and supporting your position, be sure to address the most compelling reasons and/or examples that could be used to challenge your position.

The phrase "strong beliefs" may bring to mind images of heroes, people who have fought valiantly for what they knew to be right, or it may bring to mind images of tyrants, people whose beliefs were so strong (if misguided) that they were able to commit atrocities without regard for others. Whether such figures fall on the right side of history or not, strong beliefs often brook no adjustment and permit no new information to be considered. However, some beliefs are strong for good reason—who is not possessed of a strong belief that the earth is round, for instance? Strong beliefs do prevent people from thinking clearly about issues when those beliefs are based on emotion, group loyalty, or tradition; however, strong beliefs need not cloud our thinking when those beliefs are a genuine product of a logical, ongoing search for truth that is open to revision and new evidence.

Seventeenth-century Italian astronomer Galileo Galilei alleged that the earth moved around the sun, rather than the reverse; for this heliocentric theory he was tried by the Catholic Church, convicted of heresy, and placed under house arrest for the rest of his life. Leaders of the Church held the strong belief that Earth must be at the center of the universe. When presented with evidence that the orbits of the planets seemed to go every which way in this model (yet Galileo's model showed the planets moving, more sensibly, in ellipses), the Church did not admit this new evidence into its thinking. Of course, Galileo himself was possessed of strong beliefs, and although he was forced to publicly recant, he did not actually change his view. Yet Galileo's belief was not dogmatic; it was based on years of astronomical observation and careful calculations. Furthermore, Galileo, a Catholic, began with a geocentric worldview; his very heliocentric position was proof of his willingness to change his mind in the face of new evidence.

While Church leaders possessed strong beliefs that brooked no adjustment, Rene Descartes was a devout religious thinker whose strong beliefs did not cloud his thinking. The purpose of Descartes' famous "I think, therefore I exist" was to create a system of logic that would allow him to clear away that which he only thought he knew (but didn't actually know for sure), so he could logically build a case for his religious belief. Adopting a position of ultimate skepticism, Descartes asserted that all he really knew was that he existed. He then reasoned, logically, from that point. Whether one agrees with Descartes' conclusions, his "Meditations" is a masterwork of clear and rigorous thinking.

Just as Descartes was willing to toss aside all he thought he knew in pursuit of verifiable truth, thinkers on moral issues, such as slavery, have demonstrated that strong beliefs cloud our thinking if we don't admit of new evidence, but can be a force for good if we do. In the United States prior to the Civil War, pro-slav-

ery forces argued that the great society of ancient Athens had been built on a framework of slavery. When presented with new information, such as that Greek slavery was very different from the slavery practiced in the U.S., or Sojourner Truth's poignant "Ain't I a Woman?" address, reprinted across the nation – most did not change their minds. Of course, some did, and the North had no shortage of outspoken abolitionists. The Civil War was a war of strong belief against strong belief; the side most willing to change its mind in the face of moral argument was, rightfully, the side that won.

All people are created equal, but all strong beliefs are not. Strong beliefs based on evidence and logic are strong beliefs that are nevertheless changeable, and need not muddy our thinking. It is dogmatism that is the enemy, not strength of conviction.

Comments:

This is a lengthy, example-based essay that gives a balanced, nuanced position on the topic. "Strong beliefs prevent people from thinking clearly about issues" is a fairly extreme statement, so a well-developed thesis here is a good strategy. The introduction is long in order to give time to develop that thesis: *"Strong beliefs do prevent people from thinking clearly about issues when those beliefs are based on emotion, group loyalty, or tradition; however, strong beliefs need not cloud our thinking when those beliefs are a genuine product of a logical, ongoing search for truth that is open to revision and new evidence."*

The first body paragraph is sophisticated—it actually gives two closely related examples, or uses a single example to support the thesis in two ways by showing that the Church's strong belief was indefensible, but Galileo's strong belief was justifiable.

The second body paragraph is somewhat weaker, but there is a nice transition between the two paragraphs (*While Church leaders possessed strong beliefs that brooked no adjustment, Rene Descartes...*), and the writer balanced out an example about religious belief gone wrong with an example of religious belief the writer thinks falls on the other side of the thesis.

The third body paragraph is fine, although it doesn't seem to fit the topic as well as the first two; the writer makes no distinction between "new information" such as astronomical observation and "new information" of a moral sense. However, the slight shift in emphasis allows the writer to incorporate other examples recalled from his or her college course on pre-Civil-War U.S. history.

The conclusion flows nicely from the third example (although this is not necessarily expected in an essay). It is brief and to the point, and restates the thesis in different words.

Though the essay doesn't really take a side, it does make very clear what the strongest arguments both for and against the prompt are, and thus succeeds adequately in addressing the specific instructions.

The writer's language and main ideas are clear. The second and third examples are not as strong as the first, but this essay's main strength is its well-developed main idea, and sophisticated attempt to validate a two-part thesis with relevant examples.

This essay is also not perfect, but would likely receive a 6.

More Sample Issue Essays

For sample Issue Essays—with comments provided by the people who grade the real GRE—see *The Official Guide to the GRE Revised General Test*—Analytical Writing section, beginning on page 11.

How to Prepare

1) Read a variety of sample essays.

2) Brainstorm a large number of topics from ETS's published topic pool:

http://www.ets.org/gre/revised_general/prepare/analytical_writing/issue/pool

3) Write several practice essays under timed conditions, also using topics from ETS' published topic pool. Don't select the topics you most *want* to write about—just scroll down the list and do the first topic you land on, or ask someone else to assign you a topic. Write your practice essays on a computer, using only the functions available to you on the real exam (i.e., turn off spell check and grammar check).

4) Take a full-length Manhattan GRE practice exam (included with your purchase of this book!), and don't skip the essay section!

ANALYZE AN ARGUMENT

The Analyze an Argument task gives you 30 minutes to plan and write a critique of an argument presented in the form of a short passage. A critique of any other argument will receive a score of zero. To score well, you need to do three things. First, analyze the line of reasoning in the argument (which will always be faulty). Then, explain the logical flaws and assumptions that underlie that reasoning. Finally, you must discuss what the author could add in order to make the conclusion of the argument more logically sound.

It is absolutely critical that you recognize that you are NOT being asked to present your own views on the subject of the argument.

Argument Essay Ground Rules

The topic that you actually see on the real test will be chosen from a list of topics available on ETS's website:

http://www.ets.org/gre/revised_general/prepare/analytical_writing/argument/pool

Yes, that's right! You can view all of the possible topics ahead of time. The topic you end up writing about will be one of the ones on the list at the page above, possibly with minor wording changes.

Like the Analyze an Issue task, the Analyze an Argument essay requires you to respond to specific instructions. This change was effected in order to obviate the practice of using a pre-written response and simply swapping in words related to the specific argument presented. In the Official Guide, ETS lists eight possible sets of instructions that could accompany an argument essay prompt. However, the eight of them are even less interesting than the six provided for the issue essay! Not one of them demands anything that wouldn't be featured in any successful argument essay on the given prompt. Here they are, from page 25 of *The Official Guide to the GRE Revised General Test*. You would be given an argument followed by one of these:

1. Write a response in which you discuss what specific evidence is needed to evaluate the argument and explain how the evidence would weaken or strengthen the argument.

2. Write a response in which you examine the stated and/or unstated assumptions of the argument. Be sure to explain how the argument depends on these assumptions and what the implications are if the assumptions prove unwarranted.

3. Write a response in which you discuss what questions would need to be answered in order to decide whether the recommendation and the argument on which it is based are reasonable. Be sure to explain how the answers to these questions would help to evaluate the recommendation.

4. Write a response in which you discuss what questions would need to be answered in order to decide whether the advice and the argument on which it is based are reasonable. Be sure to explain how the answers to these questions would help to evaluate the advice.

5. Write a response in which you discuss what questions would need to be answered to decide whether the recommendation is likely to have the predicted result. Be sure to explain how the answers to these questions would help to evaluate the recommendation.

6. Write a response in which you discuss what questions would need to be answered in order to decide whether the prediction and the argument on which it is based are reasonable. Be sure to explain how the answers to these questions would help to evaluate the prediction.

7. Write a response in which you discuss one or more alternative explanations that could rival the proposed explanation and explain how your explanation(s) can plausibly account for the facts presented in the argument.

8. Write a response in which you discuss what questions would need to be addressed in order to decide whether the conclusion and the argument on which it is based are reasonable. Be sure to explain how the answers to the questions would help to evaluate the conclusion.

Again, there's no way of knowing yet how important the specific instructions will be in determining test takers' scores. In reality, a well-written essay in which you locate logical flaws in the argument and then explain how they could be fixed will likely score highly. That said, you should of course read the specific instructions and make sure that they are addressed, just to be on the safe side.

The Construction of Arguments

It may be helpful to quickly diagram an argument to reveal its structure, similar to the way we used a T-diagram to help with Argument Structure Passages earlier in the book.

When you diagram, the point is to put the conclusion at the top, and the supporting arguments (premises) below in a logical way—the way they are being used to support the argument. Sometimes, the diagram will look a bit strange because the argument itself is a bit strange—and therein probably lies a flaw. Feel free to note your questions in parentheses as you go.

Let's try one:

> *The town of Arcana should institute an 11pm curfew for teenagers to curb crime and improve academic performance. Many crimes are being committed by young people after dark, and a curfew would both make such crimes impossible, and provide an extra legal offense with which to charge those who do break the law. Furthermore, many young people study less than one hour per night. An 11pm curfew would improve students' grades.*

<u>11pm curfew for teens will decrease crime, improve academics</u>

crimes after dark
(same as "11pm"?)

teens study < 1 hr
(they're going to start studying at 11 now?)

curfew → "impossible"
to commit crimes

→ extra charge

(if it's impossible, who
would we be charging?!)

Feel free to make use of a two-column format, liberal use of arrows, etc—whatever makes visual sense of the argument.

Once we've diagrammed (either on paper or mentally), it's time to brainstorm the flaws. How do we find them? Fortunately, most of the mistakes have been made before....

Argument Essay: Flaws to Watch Out For

The following is a list of common fallacies found in GRE arguments. We will give numerous example arguments, each of which may have several problems. After you read through the flaws, we'll practice finding some of them in real GRE arguments.

Note that the list below is quite long! You don't have to "get" every one, nor do you have to memorize the list. This is just to get you thinking about some of the kinds of things to look out for. You do not need to memorize our names for the flaws, nor should you actually use the names in your essay. Just deconstruct the argument, pointing out the sorts of things we point out below.

In a typical GRE argument, we'd expect to find 1–5 of these flaws. It is also possible that some GRE arguments may possess flaws not listed below—as with anything, there is an infinite number of ways to mess something up.

Unjustified Assumptions – The argument is based on a questionable assumption. That is, in order for the argument to be true, the author is depending on a premise that he or she didn't write down and hasn't proven. Thus, the conclusion can't be validated unless the assumption(s) can be proved to be true.

> *The Urban Apartment Towers complex has seen a number of police visits to the property recently, resulting in the police breaking up loud parties held by young residents and attended by other young people. These police visits and the reputation for loud parties are hurting Urban Apartment Towers' reputation and ability to attract new residents. To reduce the number of police visits and improve profitability, Urban Apartment Towers plans to advertise its vacant apartments in a local publication for people age 50 and up.*

What is this argument assuming but not proving? That *people age 50 and up are less likely to have loud parties or attract police visits.* That doesn't sound like a totally unreasonable assumption, but it is an assumption nevertheless, and it is the job of the arguer to prove it (and your job to point out that the arguer hasn't done so). Perhaps older residents would attract visits of another type (e.g. healthcare personnel) that could also impact the reputation of the complex.

Skill & Will – The argument assumes that people have the ability (skill) to do something or the motivation (will) to do it, when this has not been proven to be the case. The recommendations that "Everyone should exercise two hours

per day," and "Children should be offered green vegetables three times daily" run into problems regarding the ability of people to exercise that much (what about people who are already ill?) and the desire of children to eat the vegetables.

The *Urban Apartment Towers* argument above also has both a "skill" problem and a "will" problem. Maybe over-50 people in the local area are largely on a fixed income and cannot afford to live in the Towers. And why would they want to? It's not clear that people over 50 have much motivation to live in an apartment complex where the police are always raiding loud parties.

Extreme Language – The argument (usually the conclusion) uses language so extreme that the premises cannot justify the conclusion.

> *People who jog more than 10 miles per week have a lower incidence of heart disease than people who exercise the same amount on stationary bicycles. Therefore, jogging is the best method of exercise for reducing heart disease.*

The conclusion is the final sentence: *Jogging is the best method of exercise for reducing heart disease.* The word "best" is quite extreme! The best method ever? Better than swimming, tennis, and a million other things? Proving that jogging is better than stationary bicycling (and there are some problems with that as well) just proves that jogging is "better" than one thing, not the "best."

Other extreme words to watch out for include the following: *only, never, always, cannot, certainly.*

Terms are Too Vague – Just as you are on the lookout for language that is too extreme, you're also on the lookout for language that is too vague.

The *People who jog* argument above has this problem. What on earth does it mean to "exercise the same amount" as someone who is jogging 10 miles? Does it mean biking for the same amount of *time* or the same *distance*? The same number of calories burned? Since it's much faster to ride 10 miles on a stationary bike than to jog 10 miles, if the arguer means that the distances are the same, then there's another reason (besides the author's conclusion) that the joggers have less heart disease: they are exercising more hours per week.

Predicting the Future – There's nothing wrong with trying to predict the future, of course; it's hard to run a government (or anything) without doing so. However, whenever an argument tries to predict the future, that's your opportunity to point out that the future could actually turn out some other way. Anyone who tries to predict the future is automatically introducing a level of uncertainty into his or her argument.

> *The police chief in Rand City, a major urban metropolis, has proposed cutting down on speeding by doubling the fines levied on those who are caught. Speeding has been a major problem in Rand City, where over 5,000 tickets are issued each month. Of those who are issued tickets, over 95% mail in the fines, while less than 1% contest the charges in court, thus indicating the offenders' admission of guilt. Doubling the fines for speeding will substantially reduce speeding in Rand City.*

The arguer is trying to predict the future: *Doubling the fines will substantially reduce speeding.* To find a weak link in this chain of events, ask yourself what could happen in between "the fines double" and "people speed less." What else could happen? What about "the fines double" and then "people speed just the same but don't pay their tickets"? What if the fines are so low already (hence the lack of motivation to contest the charges) that doubling them won't make a difference? You can think of lots of ways that the first part of the conclusion could lead to something other than the second part of the conclusion.

What's Their Motivation? – Whenever an argument is in the form of an advertisement or company announcement, you get to ask, "What's the speaker's motivation?" Is the speaker trying to promote a medication, make a company look good, sell something, or get elected?

The *police chief in Rand City* argument above potentially has this problem. What motivation does the police chief have in doubling traffic fines? Probably an honest desire to reduce speeding—but maybe a desire to increase the police budget by increasing what has historically been a reliable source of funding.

The Troubled Analogy – There's nothing wrong with a good analogy, of course, but analogies in GRE arguments are never good. Every time you make an analogy, you're saying that something is like something else—except that it isn't *exactly* like that, or you'd just be talking about the original topic. It's your job to find and exploit the dissimilarities.

> *Bowbridge University, a prestigious institution with a long history of educating great scholars and national leaders, launched a distance learning program five years ago. Bowbridge students were very happy with the flexibility afforded to them by the program; for instance, they could continue studying with professors on the Bowbridge campus while conducting research, traveling, or volunteering anywhere in the world. A study showed that the quality of education, as measured by students' grades, did not decrease. Thus, if the tuition-free Local City College implements a distance learning program, student satisfaction will increase without compromising quality of education.*

Is Bowbridge Univerisity similar to Local City College? There are a lot of assumptions there. We're told that Bowbridge is prestigious, and that its students travel, volunteer, and conduct research around the world. They sound like a wealthy bunch! The students at the free Local City College? Probably not as wealthy. Maybe they don't even own computers. Do they need distance learning? It's not clear that someone who attends a "local" college would want—or have the means—to attend that college from halfway around the world.

In the end, we don't know that much about Local City College. It's not our job to prove that distance learning *won't* work there; it's our job to point out that the arguer has not established enough similarities to make a good analogy between the two institutions.

Confusing Signs of a Thing for the Thing Itself – Medical tests often report false positives, while failing to catch everyone who actually has the disease. The number of people who test positive for a disease is not identical to the number of people who have the disease.

This effect is especially acute when people have an incentive (such as money) to over-report something, or an incentive (such as fear or laziness) to under-report something. For instance, reports of crimes such as littering and jaywalking are extremely low—that doesn't mean people aren't committing those crimes all the time. Reports of whiplash from car accidents tend to be highly inflated, since victims are often in a position to gain money from insurance companies. Reports of workplace harassment may be lower than actual incidents of harassment because workers fear losing their jobs or worsening the problem.

The argument above, *Bowbridge University*, has this problem. "The quality of education, as measured by students' grades, did not decrease." Maybe professors grade online students more leniently, or give them easier assignments. Grades are not the same as "quality of education."

Another common variation on this problem assumes that, because a law exists, people must be following it. *A law is not the same as compliance with a law.* One GRE argument tells us that the city has instituted water rationing and that local businesses are doing worse, and concludes that water rationing is hurting businesses. However, the fact that a regulation exists doesn't mean it is being followed—to establish causality, the arguer would first need to show that

businesses are even obeying water rationing in the first place (If there's no enforcement, it's entirely likely that at least some businesses would simply ignore rationing.)

Short Term vs. Long Term – Something that's good in the short term, under certain circumstances (antibiotics, for instance) may not be good for you in the long term. Something that is a good idea in the short term (working all night to rescue people in an emergency) might not even be possible in the long term.

Similarly, something that's good or possible long-term may not be good or possible short-term. Eating a carrot a day may be beneficial for your eyesight over many years, but it won't help you pass your pilot's exam next week.

> *A study of 120 elderly, hospital-bound patients in the United Kingdom showed that daily consumption of Nutree, a nutritional supplement containing vitamins, fiber, and sugar, increased by an average of four months the typical life expectancy for people of the same age and physical condition. Thus, anyone who wants to live longer should drink Nutree every day.*

120 elderly, hospital-bound patients did it, so you should too? There are several problems here. (The next three flaws are also about this argument.) But let's look at short term/long term. People who were already elderly and living in the hospital drank a sugary beverage every day and lived four months longer. The fact that we've already calculated their life expectancy seems to imply that all of the people in the study have already died. Drinking a sugary beverage every day for a short period of time might be beneficial to some people, but what if you start drinking it when you're 25? Maybe that much sugar isn't good for you over several decades.

Sample Isn't Representative – If the GRE mentions a study, chances are that the sample is not representative. One in the argument pool refers to "French women in their eighties who were nursing-home residents." Wow, what a very specific group! It's your job to point out that what works for French female octogenarians might not work for non-French people, men, and people under 80.

Of course, the argument above, *A study of 120 elderly, hospital-bound patients,* has this problem.

Sample Is Too Small – If a GRE argument mentions how many people were in a study, it's your job to say that the study should've been bigger. *A study of 120 elderly, hospital-bound patients* has this problem.

No Control Group – A good study should have a control group—that is, a group of people who are as similar as possible in every way, and differ from the test group by only one variable.

You can't just give people a new medicine and measure whether their condition improves; you have to get together a big enough group of people who meet certain conditions (such as having a particular illness at a particular stage), divide the people into two groups (balanced by gender, age, and a host of other factors), and give the drug to only one group. It's important to make sure that the people receiving the drug do not just get *better,* but *better than the other group.* After all, what if it's the sort of illness that goes away on its own? Maybe some outside force (the changing seasons?) will cause improvement in both groups. It's your job to point out when a study lacks a control group, and what impact this might have on the study's findings.

A study of 120 elderly, hospital-bound patients has this problem. The argument makes reference to another group of people of the same age and physical condition, but does not specify whether they are hospital bound U.K. residents. Where is the group of elderly, hospital-bound U.K. residents who did not drink Nutree over the same period of time? Maybe they would also have exceeded *"the typical life expectancy for people of the same age and physical condition."* Maybe the Nutree is irrelevant, and it was just being in the hospital that kept people alive that extra four months.

The Ever-Changing Pool – Most groups of people have a rotating cast of members. If a civic club voted in favor of something yesterday and against it twenty years ago, we wouldn't automatically conclude that people in the club changed their minds over time; it's pretty likely that the club includes different people than it did back then.

> *The following is a letter to the editor of a city newspaper:*
>
> *A petition is circulating in our city opposing the building of a new sports center at State University, on land now occupied by abandoned strip malls. Just five years ago, many city residents opposed the building of the new State University dormitory complex, yet in a poll just this year, 80% of respondents said they thought building the dormitory complex had been a good idea. If the people who currently oppose the new sports center just wait and see, they will change their minds.*

Five years ago, people opposed the new dorm, and now 80% of respondents to a poll like the dorm. Are the poll respondents the same population as the voters? (For instance, if the poll was conducted on or near campus, a high percentage of students being polled would certainly skew results).

Even if the poll were representative of the city's current residents, it's not clear that they are the same residents as five years ago. Maybe some residents disliked the college's expansion plans enough to move out of town. Maybe the new dorm allowed the college to admit significantly more students, thus merely diluting the pool of people who disliked and still dislike the dorm. Remember to look for a "survivor bias"—the people who stuck around didn't hate the dorm enough to leave.

Correlation Does Not Equal Causation – Just because two things are happening at the same time doesn't mean one causes the other.

> *Researchers have noted that cats that eat Premium Cat Food have healthier coats and less shedding. While Premium Cat Food costs more, the time saved cleaning up pet hair from furniture and rugs makes Premium Cat Food a wise choice.*

Two things are happening at the same time: cats are eating Premium food, and they are shedding less. Does that mean the food causes the reduced shedding?

One thing to consider is if the relationship is reversed (i.e. B is causing A as opposed to A causing B). Here, it's unlikely that it's the reverse (less shedding causes cats to eat Premium Cat Food?). However, there may be a third factor at work, which you should always look out for.

In this case, it's actually pretty likely that some outside cause is causing both the eating of Premium food and the reduced shedding.

For instance, Premium food sounds pretty expensive. Perhaps people who can afford to purchase Premium food for their cats (and choose to do so) also provide their cats with grooming, top-notch health care, or other amenities that reduce shedding. Perhaps well-heeled individuals tend to have special breeds of cats that naturally shed less. The possibility of this sort of third factor is very common on the GRE when there is a correlation.

Nothing is Quantified – Sometimes, we can get away without attaching numbers to things. Most people would be happy to be "healthier" or "richer," even if we can't measure that exactly. However, quantification (expressing things as numbers) becomes important when we try to argue something like, "*the eventual savings will outweigh the startup costs.*" Be on the lookout for this type of situation—we are trying to compare two things that *can* be quantified, but aren't.

The argument *Premium Cat Food* has this problem. "Healthier coats and less shedding" sounds like a nice enough benefit without needing to have numbers attached, but we run into problems with, *"the time saved cleaning up pet hair from furniture and rugs makes Premium Cat Food a wise choice."*

Really? To validate this claim, we would need to know 1) how much more the cat food costs than the cat food the pet owner currently buys, 2) how much time the pet owner spends cleaning up cat hair, and 3) the monetary value of the pet owner's time.

Of course, all of these factors vary from pet owner to pet owner, so even if we could get all the facts and figures, it would certainly not be true that the premium food would be a "wise choice" for everyone.

How Was It Before? – Model Heidi Klum once responded to a fan's question about getting back into shape after pregnancy with the question, "Well, how were you before?" It's hard to judge the present, or predict the future, without information about the past.

> *A youth group applied for and received a permit to use the city park for a Culture Festival, which took place last weekend. On Wednesday, the Environmental Club, a group of local volunteers, visited the park and picked up 435 pieces of trash. The presence of such a quantity of rubbish signals a clear lack of respect for the park. Clearly, the youth group should be denied permits to use the park for any future events.*

Here, it is unclear whether the 435 pieces of trash were left by the youth group, or if they were there beforehand. Who counts trash like that anyway? (At least they're quantifying).

Alternate Cause – Just because two things happened in a certain order doesn't mean one caused the other. Could some outside force be the cause?

The *435 pieces of trash* argument above has this problem. Maybe the trash was left by other groups that used the park (perhaps on Monday or Tuesday before the Environmental Club arrived?). There are many possible scenarios. Perhaps the trash was blown in by the wind.

Alike Doesn't Mean Identical – People who (or things that) are alike in some ways are undoubtedly different in others.

> *Cetadone, a new therapy for the treatment of addiction to the illegal drug tarocaine, has been proven effective in a study centered around Regis Hospital in the western part of the state of New Portsmouth. The study involved local tarocaine addicts who responded to a newspaper ad offering free treatment. Participants who received cetadone and counseling were 40% more likely to recover than were patients assigned to a control group and receiving only counseling. Conventional therapies have only a 20% recovery rate. Therefore, the best way to reduce deaths from tarocaine overdose throughout all of New Portsmouth would be to fund cetadone therapy for all tarocaine addicts.*

Are tarocaine addicts in western New Portsmouth the same as tarocaine addicts in the rest of the state? Perhaps one area is rural and one is urban, or the demographics of different parts of the state vary. Furthermore, the addicts in this study seem pretty functional and motivated—they managed to successfully respond to a newspaper ad, and apparently weren't paid, so their motivation seems to have been to recover from addiction. Maybe the addicts who do well on Cetadone are not the same addicts in danger of a fatal overdose.

While drug addiction may seem to be a defining feature, the only thing that we can assume is uniform about tarocaine addicts is that they are addicted to tarocaine—anything else is up to the speaker to prove.

Percents vs. Real Numbers (and Other Mathematical Confusion) – If David pays 28% of his income in taxes and Marie pays 33% of her income in taxes, who pays more money to the government? Without knowing how much the two people make, it's impossible to say. Don't confuse percents with actual numbers of dollars, people, etc.

The *Cetadone* argument above has big-time math issues. 40% certainly looks like a higher number than 20%. And there are no real numbers of people here anywhere, so we're not confusing a percent with a real number.

However, the 20% is an actual *recovery rate for* conventional therapies.

The 40% is a *percent increase on an unknown figure*—the recovery rate of the control group (which received counseling—not necessarily a conventional therapy). We have no way to compare this 40% increase to an actual 20% recovery rate. For instance, what if the control group had a 50% recovery rate? Then the cetadone group would have 70% recovery rate (1.4 x 50). But what if the control group had a 1% recovery rate? Then the cetadone group would have a 1.4% recovery rate, making it much less successful than conventional therapies.

In sum, if any numbers are presented in an Argument topic, see whether they are being cited in a logical way. This is the exact same reasoning about percents and percent change that you will need for the Data Interpretation part of the exam (and of course, the math on the actual math section is much harder than anything that would ever occur in an essay topic), so it pays in numerous ways to have a solid knowledge of percents.

Don't Forget to Strengthen the Argument: Just Flip the Flaw

To discuss in your essay how the argument might be strengthened, just flip the flaw around. For instance:

Nothing is Quantified?
This argument could be improved by quantifying X, Y, and Z…

Possible Alternate Causes?
This argument could be improved by investigating and ruling out alternate causes such as…

Correlation Does Not Equal Causation?
This argument could be improved by proving that X causes Y through a controlled study…

No Control Group, Non-Representative Sample, Too-Small Sample?
This argument could possibly be validated by a new study having the following qualities…

Brainstorming the Argument Essay

Look back at the list of flaws and try to find several that apply to the following argument:

> *Invoice Regulators, Inc. (IRI) can make your company more profitable. IRI examines our client firms' outgoing invoices and vendor receipts to help clients recoup money owed and refunds due. One client, a family firm with a 100 year history, discovered $75,000 worth of uncashed checks in an employee's desk drawer, and others have also made large gains. 80% of our client firms have experienced an increase in sales during the quarter our services were acquired. Hire IRI to improve your firm's profitability.*

Did you make your own list of flaws? Jot some down before you keep reading.

Here's what we came up with for this argument:

*Manhattan*GRE Prep
the new standard

Correlation Does Not Equal Causation – 80% of client firms had a sales increase around the time IRI was hired. So what? Firms often have sales increases; one thing didn't necessarily cause the other.

Alike Doesn't Mean Identical/ Unjustified Assumptions – The argument assumes that other businesses have outgoing invoices in the first place, and that, quite frankly, the business owners are a bit incompetent. It does not seem likely that the "family firm with a 100 year history" and a drawer full of forgotten money is representative of other companies. We see **Small Sample / Unrepresentative Sample** issues here as well.

Short Term vs. Long Term – The promise to "make your company more profitable" implies an ongoing financial improvement. The two cases cited seem temporary—the $75,000 is a one-shot deal, and the "increase in sales during the quarter" makes no mention of some improved, systemic way to enhance ongoing profitability.

Terms are Too Vague / Nothing is Quantified – Other clients have made "large gains." How large? Big enough to offset the cost (which was never mentioned) of IRI's services? What percent of clients experience the large gains?

What's Their Motivation? – Obviously, this is an advertisement. But it doesn't hurt to point out that IRI clearly has its own financial interests in mind here.

We also noticed another big problem that isn't named in this chapter, but is specific to this argument:

Confusing Sales with Profitability – Here, the argument confuses increased profitability (which is at least temporarily achievable by cashing a drawer full of checks or chasing refunds) with sales. Perhaps IRI costs more than the sales increase, and would thus hurt profitability.

Once you've identified the flaws, make a quick outline. (Don't use our names for the flaws—just write down what you're going to say.)

If you have more than four or so flaws to write about, you may wish to group any that are very similar, or simply omit the weakest.

You also want to put your ideas in a logical order so that your argument is persuasive and so that you can write nice transitions from one idea to the next.

Here is one sample outline:

>   the "checks in the drawer" client ≠ representative of other potential clients
>   idiots!
>   even if not idiots, one biz is insufficient evidence
>   not all biz even have outgoing invoices
>
>   claims of "other biz" are vague, nothing quantified
>   gains big enough to outweigh costs of IRI? (what ARE costs of IRI?)
>
>   claims of enhanced profitability even for existing clients are suspect
>   sales ≠ profitability
>   sales "in same quarter" – not even clear it's AFTER IRI
>   even if it were, correlation ≠ causation!
>
>   "profitability" implies ongoing

If this seems like a lot to write before even getting started typing, don't worry—we wrote a bit more here than you would probably write, since you're only writing for yourself.

Make sure that you're not just throwing disconnected ideas on the page. Remember the ***dinner table test*** from the section on the Issue Essay. Make sure that, in deconstructing a bad argument, you yourself are making a good argument.

From a "debater" perspective, here is our argument (this isn't something we'd actually write down, since we're about to type the real essay, but your outline should reflect a coherent argument that you've formed mentally before you begin to write):

I.   Just because hiring IRI has been profitable for some clients doesn't mean it would be profitable for others.

II. However, it's not even clear that IRI *has* been profitable for anyone, since we don't have any actual numbers to quantify most of the firms' gains, and we don't know what it costs to hire IRI.

III. The claims of profitability for existing clients are also suspect because IRI has confused sales with profitability, taking credit for something that is irrelevant to IRI's services and that possibly even began before IRI was hired.

IV. Profitability implies an ongoing financial improvement. IRI fails to define the period. A one-shot cash infusion is not the same thing as enhanced profitability.

The above statements are the parts of the argument each body paragraph will make. Note how the order seems "right"—we go from arguing that IRI won't be profit-enhancing for everyone, to questioning whether it's profit enhancing for anyone at all. II and III make the same point from different angles and clearly should come one after the other.

In the outline/argument above, we left out "What's their motivation?" (the idea that, because the text is from an ad, the speaker is biased). This point seems way too obvious to write an entire paragraph about, although mentioning it would be perfectly appropriate in an introduction. Also note that in our outline, we wrote "idiots!" Feel free to write stuff like this in your own notes, but don't use that type of language on the GRE. When we really write the essay, we'll say something about "a possibly incompetent employee."

Note that we didn't bother to write down a thesis. The thesis for an Argument essay will pretty much always be something like, "The argument rests on questionable assumptions, suffers from vaguely-defined terms, and contains numerous logical flaws that make it impossible to validate the conclusion."

About Timing: On the real test, you should spend 2–3 minutes on the entire process of diagramming, brainstorming flaws, and organizing your thoughts into a coherent and persuasive outline. However, for now, it would be reasonable to practice brainstorming taking a bit more time (say, 5-6 minutes), knowing that with practice you'll get better and faster at spotting flaws.

A brief mention of specific instructions: While the specific instructions may ask you to add something into your essay that you wouldn't necessarily have included otherwise, there shouldn't be any need to radically change an essay from the standard format described here in order to obey the specific instructions. Generally, adding a single sentence to each paragraph, or even a few words, will suffice. For example, one set of instructions says this:

"Write a response in which you discuss what questions would need to be answered in order to decide whether the prediction and the argument on which it is based are reasonable. Be sure to explain how the answers to these questions would help to evaluate the prediction."

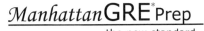

Notice that the instructions don't really recommend anything that a well-written essay wouldn't do anyway. Therefore, feel free to write your outline without even worrying about the instructions, then simply check to be sure there will be space to include whatever little details the specific instructions requested (five out of eight of the specific instruction prompts involve responding to "questions that need to be answered," for example).

About Brainstorming Practice: Some practice with brainstorming will also speed up the process. You may find some flaws seem to occur more often than others (that's definitely true). If you find yourself brainstorming or writing three "correlation does not equal causation" essays in a row, there's nothing wrong with that. The GRE writers implant the same flaws into their argument topics over and over.

You can practice brainstorming by visiting this link and exploring the pool:

http://www.ets.org/gre/revised_general/prepare/analytical_writing/argument/pool

Try diagramming the argument, finding flaws, and organizing an outline, as described above, for some of the topics listed.

Don't just pick out the topics that you most want to write about! Force yourself to start at the beginning, or scroll down a bit and do the first topic you see.

Okay. We've done a bunch of preparation. Let's talk about how to write this thing.

Argument Essay Outline

I. Introduction: In the intro, you should discuss the argument at hand and give your "take." Do not repeat the argument; the grader is already very familiar with it.

> *Candidates for office are often prompted to make unlikely promises to gain support. While it is clear that the people of Brownsville would like more jobs to be created, it is unlikely that the mayoral candidate's plan will bring about the intended effect.*

You are then going to establish your "take" or thesis. Unlike in the Issue essay, where you were instructed to brainstorm both sides and construct a sophisticated, nuanced main idea, here your main idea is much easier. It's pretty much always going to say that the argument has some serious problems:

> *While the mayor's goals may be admirable, his plan rests on a number of unjustified assumptions and fails to take into account other factors affecting job creation in a seaside resort town.*

Another example of an introduction paragraph:

> *A study has recorded a variety of health benefits occurring at the same time as the consumption of soy beverage by a small, homogeneous study group. While it may actually be the case that drinking 12 ounces of soy beverage per day slows the progress of arthritis, the study presented does not actually prove this to be the case; the study's limited sample size, lack of a control group, and confusion of reported symptoms with internal body processes all serve to seriously compromise the study's conclusion.*

Notice that each of these main ideas began with acknowledging some small positive—at least the mayor's intentions are good! Soy beverage *might* still be beneficial! This is a good way to add some nuance to your main idea.

II. Body: Explain one main point in each of 2–4 paragraphs.

Each of the flaws you decided, from your brainstorming process, to write about should become the main point of a body paragraph. Or, if you decide to group more than one flaw into a paragraph, make sure that the two flaws are very closely and logically related; for instance, "the sample size is too small" and "the sample is not representative" are good candidates to be grouped into a single paragraph. Generally, though, keep it to one main point per paragraph. GRE graders have given high scores to Argument essays that include as many as six body paragraphs—in such a case, many of the body paragraphs are quite short.

Arrange your main points in a logical way, and use **transitions** to segue from paragraph to paragraph. Transitions are usually located in the first sentence of a new body paragraph. For instance, if you have just written a paragraph about how a study's sample size was too small and not representative, you might begin the next paragraph with something like:

> *Not only should it be apparent that a study based on a sample of 80 Korean women is not necessarily applicable to humanity at large, it is also the case that, due to the lack of a control group, we are unable to evaluate the results of the study for even this extremely limited sample.*

Here we have segued from talking about the sample's size and makeup to talking about a problem related to working even within the small and limited sample. This is a logical progression of ideas; the use of such transitions throughout an essay creates a sense of coherence and fluency.

Don't forget to **improve the argument.** There are (at least) three possible ways to arrange your argument to incorporate this component.

1) Each time you mention a flaw, follow up with how to fix it. The "improve the argument" component would therefore be part of each body paragraph.

2) Write two or more body paragraphs about the argument's flaws, and follow up with one body paragraph on how to fix those flaws.

3) Use the body paragraphs entirely to discuss the flaws, and save the discussion of how to fix those flaws for the conclusion. This may be the best plan for anyone frequently stuck for a conclusion. Keeping the "improve the argument" component brief is also a good way to keep from sounding repetitive.

So, don't forget to "improve the argument," even if only for a sentence or two in the conclusion.

DON'T SPEND TOO MUCH TIME MAKING A SINGLE POINT OR YOU WILL RUN OUT OF TIME!

III. Conclusion: In the conclusion, you should re-summarize your critique. The conclusion does not have to be lengthy: simply re-state your thesis or main idea in different words, and state or re-state what would need to be done to improve the argument. Ending with ideas for improvement gives a nice, positive note at the end:

> *The candidate for mayor who proposed bringing a big-box home improvement store to Brownsville may have been motivated by the admirable goal of creating jobs in an economically distressed area. However, the candidate failed to take into account job loss from local hardware stores that would likely be run out of business, as well as the cost to the city of tax incentives that are likely to outweigh the store's economic*

boost. If we are to believe in the candidate's plan—and the candidate—further research and more rigorous quantification will be required.

Ideally, the conclusion should sum things up while offering some special perspective or insight. In any case, try to avoid having your conclusion sound repetitive or unnecessary. If in doubt, keep it short.

Style Points

Debate Team Persuasion Tactics: It's possible to say the exact same thing in a way that is not very persuasive, and in a way that is. Say you are trying to argue against the school superintendent's plan for year-round school:

1) The superintendent has not proven that her plan will achieve the goal of improving academic performance. However, it may serve the function of reducing crime.

2) While the superintendent's plan may indeed reduce crime, she has not proven that her plan will achieve the stated goal of improving academic performance.

Which version sounds worse for the superintendent? The last one, right? *If you have two opposing things to say, put the one that's on your side last.* This makes the one that isn't on your side seem less important. The order should be (1) Concession, then (2) your Assertion.

If you have a fairly weak point, use that point's weakness to your advantage to emphasize how strong your next point is! For instance, say we were only able to come up with three flaws for a particular argument, and one of them is pretty weak, but we can't toss it out because then we won't have enough to write about. Put the weakest point in the middle (if that won't disrupt the flow of the argument), and use it to underscore the final, biggest point.

For instance, say your second (weak) point is that the company president is trying to predict the future, and no one can really predict the future. Say your third (strong) point is that the company president is basing his predictions on an analogy with another company—and that company is completely different from his own company. Here's a snippet of that essay (the entire second paragraph and the beginning of the third), written in a persuasive way:

> The company president's argument is also weak because it attempts to predict the future, and to predict it absolutely. He even goes so far as to say that the company will "certainly" meet its sales target. But what if the lead salesperson gets sick, or what if a nationwide crisis suddenly causes sales to plummet? The president's conclusion is dubious because he is making an unwisely extreme assertion that simply cannot be validated.

> Even if we were to accept the presence of some uncertainty in predicting the future, the most grave flaw in the president's argument is its dependence on a highly questionable analogy...

The second paragraph isn't wonderful. But notice how we set it up to create a nice transition into the third, stronger paragraph. We do this all the time when we're arguing in real life – "But if that's not good enough for you, try this!"

Tone: There's no rule against saying "I," but don't be too informal. Avoid conversational asides, and don't try to be funny. Keep the tone serious and academic. When you're referring to an argument and it's not clear who's talking, you can refer to that person as "the speaker."

Varied Diction: Throughout the essay, you will say the same thing several times. Don't use the exact same words! That is, paraphrase yourself. If in the introduction, you wrote:

> While it is indisputable that a new train line would create some new jobs in Arrin City, the mayor's argument that the train line will improve the city's overall financial health is flawed due to a variety of counterfactors, including possible job loss in other sectors, that the mayor has neglected to take into account.

…then in your conclusion, you might write:

> The mayor's contention that a new train line would improve the city's financial health is sadly misguided; while undoubtedly there would be some benefits, such as new jobs directly serving the train line, the financial benefit of those jobs would likely be dwarfed by other financial losses sustained in the wake of the train line's implementation.

Note that we switched in "undoubtedly" for "indisputable," and switched up the wording by shuffling the three ideas in the sentence ("some new jobs, mayor is wrong, other factors" vs. "mayor is wrong, some new jobs, other factors").

However, while you do want to avoid saying "indisputable" over and over when there are so many other good words (undeniable, unquestionable, irrefutable, incontrovertible, indubitable) you could use in its place, don't worry about repeating words such as "train" and "mayor." There's absolutely nothing wrong with using the word "train" many, many times in an essay about whether a new train line should be built.

Varied Sentence Structure: Aim for a mix of long and short sentences. Throw in an occasional semicolon, colon, hyphen or rhetorical question.

Vocabulary: Use GRE-type words in your writing (but only if you're sure you can use them correctly!). Some good vocab words to think about are those about arguments themselves, since those will work in nearly any essay. Some examples:

> *aver, extrapolate, contend, underpin, claim, hypothesize, rebuttal, postulate, propound, concur…*

Transitions: A top-scoring essay has body paragraphs that lead logically into one another. You can create this chain of logic by arranging your examples or reasons in a progressive way and by using transition phrases and similar signals. The simplest transitions involve phrases such as "On the other hand…" or "Finally…" A more sophisticated transition might take the form:

> *In addition to the loss of income from tolls paid by drivers, another potential loss of income to the city is from parking fees.*

Transitions are usually located in the first sentence of a new body paragraph.

Finally, as a reminder: *length* on the GRE essay is highly correlated with scores. Write as much as you can in the time allotted. If you had a choice between painstaking checking your spelling and writing another paragraph, it would probably be best to write another paragraph.

Trouble Getting Started? Remember, you're writing on a computer. If you "freeze" when trying to start your introduction, write something else first! Just pick whichever body paragraph seems easiest to write and dive in! You can certainly cut and paste as needed. In the worst case, use a "starter" sentence to turn the engine over in your mind: "This is a dumb idea because…" or "This is a great idea because…" Just keep an eye on the clock and make sure you leave enough time for both an intro and a conclusion.

A Note on Proofreading: Very few test takers will have time for significant proofreading. Keep in mind that the graders are aware of your time constraints. They are not judging your spelling or punctuation, except where it muddies your meaning. In fact, the most important part of proofreading on the revised GRE is to check that you responded to the specific instructions that were presented in the prompt. Beyond that, focus on making sure your points are clear.

Sample Essays

> **Invoice Regulators, Inc. (IRI) can make your company more profitable. IRI examines our client firms' outgoing invoices and vendor receipts to help clients recoup money owed and refunds due. One client, a family firm with a 100 year history, discovered $75,000 worth of uncashed checks in an employee's desk drawer, and others have also made large gains. 80% of our client firms have experienced an increase in sales during the quarter our services were acquired. Hire IRI to improve your firm's profitability.**
>
> Write a response in which you discuss what questions would need to be answered in order to decide whether the recommendation and the argument on which it is based are rea-sonable. Be sure to explain how the answers to these questions would help evaluate the recommendation.

One ought to consider the claims of any advertisement with skepticism, and the entreaty to acquire Invoice Regulators' services is no different. IRI offers to examine a firm's invoices and receipts, and asserts that these services will enhance profitability. The argument is dubious; it rests on a questionable analogy, suffers from a lack of quantification, confuses sales with profitability, and makes unwarranted claims of causality.

IRI's ad relates the peculiar story of a company employee who neglected to cash $75,000 in checks. We don't know anything else about this company, or whether what worked for that type of business would work for other types of businesses—some types of businesses, such as retail stores, collect money on the spot, so it is unclear whether IRI's services could enhance such firms' profitability. However, we need not even go that far—very few employees could forget $75,000 in a desk drawer, and very few firms would need outside assistance to notice that such a sum had gone missing. But are there any other businesses that have had similar lucky discoveries because of IRI's help? The argument fails to extend the analogy from this "family firm with a 100 year old history" to any other types of businesses, or even to more competently managed businesses of the same type.

One might object that IRI has made "large gains" for other clients. However, this claim is vague. What are "large gains"? What kind of companies were these, and would their results apply to other companies? This claim utterly lacks quantification, an argumentative offense made all the more egregious when we consider that "gains" are not the same as "profitability." For the gains to translate into profitability, we would need to know the cost of IRI's services, and whether the gains outweigh the cost.

IRI goes on to claim that 80% of clients achieved an increase in sales. However, just because increased sales happened around the same time as hiring IRI does not mean that IRI is responsible for the sales. The ad never explains how reviewing invoices and receipts could have an effect on sales. Is there any evidence to directly link the increase in sales to IRI's intervention? In fact, the ad doesn't even say that the sales increase happened after IRI was hired—just "in the same quarter." Maybe the causal relationship actually runs the opposite way—perhaps it was the increased sales that gave the companies the funds to hire IRI in the first place.

IRI is soliciting new clients based on an advertisement that makes an extremely weak analogy from a single case study, fails to quantify gains made or costs incurred by clients, confuses sales and profit, and assumes a model of causality for which there is no evidence. To better evaluate IRI's argument, the reader would need to know whether IRI has helped businesses similar to her own and whether IRI's success at those companies could be reasonably predicted to be repeated, as well as the cost of IRI's services so that the two costs could be weighed. The ad would be further improved by the omission of the irrelevant claim about sales; perhaps the space could be better used to quantify other claims central to evaluating IRI's services.

Comments:

This is a fairly lengthy essay that comprehensively covers the errors made in the argument. The language is clear, and the main idea ("The argument is dubious; it rests on a questionable analogy, suffers from a lack of quantification, confuses sales with profitability, and makes unwarranted claims of causality") gives a good roadmap of the rest of the essay.

The transitions between paragraphs are nice, especially "One might object…," which astutely anticipates the objection that more than one company was mentioned, but then points out that the mention was so vague as to be useless.

The coverage of causality in the third body paragraph was good, especially the counterexample ("perhaps it was the increased sales that gave the companies the funds to hire IRI in the first place").

The conclusion thoroughly covers how the argument could be improved, including the omission of irrelevant claims.

Notice how each body paragraph presents at least one question that the author of the argument would need to address, as requested in the specific instructions.

This essay, while not perfect, would likely score a 6.

> *The following appeared as a letter to the editor of National Issues magazine in the country of Ganadia.*
>
> **Last month, National Issues ran an article about the decline—as measured by shrinking populations and the flight of young people—of small towns in Ganadia. Here in Lemmontown, a small resort town on the ocean, we are seeing just the opposite: citizens from the neighboring towns of Armontown and Gurdy City are moving here at a record rate. Furthermore, greater than ever numbers of high school graduates in Lemmontown are choosing to stay in Lemmontown, as the building of new hotels has created a significant number of jobs. All along the eastern seaboard are similar stories. Small towns in Ganadia are not in decline.**
>
> Write a response in which you discuss one or more alternative explanations that could rival the proposed explanation and explain how your explanation(s) can plausibly account for the facts presented in the argument.

A letter to the editor of National Issues magazine takes issue with the magazine's claim that small towns in Ganadia are declining. It seems that the writer is from a small town that is not declining. Of course, the magazine's contention was almost certainly that small towns, on average, are declining; a single counterexample does not disprove that claim. The arguments' other flaws stem from the same central problem: Lemmontown is just one town, and not necessarily a very representative one.

The writer explains that Lemmontown is a resort town on the ocean. Resort towns depend on income flowing in from visitors, and the seaside (or whatever else visitors are there to see) is an asset that most towns do not have. These atypical resort assets are directly cited as the driver behind the jobs that are keeping young people in Lemmontown. Non-resort towns would not likely experience a similar effect. To set the argument on more sound footing, the writer would need to demonstrate that Lemmontown is typical of other Ganadian towns.

Of course, the writer does mention two other towns: Armontown and Gurdy City. While the writer means to cite those towns as evidence that Lemmontown is doing well, he or she inadvertently weakens the argument by giving two counterexamples: both Armontown and Gurdy City are losing residents, in accordance with the trend cited by National Issues. In fact, of the three towns the writer references, two of them are losing people. To strengthen the argument, the writer would have to prove that there are more Lemmontowns (so to speak) than Armontowns and Gurdy Cities, or that Armontown and Gurdy City are not small towns.

Finally, the writer points out that "all along the eastern seaboard are similar stories." This assertion is vague. Are there enough stories of non-declining small towns to outweigh accounts of declining small towns? The claim lacks quantification. Also, the eastern seaboard is not necessarily representative of the rest of Ganadia. Perhaps the seaboard is full of thriving resort towns, but the bulk of Ganadia's small towns exist in the interior and on the west coast, where conditions are worse. To validate his or her claims, the writer would need to quantify the claim that eastern seaboard success stories are more numerous than accounts of small towns in decline.

The letter to the editor takes exception to a general claim by providing a specific exception. One anecdote does not make an argument. The argument as written fails to establish that Lemmontown's happy situation is representative of Ganadian towns at large.

Comments:

This is a moderately lengthy essay that effectively takes apart the writer's attempt to use an anecdote to disprove a general trend. "The arguments' other flaws stem from the same central problem" is an apt description and ties the essay into a coherent whole.

The essay follows the structure of detailing a problem in each body paragraph and then offering suggestions for improving the argument within the same paragraph. Thus, the conclusion is fairly short, which is fine.

The language is clear, and adequate transitions between body paragraphs are provided.

Notice that each paragraph succeeds in giving an alternative explanation for a given fact, as requested in the specific instructions.

This essay, while not perfect, would likely score a 6.

More Sample Argument Essays

For sample Argument Essays—with comments provided by the people who grade the real GRE—see *The Official Guide to the GRE Revised General Test* – Analytical Writing section, beginning on page 11.

How to Prepare

1) Read a variety of sample essays.

2) Brainstorm a large number of topics from ETS's published topic pool:

   http://www.ets.org/gre/revised_general/prepare/sample_questions/analytical/issues/_writing/argument/pool

3) Write several practice essays under timed conditions, also using topics from ETS's published topic pool. Don't select the topics you most *want* to write about—just scroll down the list and do the first topic you land on, or ask someone else to assign you a topic. Write your practice essays on a computer, using only the functions available to you on the real exam (i.e., turn off spell check and grammar check).

4) Take a full-length Manhattan GRE practice exam (included with your purchase of this book!), and don't skip the essay section!

GRE ISSUE ESSAY QUOTES

An excellent way to go "above and beyond" on the Issue essay is to strategically deploy a relevant quote. The following quotes by notable thinkers have been selected for brevity as well as for relevance to common GRE essay themes: just government, human virtues, altruism, the value of progress, the purpose of education, etc.

Try completing several practice essays while "cheating" off this guide; you're looking to drop one quote per essay, usually in the introduction or conclusion.

While writing practice essays, see which quotes appeal to you and seem easy to memorize. Your goal for this activity is to memorize 5–6 of your favorite quotes such that you'll be able to make one of them fit on test day. That said, **do not stress** about having a quote—if this feels unnatural or cumbersome to you, feel free to skip it.

Albert Einstein:
"Any intelligent fool can make things bigger, more complex, and more violent. It takes a touch of genius—and a lot of courage—to move in the opposite direction."
"Two things are infinite: the universe and human stupidity, and I'm not sure about the universe."

Calvin Coolidge (30th U.S. President, advocate of small government):
"The world is full of educated derelicts."
"The slogan 'Press on' has solved and always will solve the problems of the human race."

Samuel Beckett (Irish avant-garde writer, highly minimalist, known for bleak outlook):
"We lose our hair, our teeth! Our bloom, our ideals."
"What do I know of man's destiny? I could tell you more about radishes."
"Nothing happens, nobody comes, nobody goes, it's awful."
"There's man all over for you, blaming on his boots the fault of his feet."
"The tears of the world are a constant quality. For each one who begins to weep, somewhere else another stops."

Oscar Wilde (Irish writer and prominent aesthete):
"The public have an insatiable curiosity to know everything. Except what is worth knowing."
"Democracy means simply the bludgeoning of the people by the people for the people."
"Discontent is the first step in the progress of a man or a nation."

Camille Paglia (modern-day American author, professor, "dissident feminist"):
"Education has become a prisoner of contemporaneity. It is the past, not the dizzy present, that is the best door to the future."
"Popular culture is the new Babylon, into which so much art and intellect now flow."

Martin Luther King, Jr.:
"We may have all come on different ships, but we're in the same boat now."
"He who passively accepts evil is as much involved in it as he who helps to perpetrate it."
"The question is not whether we will be extremists, but what kind of extremists we will be."
"Freedom is never voluntarily given by the oppressor; it must be demanded by the oppressed."
"Everybody can be great... because anybody can serve."
"Injustice anywhere is a threat to justice everywhere."

Voltaire (French Enlightenment writer, philosopher, advocate of civil liberties):
"As long as people believe in absurdities they will continue to commit atrocities."
"It is hard to free fools from the chains they revere."
"I disapprove of what you say, but I will defend to the death your right to say it."
"It is dangerous to be right when the government is wrong."

Julius Caesar:
"Men willingly believe what they wish."
"As a rule, men worry more about what they can't see than about what they can."

Virgil (classical Roman poet):
"Who asks whether the enemy were defeated by strategy or valor?"
"Evil is nourished and grows by concealment."

Franz Kafka (one of the most influential fiction writers of the early 20th century, author of *The Trial*):
"There are questions we could not get past if we were not set free from them by our very nature."

Winston Churchill (led the U.K. during WWII):
"I have nothing to offer but blood, toil, tears, and sweat."
"Without victory there is no survival."

Napoleon Bonaparte:
"Men are moved by two levers only: fear and self-interest."
"A people which is able to say everything becomes able to do everything."
"Greatness be nothing unless it be lasting."

Jean-Paul Sartre (20th century French existentialist writer/philosopher):
"Once you hear the details of victory, it is hard to distinguish it from a defeat."
"I hate victims who respect their executioners."
"All human actions are equivalent… and all are on principle doomed to failure."
"Hell is other people." (from the play "No Exit")

John F. Kennedy (35th U.S. President):
"Do not pray for easy lives. Pray to be stronger men."
"Efforts and courage are not enough without purpose and direction."

Theodore Roosevelt (26th U.S. President):
"Far and away the best prize that life offers is the chance to work hard at work worth doing."

Woodrow Wilson (28th U.S. President, leading intellectual of the Progressive era):
"No nation is fit to sit in judgment upon any other nation."

Ralph Waldo Emerson (19th century American transcendentalist author, proponent of individualism):
"It is said that the world is in a state of bankruptcy, that the world owes the world more than the world can pay."
"Can anything be so elegant as to have few wants, and to serve them one's self?"

Daniel Webster (leading American statesman during Antebellum period):
"Liberty exists in proportion to wholesome restraint."
"A mass of men equals a mass of opinions."
"Whatever government is not a government of laws, is a despotism, let it be called what it may."

Tom Stoppard (20th century playwright renowned for use of humor):
"Life is a gamble at terrible odds, if it were a bet, you would not take it."

Sinclair Lewis (20th century American novelist, author of *Babbitt*):
"Pugnacity is a form of courage, but a very bad form."

Thomas Jefferson:
"The will of the people is the only legitimate foundation of any government, and to protect its free expression should be our first object."

Florence Nightingale (English nurse, came to prominence tending to soldiers during Crimean War):
"I think one's feelings waste themselves in words; they ought all to be distilled into actions which bring results."
"How very little can be done under the spirit of fear."
"The martyr sacrifices themselves entirely in vain. Or rather not in vain; for they make the selfish more selfish, the lazy more lazy, the narrow narrower."

Virginia Woolf (20th century English modernist writer, author of *The Hours*):
"Really I don't like human nature unless all candied over with art."

Socrates (ancient Greek philosopher, teacher of Plato):
"Life contains but two tragedies. One is not to get your heart's desire; the other is to get it."
"The only good is knowledge and the only evil is ignorance."
"From the deepest desires often comes the deadliest hate."
"I am not an Athenian, nor a Greek, but a citizen of the world."
"Nothing is to be preferred before justice."
"Let him that would move the world, first move himself."

John Locke (17th century English philosopher influential in the Enlightenment):
"The action of men are the best interpreters of their thoughts."

Thomas Hobbes (17th century English philosopher):
"Leisure is the mother of Philosophy."
"The life of man: solitary, poor, nasty, brutish, and short."

Henry David Thoreau (transcendentalist writer, author of *Walden*):
"The mass of men lead lives of quiet desperation."
"Distrust any enterprise that requires new clothes."
"If you have built castles in the air, your work need not be lost; that is where they should be. Now put the foundations under them."

Immanuel Kant (18th century German philosopher):
"Out of timber so crooked as that from which man is made nothing entirely straight can be carved."
"Live your life as though your every act were to become a universal law."

Gertrude Stein (avant-garde American writer who lived as an expatriate in France):
"Money is always there but the pockets change."

Mohandas Gandhi (political and spiritual leader of Indian Independence Movement):
"There is more to life than simply increasing its speed."
"God comes to the hungry in the form of food."
"Non-cooperation with evil is as much a duty as is cooperation with good."
"I suppose leadership at one time meant muscles; but today it means getting along with people."

William Shakespeare:
"There's small choice in rotten apples." (From *The Taming of the Shrew*)
"Sweets grown common lose their dear delight." (From Sonnet 102)
"The worst is not, so long as we can say, 'This is the worst.'" (From *King Lear*)
"When sorrows come, they come not single spies, but in battalions." (From *Hamlet*)

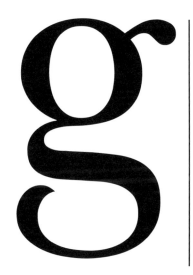

Appendix
of
READING COMPREHENSION & ESSAYS

VOCABULARY
AND READING
COMPREHENSION

In This Chapter . . .

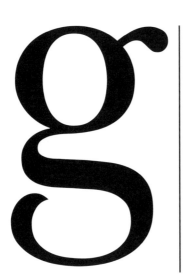

- Pure Jargon

- Semi-Jargon

- Glued-Together Words

- Common Words Used in Fancy Ways

- Vocab You Oughta Know

Appendix: Vocabulary and Reading Comprehension

Compared with the other Verbal question types, Reading Comprehension is less concerned with your knowledge of vocabulary. Every specialized term is defined to a sufficient degree within the passage. Moreover, even difficult "normal" words are used in context; as a result, you have an enormous leg up on knowing what the words mean.

That said, Reading Comprehension can still try to scare you off with puffed-up vocabulary and difficult idioms. For a comprehensive lesson on learning vocabulary and idoms, see our *Text Completion & Sentence Equivalence Strategy Guide*. In the meantime, we'll quickly introduce you here to some "ten-dollar words" that have appeared in previous GRE passages.

1. Pure Jargon

Pure Jargon words are specialized terms that the passage defines on the spot, almost always within the same sentence. There is no expectation that you've ever seen these words before.

> *...afterward, the politician began to practice* **Priusism**—*a philosophy espousing the use of low-emission vehicles...*

> *...he also began to eat low-carbon vegetables, such as* **aconiteotes** *and* **pleonasmides**...

(In case you weren't sure, the bolded terms are completely made up!)

Pure Jargon terms can refer to particular animals, plants, minerals, or chemicals that play some kind of role (important or trivial) in the story. Or they might represent medical conditions, social movements, foreign words, and so on.

Here are some examples from published GRE passages. We will *not* define these words here, nor should you go look them up (even if you recognize a few). After all, they will be defined in the passage!

> *Achondrite*
>
> *Appendicularian*
>
> *Chondrule*
>
> *Flux* (in metallurgy)
>
> *Hypercholesterolemia*
>
> *Igneous*
>
> *Leitourgia*
>
> *Phytoplankton*
>
> *Saint-Simonianism*
>
> *Shergottite*
>
> *Siderophore*
>
> *Zooplankton*

To deal with a Pure Jargon term, first assess how important it is. If it's just a side example, ignore it. But if it seems to play a big role in the passage, then abbreviate it to a single capital letter in your notes.

For instance, in one published GRE passage, *shergottites* are very important. In fact, they present the central puzzle of the passage.

When you read that passage, you could write this: *S's = big puzzle*

Notice that you can get a sequence of these Pure Jargon terms: X is used to define Y, which then is used to define Z. In the *shergottite* passage, first *igneous* is defined, then *achondrites* and *chondrules*, and finally *shergottites* are defined as a particular type of *achondrite*. There's nothing crazy here. Just keep track of the sequence!

2. Semi-Jargon

Semi-Jargon words are "sort of" specialized words. You may have heard or seen these words before. The passage may not stop to define these words, but it will give you enough within a couple of sentences to figure out a working definition.

Here are a few examples of Semi-Jargon words from published GRE passages, together with the working definition you can piece together from context:

Empiricism = a philosophy of using observations to gain knowledge

Isotope = some kind or version of a chemical element

Lymphocyte = something from the immune system that attacks foreign stuff in the body

Magistrate = some kind of public official

With Semi-Jargon words, you need to be okay with partial, incomplete definitions. It may bother you that you don't know or remember more. Relax: you can rely on the contextual meaning.

3. Glued-Together Words

You've probably never seen Glued-Together words before, but you can figure them out by breaking them apart. Glued-Together words mean exactly what you'd guess they mean. They look fancy and imposing, but don't be intimidated. Just break them into parts. You might need to use a Latin root or two, but you won't come across any tricks.

Here are some examples from published GRE passages:

Circumstellar = around a star

Deradicalized = something made not radical or extreme

Geochemical = having to do with geology and chemistry

Historicophilosophical = both historical and philosophical

Knowingness = quality of knowing something

Presolar = before the sun

Sociodemographic = having to do with both sociology and demography, the study of populations

Spherule = tiny sphere or globule

4. Common Words Used in Fancy Ways

This isn't a big category, but it's worth watching for. You may come across a common word that momentarily confuses you, because it's used in a "literary" way, not the way you'd use it in speech.

Here are a couple of examples:

> *Argue* = argue for
>
> *The absence of rhyme argues a subversion… = the absence of rhyme argues FOR a subversion…*
>
> *Minute* = small
>
> *Minute quantities… = small quantities…*

If a common word trips you up, simply ask yourself how else you might use it in writing.

5. Vocab You Oughta Know

This category is the most dangerous, because although the passage will still give you context, it will give you less context for them than for the Pure Jargon or Semi-Jargon words. In fact, if you aren't sure what these words mean, you might struggle briefly as you sort out the possible meanings.

However, if you know these words outright, you will move faster through passages. Moreover, these words are ones you're generally studying for the rest of the Verbal section, so you should be in good shape anyway!

Here are a few favorites (ones that have shown up in more than one published passage):

> *Ephemeral* = short-lived, vanishing
>
> *Fluctuation* = a change up & down, variation
>
> *Ideology* = system of beliefs (also *ideological*)
>
> *Unequivocal* = without a doubt, unambiguous (also *unequivocally*)

Here are several others that have appeared in published passages. You probably already know many of them in context. If you're not sure, look the word up and write a definition.

Abolitionist	Doctrinaire	Nostalgia	Subvert
Acquisitiveness	Dubious	Oligarchy	Suffrage
Adherent	Eclectic	Par (on a par with)	Synchronized
Admonish	Egalitarian	Periodic/periodically	Syntax
Ambivalence	Emancipator	Physiological	Synthesis
Annex	Emergency	Plutocratic	Taxonomy/taxonomic
Annihilate	Enigma	Polemic	Temperament
Annul	Equivalence	Postulate	Temperance
Antipathy	Escape velocity	Pragmatic	Terrestrial
Antithetical	Ethos	Predatory	Thenceforth
Aristocracy	Evolution/evolve	Premised	Thesis
Ascribe/ascription	Expansionist	Pristine	Transient
Assimilation	Expediency	Progeny	Transmute
Benefactor	Hallucination	Proletariat	Transplantation
Benevolent	Heterogeneous	Qualified (restricted)	Undifferentiated
Benign	Iconoclastic	Recalcitrant	Unfettered
Categorization	Impinge	Receptivity	Utopian
Cavalier	Induce	Refute	
Coercion	Inextricably	Reminiscent	
Coexistence	Ingenuity	Reverie	
Cognitive	Inordinate	Sanction	
Composition (in art)	Intrepid	Satiric/satirist	
Contemplative	Intractable	Scrutiny	
Countenance	Juxtapose	Smelt	
Counterpoint	Mantle (of the earth)	Socialism	
Decry	Mediated	Static	
Deride	Mercurial	Subjugation	
Deterrence	Militarist	Subjectivity	
Discreditable	Mores	Subordinate/ subordination	
Dispersal	Nebula (in astronomy)		

mbaMission

Every candidate has a unique story to tell.

We have the creative experience to help you tell yours.

We are **mbaMission**, published authors with elite MBA experience who will work with you one-on-one to craft complete applications that will force the admissions committees to take notice. Benefit from straightforward guidance and personal mentorship as you define your unique attributes and reveal them to the admissions committees via a story only you can tell.

We will guide you through our "Complete Start to Finish Process":

- ☑ Candidate assessment, application strategy and program selection
- ☑ Brainstorming and selection of essay topics
- ☑ Outlining and essay structuring
- ☑ Unlimited essay editing
- ☑ Letter of recommendation advice
- ☑ Resume construction and review
- ☑ Interview preparation, mock interviews and feedback
- ☑ Post-acceptance and scholarship counseling

Monday Morning Essay Tip: Overrepresenting Your Overrepresentation

Many in the MBA application pool—particularly male investment bankers—worry that they are overrepresented. While you cannot change your work history, you can change the way you introduce yourself to admissions committees. Consider the following examples:

Example 1: "As an investment banking analyst at Bank of America, I am responsible for creating Excel models...."
Example 2: "At 5:30 pm, I could rest easy. The deadline for all other offers had passed. At that point, I knew...."

In the first example, the candidate starts off by mistakenly introducing the reader to the very over-representation that he/she should be trying to avoid emphasizing. In the second example, the banker immerses the reader in an unraveling mystery. This keeps the reader intrigued and focused on the applicant's story and actions rather than making the specific job title and responsibilities the center of the text. While each applicant's personal situation is different, every candidate can approach his/her story so as to mitigate the effects of overrepresentation.

To schedule a free consultation and read more than fifty Monday Morning Essay Tips, please visit our website:
www.mbamission.com

Finally, a GMAT® prep guide series that goes beyond the basics.

Number Properties, Fourth Edition
ISBN: 978-0-9824238-4-4
Retail: $26

Fractions, Decimals, & Percents, Fourth Edition
ISBN: 978-0-9824238-2-0
Retail: $26

Equations, Inequalities, & VICs, Fourth Edition
ISBN: 978-0-9824238-1-3
Retail: $26

Word Translations, Fourth Edition
ISBN: 978-0-9824238-7-5
Retail: $26

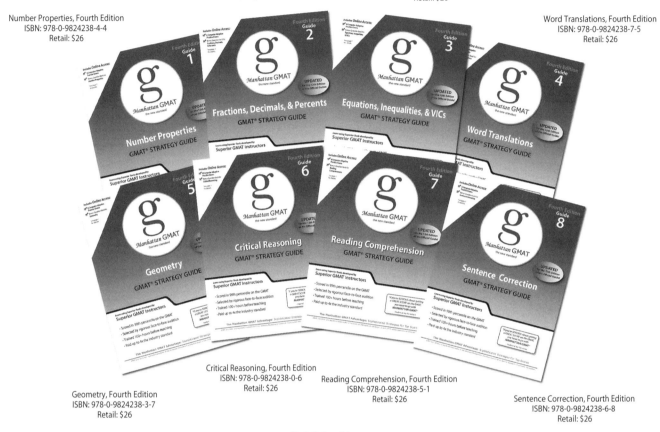

Geometry, Fourth Edition
ISBN: 978-0-9824238-3-7
Retail: $26

Critical Reasoning, Fourth Edition
ISBN: 978-0-9824238-0-6
Retail: $26

Reading Comprehension, Fourth Edition
ISBN: 978-0-9824238-5-1
Retail: $26

Sentence Correction, Fourth Edition
ISBN: 978-0-9824238-6-8
Retail: $26

Published by

Manhattan GMAT

 You get many more pages per topic than you find in all-in-one tomes.

 Only buy those guides that address the specific skills you need to develop.

 Gain access to Online Practice GMAT Exams & Bonus Question Banks.

COMMENTS FROM GMAT TEST TAKERS:

Now Available at your local bookstore!

"Bravo, Manhattan GMAT! Bravo! The guides truly did not disappoint. All the guides are clear, concise, and well organized, and explained things in a manner that made it possible to understand things the first time through without missing any of the important details."

"I've thumbed through a lot of books that don't even touch these. The fact that they're split up into components is immeasurably helpful. The set-up of each guide and the lists of past GMAT problems make for an incredibly thorough and easy-to-follow study path."

GMAT and GMAC are registered trademarks of the Graduate Management Admission Council which neither sponsors nor endorses this product.